The East India Company in Persia

The East India Company in Persia

*Trade and Cultural Exchange in
the Eighteenth Century*

Peter Good

I.B. TAURIS
LONDON • NEW YORK • OXFORD • NEW DELHI • SYDNEY

I.B. TAURIS
Bloomsbury Publishing Plc
50 Bedford Square, London, WC1B 3DP, UK
1385 Broadway, New York, NY 10018, USA
29 Earlsfort Terrace, Dublin 2, Ireland

BLOOMSBURY, I.B. TAURIS and the I.B. Tauris logo are trademarks of Bloomsbury Publishing Plc

First published in Great Britain 2022
This paperback edition published 2023

Copyright © Peter Good, 2022

Peter Good has asserted his right under the Copyright, Designs and Patents Act, 1988, to be identified as Author of this work.

For legal purposes the Acknowledgements on pp. ix–x constitute an extension of this copyright page.

Series design by Adriana Brioso
Cover image © Tuul and Bruno Morandi/Alamy Stock Photo

All rights reserved. No part of this publication may be reproduced or transmitted in any form or by any means, electronic or mechanical, including photocopying, recording, or any information storage or retrieval system, without prior permission in writing from the publishers.

Bloomsbury Publishing Plc does not have any control over, or responsibility for, any third-party websites referred to or in this book. All internet addresses given in this book were correct at the time of going to press. The author and publisher regret any inconvenience caused if addresses have changed or sites have ceased to exist, but can accept no responsibility for any such changes.

A catalogue record for this book is available from the British Library.

A catalog record for this book is available from the Library of Congress.

ISBN: HB: 978-1-3501-5227-4
PB: 978-0-7556-4626-5
ePDF: 978-1-3501-5229-8
eBook: 978-1-3501-5228-1

Typeset by Newgen KnowledgeWorks Pvt. Ltd., Chennai, India

To find out more about our authors and books visit www.bloomsbury.com and sign up for our newsletters.

Contents

Acknowledgements	ix
Author's Notes	xi
Prologue	xv
Introduction	1
1 Life in the Company's Persian factory	27
2 Governance, information management, reporting, communication and control	43
3 Trade's increase: The Company's commerce in Persia	73
4 A navy for hire: The continuing maritime operations of the East India Company in the Persian Gulf 1727–43	97
5 Brokers, Khwajas and country Christians: The Company's employment of non-Europeans in Persia	127
Conclusion	153
Notes	159
Bibliography	183
Index	193

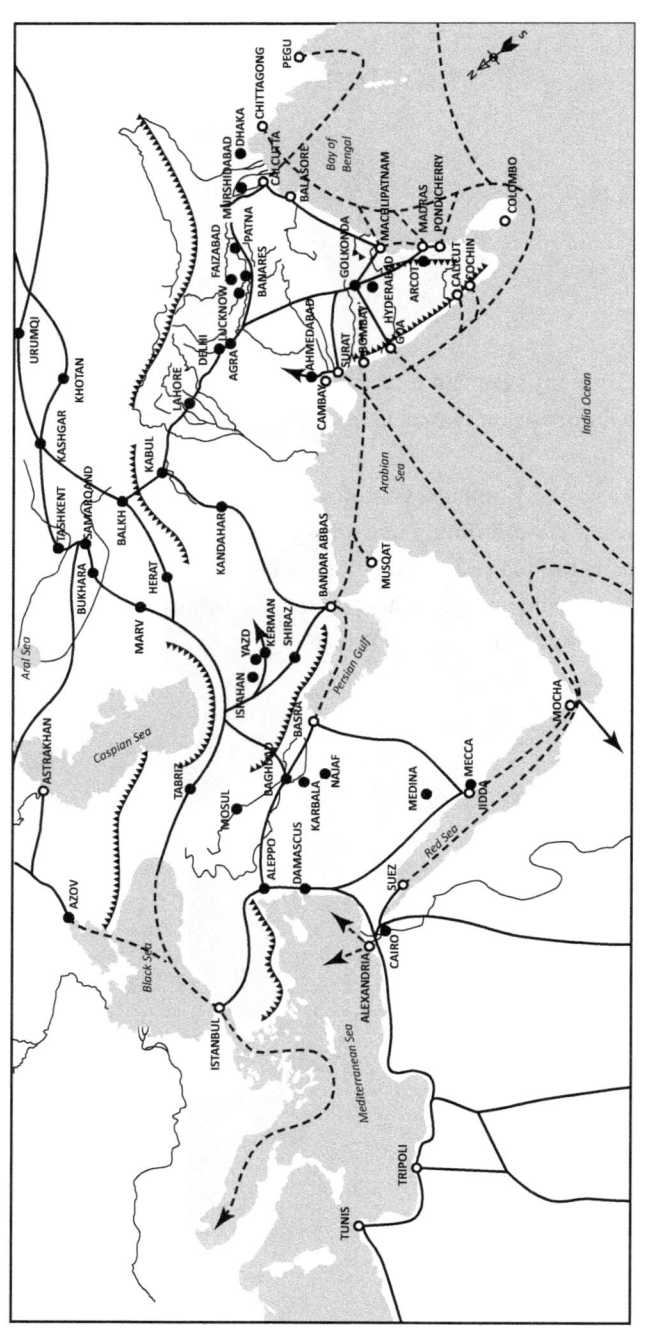

Map 1 Land and maritime trade routes around the Indian Ocean.

Map 2 The Iranian Plateau and its environs.

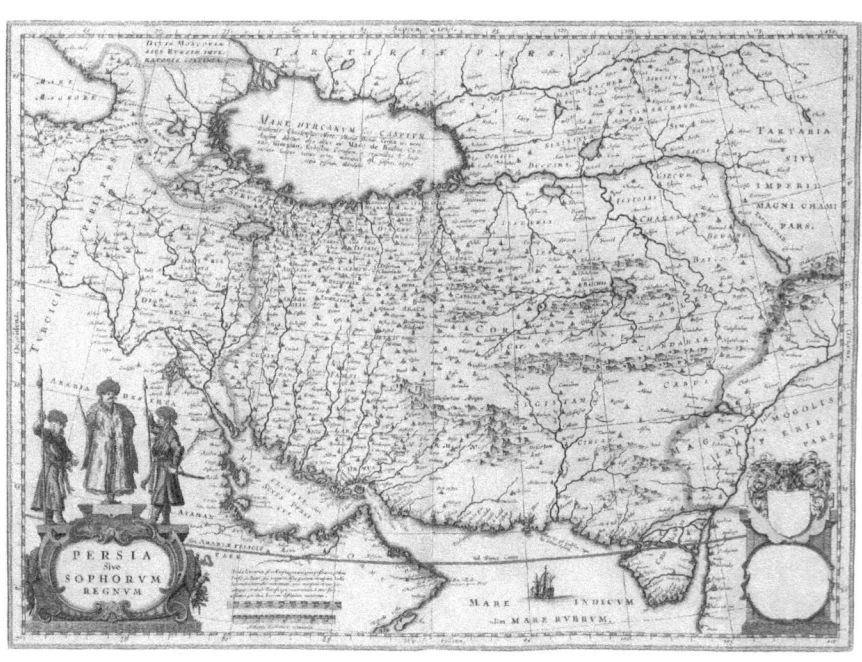

Map 3 Map of Persia 1645. (Photo by: Picturenow/Universal Images Group via Getty Images)

Acknowledgements

I have been lucky over the last decade to bring this project to fruition in great and generous company. My first thanks go to my supervisory team Mark Frost (University of Essex, now UCL) and Margaret Makepeace (The British Library). Both Mark and Margaret's knowledge, expertise, humour and, most of all, patience guided me through the PhD process from start to finish and this book is the result. While studying for my PhD, from which this text is derived, I was welcomed into two teams: the Qatar Digital Library team at the British Library and the Department of History at the University of Essex, so my next thanks go to all of them, particularly Fiona Venn, Jeremy Krikler and Sean Kelley for their invaluable advice and mentoring. I would also like to thank Professor Edmund Herzig (Oxford) for a thorough and constructive viva.

I am also incredibly grateful to Professor William Pettigrew (Lancaster) and my former colleagues from the PEIC team at the University of Kent (Aske Brock, Misha Ewen, Edmond Smith, David Veevers and Liam Haydon), not only for giving me my first job in academia but also for their comments, critiques and suggestion on the various chapters of this book, not to mention their friendship. Since joining the University of Kent, I have benefitted from the generosity of many colleagues past and present, particularly Professor Jan Loop (Copenhagen), Suzanna Ivanic, Leonie James, Professor Kenneth Fincham, Sam Robinson (Southampton) and Professor Gaynor Johnson, for looking over various chapters of this manuscript. It is better for their expert eyes, firm encouragement and enthusiasm for the project. I have also had the privilege of working with Mark Williams (Cardiff) who gave invaluable insight into the chapters regarding the social life of the Company and Martha Chaiklin for her overview of the manuscript at various times. I count myself blessed to have met Martha at the Global Companies Conference held at Heidelberg in 2015, where I benefitted from the expertise and comments of Adam Clulow (Monash), Guido van Meersbergen (Warwick) and Tristan Mostert, to name but a few.

According to Professor Ali Ansari (St. Andrews) Persian Studies has been described as a niche within a niche, but I can only echo him by saying what a rich seam it is! I have nothing but admiration for my friends and colleagues who study Iran's history, cultures, arts and politics who welcomed me with open arms when first starting my PhD journey and have been stuck with me since. Fuchsia Hart and Lindsey Allen (KCL) have given generously of their time in helping to find references, particularly when lockdowns and travel restrictions made this difficult. Rowena Abdul-Razak and Khodadad Rezakhani gave me great opportunities to speak about my research on the platforms that they have created from scratch to support and showcase researchers like myself since the outbreak of the Covid-19 pandemic. I have now attended three Symposia Iranica conferences and various chapters of this book have been presented at these conferences. The feedback I have received whether from professors or PhD students has broadened my mind and improved this manuscript hugely; long may this community persist, even though I'm too old to present now.

This book would not exist were it not for the team at I.B. Tauris, Joanna Godfrey (now at Yale), Yasmin Garcha, Rory Gormley and Olivia Dellow. Naturally, any remaining errors are solely my own.

Academia can be a lonely business, a precarious and peripatetic existence, so I am forever grateful to my friends and colleagues who have ensured that I am never lonely for too long. In no particular order then: Natasha Morris, the team at Medieval and Early Modern Orients, the MA class at the University of Exeter 2011–12, Alex, Alex, Carrie, Chris, Greg, Matthew, Skevoulla, Natalie, Ranulf, Oscar.

This book is dedicated to my family: my mother and father Margaret and Simon, my sister Sarah and my grandfather Edward. Editors-in-chief, literary critics, proofreaders … baristas, you name it, they can do it. They have seen me through with their boundless energy, enthusiasm and love. So to them, last of all, thank you. In short: I am so lucky.

… Meanwhile in Bandar Abbas …

Author's Notes

Currencies

A wide variety of different coins and currencies are referred to throughout this book. These include copper, silver and gold coins minted by English, Persian, Indian and Italian states, in addition to currencies of account. The true value of Persian coinage in particular is problematic due to differing levels of debasement and means of measurement. For those interested in better understanding the financial history of Persia, I recommend *The Monetary System of Iran* by Matthee, Floor and Clawson. For the present volume, only a basic understanding is necessary, particularly concerning the relative value of the salaries earned by Company employees and to understand the volume of some of the trades and transactions undertaken.

The value of Persian coins is generally expressed through the toman, originally a gold coin worth 10,000 dinars but by this period only used as a currency of account. A shahi was both the currency of account used by the Company, sometimes expressed as *shahis factory*, and a physical coin of which 200 make a toman. There was also the mahmudi worth two shahis and the 'abbasi worth 4 shahis.[1] The rupee was calculated at 8 shahis until 1733 when it was recalculated at 10 shahis, showing a significant debasement of the silver coinage in Persia. Below is a table that shows the salary scale of the Company's Persian factory employees with relative values in shahis, rupees and pound sterling.

Position	Salary in £	Salary in Rupees	Salary in Shahis Factory
Agent	150	1,200	12,000
Senior Merchant	40	320	3,200
Senior Factor	30	240	2,400
Factor	15	120	1,200
Surgeon	60	480	4,800
Writer	5	40	400
Persian Writer	17.10s.	140	1,400
Linguist at Bandar Abbas	75	600	6,000
Linguist at Isfahan	80	640	6,400

IOR/G/29/5 f.394v Account Salary for the year commencing 1 August 1735 and ending ultimo July 1736.

Weights

Like early modern currencies, weights are rather difficult to track and accurately measure; the Company undertook periodic tests to check weights in order to rationalise what they believed they had dispatched with what was received at Bombay. There are only a few measures directly referenced in the text; the *mann-i shah* was equal to two *mann-i Tabriz*, each of 2.89 kg. Both are rendered as 'maund' by the Company's merchants, often without differentiation, although occasionally 'maund shaw' appears. The pound avoirdupois was current for the Company, weighing 0.454 kg. Bales were reckoned at 36 *mann-i Tabriz* or around 104 kg.[2]

Dates

For all references, the date written in the primary source has been used, with the exception of measuring the start of each year not from Lady Day (25 March), as was the custom before 1752, but from 1 January. This mirrors the custom of the Company, who often wrote both years into their records after January, for example, 1 March 1740/41.

Transliterations and names

For most names, I have used recognised English equivalents, Ali rather than 'Ali, Abbas rather than 'Abbās or Isfahan rather than Esfahān, or the Library of Congress system (in italics with translations) without diacritics in order to make the text as accessible and intelligible as possible to non-Persian speakers. I have also shortened some names after the first usage, for example, rendering Mohammad Taqi Khan Shirazi as 'Taqi Khan'. Where Persian names have been spelled phonetically by eighteenth-century standards, I have tried to provide the most likely rendering of them; for the names of the Banians and Armenians in particular, I have retained the spelling in the primary source.

Figure 1 Nader Shah, Shah of Iran (1736–47), date: 1688–1747 (Chronicle via Getty Images).

Prologue

In 1747, the ancient Persian city of Kerman was in flames. The population of the region had suffered weeks of dreadful violence and looting. Most of the notable residents attempted to flee but found themselves trapped. The merchants of the city were forced to pay vast sums of money to marauding troops, after which some had still been severely beaten or murdered. Meanwhile, the deputy governor of the city killed himself on being presented with a demand for 10,000 toman, a sum so vast it was inconceivable he would be able to pay it. Amidst all of this, a young Englishman, Danvers Graves, recorded the events he witnessed in increasingly shocking detail. Graves had been dispatched by the East India Company to oversee their business in Kerman, especially the lucrative purchase of wool and locally mined copper. Instead of overseeing a daily list of purchases, payments, supply contracts and enjoying local entertainments, Graves bore witness to the almost complete destruction of Kerman and its population. Kerman was indeed only the latest victim; the perpetrators of these acts of carnage and destruction were not glorious conquerors, not a foreign king or general, but the Shah of Persia himself, Nader Shah.[1]

Graves was experiencing the final act of the life of this ruler, who presided over one of the most infamous reigns in the long history of Persia. Having risen from a local military strongman to the ruler of a vast empire, Nader Shah had distinguished himself as a leader and commander. He was, especially in his later years, extremely cruel and utterly ruthless with his own people as well as his enemies. In the case of Kerman, the Shah had decided to punish the city for withholding their tax and wealth from him while he prepared for yet another military campaign. Graves' account tells how Nader Shah ordered the executions of prominent citizens, the seizure of property and wholesale destruction of any who resisted him in even the smallest of ways. The Armenian Christian Patriarch had fled Persia for the Ottoman Empire in the face of financial exactions and threats of violence, while the Company had withdrawn their servants from Persia almost entirely. Graves was faced with an army literally on his doorstep. His household servants threatened, beaten and left destitute had taken shelter with him, while his local translator had robbed him before fleeing the city.

Rather than fleeing alone, Graves stayed to protect the interests of his employers, their local assets and to preserve the lives of his local employees. After failing to secure an audience with the Shah or his officials through the proper channels, Graves turned to other means, first approaching the Shah's personal physician, the French Jesuit Louis Bazin. When the letters carried by Bazin, begging protection and clemency for the Englishman and his employees, failed, Graves tried a final, risky gambit: He walked to the compound occupied by the Shah and waited for his chance. Eventually, after being challenged by guards and officials, Graves saw the Shah walking nearby and decided that the only way he was likely to speak to him was by attracting his attention directly. Graves began loudly arguing with the guards and officials. This had the desired effect; the Shah ordered that the Englishman be allowed entry and granted him a brief audience. Graves succeeded in securing permission to pay the imagined debts the Company owed to the Shah in bills of exchange, rather than the hard cash that had previously been demanded. This bold approach did not save the Company's house in Kerman from becoming a target for further attacks. The Company's Persian servants were abducted, and later returned savagely beaten by Nader Shah's troops. For some the beatings were repeated and they were saved only by the presentation by Graves of a writ of protection granted by the Shah to the Company's servants. Graves tried to forestall any further attacks, petitioning local Persian nobles whom he had befriended, and even entertaining an Afghan commander at his own expense. The threats and extortions continued and only ended with Nader Shah's assassination at the hands of his own commanders; the ensuing chaos gave Graves enough time to save himself and his servants. In the face of all this, Graves continued to write to his superiors in the port city of Bandar Abbas, informing them of what was transpiring and his actions in trying to best serve his employers.

Graves became the Agent for Persia in 1751 but died not long after in September 1752. Danvers had three brothers: Morgan, who became a lawyer at the Inner Temple; Charles Gaspar, who joined the Church of England; and Richard, who became an Oxford academic and author, famous for his novel *The Spiritual Quixote*. While all the other brothers are listed on Richard's Wikipedia page, Danvers is notably absent; it appears that unlike his brothers, he neither attended Oxford nor joined the Bar or the Church. There is a record of Danvers' life and death in St. Lawrence's Church in the family's native village of Mickleton in Gloucestershire. In the Church is a plaque that reads,

> Sacred to the Memory of Danvers Graves Esq. Youngest Son
> of Richard Graves Esq.

A Youth deservedly lamented by his relations, his friends, and by even his country. Who, as a factor to the Honourable East India Company for 15 years

Bombay, Gombroon, Balsora, Ispahan.

Managed their affairs with Great Resolution and Fidelity,

Amidst a Thousand Dangers and Distresses,

Being more than once Plundered And many times in Danger of his Life From the Rebellious Persians,

At Length,

Being Sent into Persia as Chief Agent and Now soon to Return to his native Country, Such, Alas! Is the Uncertain Event of Human Affairs!

He was seized with a Fever and died at Gombroon in the Gulph of Persia, in the year 1752

Graves' story illuminates a number of facets: the social interaction between Persians and Englishmen, the commercial activities of the Company, practices of diplomacy and the relationships between English merchants and their local servants. It is also significant to note the vulnerability of the Company's establishment in Persia in the face of local hostility or the demands of its rulers. The letters and accounts written by Graves, along with his epitaph, are emblematic of the experience of the Company's servants in Persia in the first half of the eighteenth century. Graves' account gives a wealth of detail, from one of the few physical descriptions of Nader Shah to detailed relations of the process by which wool purchases were contracted. In many ways, the story of the fall and destruction of Kerman, and the ability of Graves to survive it are the culmination of a relationship between England and Persia that had lasted for over 130 years. Graves' knowledge of courtly practice, Persian social norms, his deployment of written agreements and his strong sense of duty towards his non-European servants are a microcosm of the wider lives of the Company in Persia, including his sudden death.

Introduction: Historiographical Essay

The Persian Gulf has been a crossroads of empires, continents and commerce for millennia, capturing the imaginations of authors, politicians and merchants from around the globe. For Europeans, whether Portuguese adventurers and explorers like Vasco da Gama (d. 1524), merchants like Jean Baptiste Tavernier (1605–1689) or the artist and gentleman traveller, Cornelis de Bruyn (1652–1727), the Gulf held a fascination grounded more in fantasy than reality. At the centre of many of these images lies the island and city of Hormuz, fabled in Europe for its fabulous wealth, bustling markets and vast maritime traffic.[1] For the English East India Company,[2] the Gulf held far more pecuniary attractions; not only was it a vital trade route between East and West, but it was also an access point to the silk of the Persian Safavid Empire, the markets of Ottoman Basra and the pearl fisheries of Bahrain.

Many studies exist on the Company's operations in India, and for good reason given its huge economic power and the long story of imperial and colonial rule there. However, the Company's other areas of interest, especially Persia, are less well studied, if at all. Despite the importance of Persian trade, the colossal scale of India's economic gravity, along with a large number of travel and other sources, has meant that it has not been reviewed alongside India in studies considering the sociocultural, religious, political and economic history of the Company. This book provides a realisation of an extensive study of available archival materials that allow considerable insight into how the Company operated in Persia. The following chapters look at Bandar Abbas as a centre of the Company's business network in a period of rapid and violent social change in Persia and a time of a growing English presence in Indian Ocean trade. The first chapter will examine the lived experience of the Company's merchants in Persia, dealing with harsh weather conditions, disease and death. The second chapter will consider how the Company's affairs in Persia were managed day-to-day, while the third chapter will look at the commercial side of the Company's operations. The Company's relationship with Persia was not solely commercial, however, as from their very earliest interactions, the Company's naval power was a matter of particular interest to the Safavids and their successors. In the fourth chapter the uses and services provided by the Company as, I have termed, a 'Navy for Hire' will be considered, not just in the sense of ships being used as military assets but also as tools of power projection and diplomatic reach. In the fifth chapter we will see that far from being an entirely English, British or even European venture, the Company was staffed by a wide range of individuals from ethnic and religious minorities comprising English merchants and Indian sailors, Eurasian soldiers, Armenian translators and Persian scribes as well as religious functionaries. This book presents the Persian factory as a constituent part of not only the Company's operations but also as an entity in its own right, connected intimately with regional political life and the commerce of the wider Gulf and Indian Ocean in its own distinct ways. It reveals how the relationship was built on mutuality, not armed or violent coercion, governed by a contract. We also see how the affairs of both Persian rulers and officials and the Company are entwined to make it possible to overcome disappointments, disputes, changes in trade, political upheaval and regime change and the endangering acts of individuals. Much of the relationship's direction was within the gift of the Persian state while the Company was left to lobby for its interests or recognition of particular requirements. The Company's presence may not have been glamorous enough to warrant the attention of Persian chroniclers, but it was demonstrably useful as a partnership between the Company and Persia that lasted for 130 years. The genesis of this enduring relationship was born in the vein of mutual cooperation and shared interest, but as we shall see, this was forged through an audacious naval and amphibious operation against a common enemy. This was not the action of an aggressive colonial European power but instead the initiative of a Persian Shah to fulfil his own ambitions taking advantage of a useful and willing minor ally on the periphery of his empire and the political landscape of the Indian Ocean.

Studies on the East India Company grew from the nineteenth- and twentieth-century interest in empire and its history. The Company is often viewed as an agent for empire, or as the means by which Englishmen 'discovered' the globe. This was facilitated by the work of William Foster, who published various collections of the Company's records, letters and papers in the first three decades of the twentieth century.[3] Following the Second World War, the approach to the history of the Company became much more concerned with questions of structure, both of the Company itself and its role in linking Europe to the powers of Asia. More recently, scholars of the Company have explored a multiplicity of aspects of the Company's business including the lived experience of Company servants and its role in the formation of empire.[4] For the purposes of this book, the work of Phillip Stern and his idea of the 'Company-State' are formative, particularly in the first two chapters which explore the lives and organisation of the Company's merchants in depth.[5] Stern has created a coherent sense of the Company's desires to control great swathes of the political and commercial lives of its subjects, from an insistence on free trade (within the Indian Ocean, at least) to measures to preserve the health of its servants. The Company in Persia could not, however, make any claims to civic control over the state of public services in Bandar Abbas or Isfahan, so this book will instead consider what measures the Company's hierarchy could put in place for the good of its servants at a great remove from the metropole of Bombay.

The Company has also served for many years as the test case for understanding the nature of the European presence in Asia. Holden Furber, writing in 1969, envisioned an 'Age of Partnership', citing the Company's many peaceful interactions with Asian powers, while Sanjay Subrahmanyam instead saw a period of 'fragile equilibrium'. Furber's work presents a rather utopian vision of this period in which 'Indian suppliers of piece-goods, Indo-Portuguese and Armenian merchants … European country captains and Indian *noquedars*' all acted in relative concert towards mutual goals and benefits.[6] Furber's assertions about a cosmopolitan network of merchants, brokers, shippers and producers are somewhat simplistic, papering over the often significant tensions that arose between constituent groups and vested interests within these networks. In Persia, for example, the Armenian community, which had long controlled the silk trade from Persia to the Ottoman Empire, was exceedingly hostile to any notion of sharing either their knowledge or allowing access to their own networks.[7] The tension here though was not between Europeans and an Orientalised 'other' but between an established merchant community and everyone else. Subrahmanyam's thesis falls too far in the opposite direction, emphasising constant conflicts between Asian states and Europeans, leading eventually to the defeat of the former by the attrition of the latter.[8] Where Furber's vision is utopian, Subrahmanyam's is exceedingly bleak, but he is not alone in this view. K. N. Chaudhuri had earlier argued that the presence of well-armed European ships in the Indian Ocean is proof of the aggressive basis of European trade.[9] These views present a black or white picture. The example of Persia presents an alternative view where the Company and successive regimes over the course of the eighteenth century sustained a peaceful and largely profitable coexistence based on the terms of principles decreed and renewed by the Safavid Shahs and their successors. Through this case study, a more nuanced shade of grey emerges between Furber, Chaudhuri and Subrahmanyam; yes, there was tension and disagreement, but these did not lead to violence; instead issues were managed through a mutually recognised and enforced mechanism over the *Longue-Durée*. Furthermore, the Company was clearly the junior partner in the relationship between it and the Persian state; it would not be until the first decades of the nineteenth century that Britain exercised any real influence over Persian politics or economics.

More recent studies of Eurasian relationships have taken a narrower focus, notably those of Adam Clulow and Bhawan Ruangsilp. Their work shows how the records and resources left by the Company can be used to gain a perspective on Asian cultures and their processes of interaction with the 'other'.[10] By combining Company sources with local ones, a synthetical understanding of both the Company and these Asian states can be constructed. Ruangsilp's example of the Verenigde Oost-Indische Compagnie, Dutch United East India Company (VOC), in Ayutthaya (Siam), where their investment in 'cultural capital', offers a clear example of how a European company and an Asian state built up a coherent relationship, without the need for violence.[11] By negotiating Siamese courtly expectations with the VOC's wider interests, the Dutch were able to build up a valuable trade in Siam, while the Siamese gained access to Dutch financial support and expertise. Clulow's work concerns the Dutch relationship with the Japanese. Here we see the Dutch in an almost total subordination to Japanese interests and practices in deference to the norms of the Tokugawa Shogunate.[12] These differing experiences show that the VOC engaged with its neighbours and interlocutors in distinct and tailored ways, informed either by 'cultural capital' or by simply being enfolded into existing subordinate and tributary relationships and structures. The nuanced fashion in which European companies approached Asian powers, and how these approaches were perceived, is vital in furthering our historical understanding of how they were able to conduct business. Both Clulow and Ruangsilp's approaches utilise Asian and European sources helping to construct a fuller understanding of the motivations of both parties. In the case of Persia, this approach is far more difficult as scholars do not have a Safavid or Persian archive with which to compare and contrast European views. While this book focusses on the experience of the Company and its merchants in Persia, rather than on the Persians themselves, by looking at the Company's accounts and additional literature, mostly in the form of European travelogues, one can identify features of Persian policy and individual agency.[13] Sadly, access to Iranian scholarship on this subject is incredibly restricted to Western scholars, further limiting any investigation into other potential sources of information or data, not to mention Iranian historiographical perspectives.

The history of the Company's trade in the Indian Ocean world more generally has been studied very closely for several decades, for instance K. N. Chaudhuri's work, covering the goods, ships and ports traded and used by the Company, has provided a platform for other scholars by exploring the trade carried out across the Indian Ocean.[14] Chaudhuri does not take account of the private trade conducted by the Company's servants; this is covered instead by the work of René Barendse.[15] While both Barendse and Chaudhuri develop the view of the Company's trade in physical commodities, as well as exploring the distribution of Company passes to native ships, neither of these authors give much agency in these trades to the native powers of Asia. Barendse argues, 'Where the Court was directly trading through a monopoly, like the Safavid Empire with silk, this was seen as an adjunct to "foreign policy". It was regarded as an exchange of gifts; where prices were based upon prestige rather than demand.'[16] Yet, as this book will show, both local and state actors in Persia were active in exercising control and manipulating trading networks and practices to their own advantage.

Rudi Matthee and Willem Floor have pioneered research into the Persian economy, as well as trade and political life. Matthee's explorations of Persian goods, as well as the political lives of Persian Shahs and statesmen, have given fresh insight into the political and economic history of Persia, while Floor's several publications concerning the Persian Gulf have done much to provide depth and detail to this region. Both scholars have studied the relationship between Persia and the VOC in great detail from an economic and political perspective. It is no surprise that these works privilege Dutch source material over English archives given the volume available. An example of this primacy is revealed in Floor's assertion that Europeans had to 'put up or shut up (or pay up)';[17] while this makes for a good turn of phrase, it misses the far more nuanced interplay of Persian state policy and English Company interests explored by this book. By investigating the Company's experience, it is evident that Persian and Company relations were much more complex than Floor avers. Floor and Matthee have likewise been instrumental in understanding Persia and its relationship to the wider Indian Ocean, as well as the wider world. This is exemplified through their contributions to the volume *Iran and the World in the Safavid Age*. Five further papers (Troebst, Faroqhi, Rota, Calmard, Marcinkowski) specifically deal with the connections between the Safavids and other European and Asian powers.[18] These chapters show Persia's place within networks of trade, patronage and diplomacy across Eurasia and the Indian Ocean, though neither in this volume or elsewhere, other than in Ferrier's dissertation and then only in the Safavid era, do we see a role for the Company.

When discussing the collapse of the Safavid Empire and its aftermath, scholars have tended to focus tightly to one figure above all, that of Nader Shah. Indeed, almost all scholarship about the post-Safavid eighteenth century up until recently has been preoccupied with the rule of this towering figure. Michael Axworthy and Ernest Tucker have both produced excellent studies of Nader Shah as an individual, while Willem Floor's publication of VOC sources on the period of Nader Shah's reign opens a European view of both the Shah and Persia during his reign.[19] Axworthy's edited volume, *Crisis, Collapse, Militarism and Civil War: The History and Historiography of 18th Century Iran*, is the only work which attempts to tackle the historiographical difficulties this period of Persia's history presents. It highlights many of the issues that arose in writing this book, particularly the dearth of European or Persian records noted by Matthee, exacerbated by the apparent disinterest of Persian chroniclers and authors in the activities of Europeans.[20] This collected volume enables a more nuanced, balanced and inquisitive view of Persia's eighteenth century which this book supports through the eyes of English observers. Matthee's assertion in his historiographical essay from Axworthy's volume that 'the role of the English in eighteenth-century Iran never much exceeded a commercial interest and was minimal (and decreasing) at best' raises some important questions about what we can learn from the Company's records.[21] While there's no doubt that the Company's interests in Persia were based on commerce, to limit their presence and experiences to purely commercial ones is too narrow. The chapters of this book will show that the Company's merchants were witnesses and participants in far more than the economic grind of the Gulf littoral or the bazaars of Isfahan, Shiraz and Kerman.

In order to find the place of the Company within this story, historians must look at the records that were left by the merchants who staffed the Persian factory. The chapters of this book explore important gaps in the current understanding of the Company's relationship with Persia using the East India Company Factory Records (IOR/G/29) as a basis. This archive has been underutilised by scholars for a number of reasons: the presence of other collections of the Company's archive, 'IOR/E/3 Correspondence with the East' in particular, and the availability of Dutch sources on the same period. The IOR/G/29 series covers the period from 1620 to 1822, though there are some significant gaps in this chronology and these dates do not correspond to specific events. The series is exceptionally rich in detail about the day-to-day business of the factory, important events and politics in Persia, the lives of those who lived and worked there, and copious data on the commodities, prices, weights and measures traded and used in Persia. The consultation books record not only the official business of the Company but also the personal lives of the factory staff, from their private sales of goods to the investigation of murders, suicide, drunkenness, elopements and fraud. The collection unfortunately has many chronological gaps, indeed, most of the seventeenth-century records are sadly lost, again limiting its potential usefulness to scholars of the Safavid period. As well as gaps in the chronology of IOR/G/29, there are other considerations; the most important of these is that the records are authored solely by Europeans. Although there are many non-Europeans working at the factory, they have very little obvious input into the collation of these records. There is, for example, little mention of the experience of the Indian soldiers and sailors who garrisoned the factory, nor of the Armenian linguists or Banian brokers. Usefully, they do contain a significant amount of detail on private events outside the purview of the Company hierarchy and demonstrate in some cases how the Company took an interest in its employees' welfare, whatever their background. It has to be also recognised that being official correspondence, the news related in these records represents the facts of events, or a version of them that would be most palatable to the Company's directors in Bombay or London. Considering this level of editorialisation one is forced to recognise that one is seeing the factory as 'a portrayal', either positive or negative depending on the ambitions, objectives or prejudice of the authors. This is no different from the Dutch archives, or the correspondence collections, however. Equally, there is nothing in these records that evokes the feelings or sentiments of those experiencing life in the Gulf factory, beyond an extremely limited impression that can be had from the use of certain language or phrases. In many ways, the lack of these personal reactions hides the true intention of the author, or the tenor of the event being recounted. As such, an amount of interpretation is required. To corroborate the evidence in this archive, as well as fill in gaps in the chronology, records from the IOR/P/341 series have been consulted. This second series is composed of the minutes of meetings held in Bombay, as well as discussions of letters and reports received there, including those from Persia. This provides us with a commentary on the correspondence sent and received from the Persian factory at a remove from the actual events, giving us a layered impression of the policies pursued by the Company at both a local level and that of the Bombay Presidency.

The period before 1722 has several useful sources which give context to the events during the period of this study and provide information about attitudes and events closer in time to those studies in the present work. These are mostly travelogues and personal accounts from European travellers, merchants, priests and diplomats from a variety of countries. After 1700, this is less the case, with fewer private accounts being written due to the increasingly poor and unstable nature of Persia at the time. The memoirs of men like John Fryer, Charles Lockyer and Alexander Hamilton,[22] all of whom worked in different capacities for the Company and conducted their own private trade, provide an insight into Indian Ocean trade, as well as comments concerning the governance of Indian and Persian states. Fryer's text includes descriptions of his travels through several Persian provinces, including the town of Bandar Abbas, while Hamilton describes sailing the Gulf and details the coastline. Other travelogues, such as those by Jonas Hanway, a merchant trading through Russia who visited the Northern provinces of Persia at the end of Nader Shah's reign, is contemporary with the events recounted here.[23]

Persian sources on this period rarely make any mention of the East India Company's business in Persia. This is a continuation of the 'aloofness' displayed by Persian chroniclers towards both Europeans and the merchant class more generally. The account of the Persian mission to Siam, documented in *The Ship of Sulaiman*, is an exception to this as the mission was carried to Thailand via India on a Company ship.[24] Hazin Lahiji, a famous poet and Persian émigré to India, devotes a few lines of his memoir recounting his journey to India to describing the Company's good treatment of him and the quality of their 'ships and packets'.[25] Persian records more generally are very little concerned with the comings and goings of the *Kullah-Pushan*,[26] with significant events, such as the Company's assistance at the battles around Hormuz, given little to no recognition. Iskandar Beg Munshi, the famous chronicler of Abbas I, devotes only a few brief sentences to the Company's involvement, most of which revolve around the English allegedly requesting protection from the Shah against Portuguese tyranny, rather than any sort of mutual agreement or partnership.[27] Chroniclers, especially official ones, are, of course, writing for a very particular and discerning audience, aiming to magnify the importance of those to whom the work is dedicated. It can therefore hardly be surprising that Iskandar Beg would not recount an equal partnership between his awe-inspiring ruler and patron and a band of European merchants, just as the chroniclers Mar'ashi Safavi and Astarabadi, when writing about Nader Shah's campaign in the Gulf, omit the Company's involvement totally.[28] In the same work, Safavi does mention that the Company has a responsibility to keep the Gulf ports free from piracy, so it is evident that the naval power of the Company was public knowledge among the literate Persian nobility.[29] The use of these works when looking at the Company in the Gulf is thus more interesting for what it does not say, rather than what it does. Persian language chronicles make limited mention of the Company's involvement in actions such as The Battle of Hormuz. However, the memoirs of state officials document this in some detail, and also the Persian court chronicles make tacit reference to the Company's contribution. The chronicles and memoirs as well as other contemporary records do not recognise the significant military relevance the Company projected. This lack of formal Persian sources, along with the large gaps in English material for this period has contributed to this era, as well as Persia itself, being neglected by scholars exploring the Company in this region.

The key document for the study of the Company and its place in Persian history is therefore the Company's English translation of the Persian *Farman* granted to the Company and then renewed multiple times between 1622 and 1747. The text of the *Farman* in the English sources is a gateway to understanding not just what the Company wanted from their relationship with the Persian state but also what the Persians expected in return and how the Persians themselves tried to divert the Company to their own purposes, whether in terms of trade, military assistance or the carrying of embassies. By considering the changing terms of the *Farman* as initiatives from both sides, rather than a list of European demands or Persian concessions, a better idea of Company–Persian interaction can be formed, which can then inform a dialogue on the nature of agreements between Asian and European powers and trading companies more broadly. The lack of copies of the Persian text of the *Farman* is symptomatic of a lack of Persian official sources for this time. The cities in which the Company did the majority of its business were sacked or burned by a series of invaders, occupiers and native forces from the Afghans and Baluchis to Nader Shah himself, making it difficult to imagine finding many sources referring to their presence there. Future research into this period will hopefully benefit from far greater and easier access to records and expertise in Iran itself.

Historical background

The Persian Gulf, or simply 'The Gulf', has served for millennia as a conduit for trade and cultural exchange.[30] The Gulf is around 990 kilometres long, from Kuwait and Iraq at the north-western end, and varies in width from 340 kilometres to 55 kilometres at its south-eastern extremity at the Straits of Hormuz between Iran and the Omani exclave of Musandam. From ancient times, the Gulf's geography made it important as a maritime route for spices, incense and other goods. This trade created the basis for numerous exchanges between peoples of many cultures and faiths travelling between the East and the West. In his introduction to *The Persian Gulf in History*, Lawrence Potter points to the Gulf as constituting 'a World of its own',[31] an insightful appreciation of the distinct sociocultural and economic features of this specific region, formed from its own unique geography, that drew in people and trade from as far away as the Iranian plateau, Mesopotamia, the Arabian Peninsula and the Indian subcontinent. The Persian Safavid Empire, to which the Gulf, at least in English eyes, nominally belonged, represented the second largest territorial empire in the Indian Ocean, after the Mughal Empire in India. Significantly, Persia was the source of a cultural tradition that spread from Istanbul to Samarkand in the form of language, poetry, music, calligraphy and architecture. In comparison to the other nations of the Indian Ocean basin, however, Persia was relatively poor in terms of precious metal, but produced a variety of important commodities with international relevance. Silk, wine, copper, carpets and textiles, dried fruits, nuts and drugs were all available in Persia and could be sold in an equally abundant range of markets, from the Arabian Peninsula and the Indian subcontinent to England, Amsterdam, Siam and Batavia. Persia also occupied a central position on several of the routes that made up the 'Silk Road', whether through the major caravan routes through Kerman and Tabriz or the maritime route in the Gulf, via Hormuz and Basra.

From the thirteenth century, the island of Hormuz, sitting at the narrow mouth of the Gulf's south-eastern end, functioned as a vital node in the trade of Eurasia. In 1296, the mainland-based Kingdom of Hormuz, which had previously occupied the area now known as Minab, was compelled by repeated harassment from the Mongols to move its capital to the island of Jarun, whereafter the island became synonymous with the name of the kingdom's former capital.[32] This move also took advantage of the decline of Kish, a more northerly island state that had controlled Gulf trade for the previous three centuries.[33] The islands maintained their independence from the large and powerful states of the Iranian plateau, becoming their own unique cultural and economic zone. Although Hormuz itself had no natural supply of fresh water, it could be supplied from the nearby island of Qeshm, which, while larger than Hormuz, was also much closer and more exposed to potential threats from the mainland. The three islands of Hormuz, Qeshm and Larak offered an opportunity for the merchant ships to shelter, resupply and ply their trade. The markets of Hormuz thus became a major emporium, where goods from Europe, Africa, India, Indonesia and China were exchanged, despite the severe limitations in the availability of arable land and fresh water. The Kingdom of Hormuz remained largely safe from external threats until the arrival of European naval power following the voyages of the famous Portuguese explorer Vasco da Gama in 1497. According to Couto and Loureiro, Hormuz became an obsession for Portuguese explorers and conquerors in the sixteenth century as they sought to control the intimate connection between the Gulf and the paths of trade in the Indian Ocean more widely. In 1507 the island was taken by the Portuguese and then permanently recaptured by them after a rebellion in 1515.[34] Despite the Portuguese occupation, Hormuz remained the key meeting point between the great empires of Asia, with the Gulf forming a porous border between the Ottoman, Safavid and Mughal Empires in the early modern period. In a wider sense, although less tangibly, the Gulf formed a frontier between these three Asian powers, where it was not only a nexus of trade but also acted as a borderland and meeting point of empires.

In 1616, the first English East India Company ship entered the Gulf and anchored off the Persian port of Jask where the Gulf of Oman joins the narrows of the Persian Gulf. The *James* carried a supply of woollen cloth, which the Company hoped would sell better in the cooler climate of the Iranian plateau than it had in India. In turn, the Company's merchants hoped to secure a cargo of Persian silk to sell back in Europe. The lure of Persian silk, along with the demand for hard-wearing and more durable woollen cloth, made the Safavid Empire particularly attractive to the Company as a place to do business. The voyage of the *James* proved modestly profitable and paved the way for a continuing trading relationship and the establishment of political connections between the Company and the Persian state. This trading relationship was the means through which they came to understand each other's mutual antipathy to the Portuguese. The Company's entrance into the Gulf took place in the latter years of the reign of Shah Abbas I (r. 1588–1629). This Shah reformed the Safavid Empire into a more coherent state after a lengthy period of war and unrest following the death of Shah Tahmasp I in 1576, who had ruled for fifty-two years. During his reign, Abbas I successfully fought off internal rivals, as well as scoring significant victories against the Uzbeks and Ottomans, the two great territorial rivals of the Safavids, opening an opportunity to secure the Gulf Coast and Hormuz from the Portuguese, a campaign in which he was to solicit directly the help of the East India Company. In 1622, according to Italian traveller Pietro Della Valle writing to his friend Mario Schipano, Abbas I was aggrieved at what he perceived as the aggressive territorial growth of the Portuguese within his empire.[35] According to Della Valle, the Shah moved against the Portuguese carefully and was quick to befriend the English in 1617 after reports reached him of these newcomers with their large, powerful ships.³⁶ As we shall see, this imperial rivalry between Persia and Portugal would be the ideal opportunity for the English to make their entry into the politics of the region.

On 14 December 1621, a fleet of English ships, commanded by Richard Blythe and John Weddell, arrived off the port of Jask, close to the mouth of the Gulf, where the Company had first traded with Persia in 1616. The fleet had been dispatched from Surat in Western India. It is not immediately clear whether the captains of the Company's ships were ordered to make war on the Portuguese on their arrival at Surat, but, by the time they arrived at Jask, they had already captured two small Portuguese ships.³⁷ The Company's ships were not just fitted for war as evidenced by the presence of merchants and Factors on board. Unfortunately, all but one of these men died, during the voyage between Surat and the Gulf.³⁸ It appears clear that the Company's ships were capable of carrying out significant military action while also providing merchants with transportation in order to further the Company's commercial aims. The arrival of the Company's fleet, coupled with its self-evident successfully aggressive stance against the Portuguese, was especially fortuitous for Abbas I of Persia, who was himself planning to strike a blow against the Portuguese.

The Shah had dispatched his trusted Armenian-Georgian General, Imam Qoli Khan, to administer the southern provinces of the Safavid Empire. Imam Qoli Khan used his position to undermine the Portuguese and, eventually, at the Shah's urging, to make common cause with the East India Company to evict the Portuguese from Hormuz entirely shortly after the battle on 22 April 1622. Gaining the cooperation of the Company was absolutely necessary for this campaign as the Persians lacked any fleet with which they could challenge the Portuguese ships moored around the island. The Company had become embroiled in the campaign due to an approach by Shah Abbas I, who was increasingly frustrated by Portuguese attempts to restrict the activity and profitability of Persian merchants in the Gulf.³⁹ It is not clear exactly when and where the negotiation for the campaign took place, though the most likely explanation is that the Company merchants dispatched to Isfahan, who were present there throughout 1621, negotiated the terms with the Shah before the arrival of the Company's trading fleet. It has been argued by various scholars, such as Niels Steensgaard and Willem Floor,⁴⁰ that the English were threatened with being cut out of the lucrative Persian silk trade were they not to comply with the Persians' request for military assistance. While this threat was no doubt credible, the Company's primary motivation for involving itself so deeply with the Persians was instead the reward of a set of wide-ranging privileges.

The Company was offered the highly lucrative status as joint revenue collectors for Hormuz, though this was later changed to Bandar Abbas when it became the major entrepôt on the South Coast of Persia. The *Farman* also rendered the Company exempt from paying customs and road tolls, *rahdari*, throughout the Safavid Empire. In addition, the Persians agreed to share half of whatever was captured on Hormuz should the island fall. The English do not seem to have hesitated in their acceptance of this offer; indeed, both fleet commanders and the Company's establishment at Surat all seem to have been keen to accept the articles in the *Farman* offered by the Shah.[41] Despite the willingness of the Company's officials to engage in this enterprise, the sailors of the fleet proved much more reticent, requiring a considerable amount of cajoling and the promise of extra pay before they acceded to take part.[42]

A letter from the Commanders of the fleet to the Company's Factors in Isfahan, dated 16 March 1622, outlines how the English ships were deployed and the role the men played in the wider siege.[43] This letter, along with others sent and received by the fleet commanders, the Company's representative in Persia and the council in Surat, makes up the primary basis for our knowledge of the events around the siege.[44] The most obvious use for the English ships was as a counter to the Portuguese fleet moored under the guns of the fortress. The letter describes how the English commanders made use of pinnaces, small sailing ships that could function either as ship's boats or as independent craft, as well as armed barges to attack the Portuguese in port. The attack resulted in the loss of a barge with two men; however, in return the Portuguese Vice Admiral's ship was holed below the waterline and subsequently capsized. The Portuguese also lost their Rear Admiral's ship when it was set ablaze and their Admiral's flagship was set on fire before being captured by the Company fleet. The captured Portuguese vessels were towed, beached and relieved of their ordnance and shot. This fleet action was followed up by a further English attack with a fire ship, which again shows the determination of the two sides to cause as much damage as possible to one another. The Commanders of the fleet reported that the Portuguese losses up until 16 March included *Tota los Sanctos, Nuestra Senora de Victoria, Sancto Pedro, Sancto Martino, Sancto Antonio and Sancto Francisco*, along with a galley and two frigates. Out of these ships, the report states that the *Tota los Sanctos* was a galleon of 1,200–1,400 tonnes with forty-five guns which had been built by the Portuguese in Goa.[45]

Meanwhile, on the island of Hormuz itself, the English set about landing eight pieces of iron artillery on the beach, presumably to keep the Portuguese occupied while the Persians dug six mines under the castle walls. The first of these was detonated on Sunday 17 April and created a practicable breach in the defences, but the Persians, led by Shah Qoli Beg, were unable, despite repeated attacks, to make good on it.[46] The second mine to be detonated was charged with powder from the English ships and lit by Thomas Barker, one of the East India Company's Factors.[47] This second mine again breached the wall, though the Persians failed to attack, leaving time for the garrison to recover.[48] Sadly for Thomas Barker, he did not survive the detonation of the mine.[49]

With no hope of support from their station in Goa, their fleet battered, burned and sunk in front of their walls, the Portuguese were now flushed from the city with women and children in tow, were cornered on a small spit of land on an island with no natural water supply.[50] The geography meant that with their naval protection gone all the English ships had to do was to stand off and pulverise the port while the Persians attempted to break into the fortification. The Portuguese garrison commander Rui Freire de Andrade decided to make terms with the Company hoping for better treatment by Christians rather than risk a massacre at the hands of the Persians. Terms were reached and on 22 April 1622 the Portuguese flag was lowered, marking an end to over 100 years of their occupancy of Hormuz. The remnant of the defending Portuguese garrison and population, in total some three thousand men, women and children, were soon ferried to Muscat, where the Portuguese had built another garrison and fortress.[51] The events at Hormuz and subsequent military clashes between the English and Portuguese in the Gulf and Indian Ocean, had they occurred in the Bay of Biscay, would have precipitated all-out war between the two countries. Technically, there was no division between the Habsburg possessions in Europe and the *Estado da India*, both being the property of the Portuguese/Habsburg patrimony of Philip III of Spain. Thus, the seizure of Hormuz and sinking of Portuguese ships was an act of war against the Portuguese Crown itself. After news of the victory of the fleet at Hormuz reached London, the Company's Court of Directors found themselves in a difficult position, not only because of Portuguese political pressure on the English Crown but also because of pressure from the Crown itself.[52] There is no evidence that the Company had discussed the Hormuz enterprise with the Duke of Buckingham, in his position as Lord High Admiral in advance,[53] and the initiative was a local decision made without the knowledge of the Company Board in London. What was to follow circumstantially demonstrates that the Crown and Admiralty were entirely unaware of the exploit and, as we shall see, lost no time in exacting a price from the Company. As indicated above, attacking and overcoming a long-established outpost possession of the most powerful nation in the Western world was never going to be without repercussions, and the news of their loss reached the Spanish in Madrid just before Christmas of 1622.⁵⁴ The English Ambassador Digby was summoned before the court and with no explanation to give he referred back to the court of King James I and told the Spanish that the Company had acted under compulsion from the Persian ruler.⁵⁵ Ordinarily this would not have sufficed and it is likely that hostilities would have ensued, but for a fortunate coincidence.

The coincidence was that King James' son Charles (later Charles I) was in Spain to woo the Spanish princess, Infanta Maria Anna, and the need for this good, Catholic dynastic match to go well smothered the immediate wrath of the Habsburgs.⁵⁶ The collapse of this match removed the necessity for the court of James I to have to resolve the Hormuz matter and the Spanish ordered their forces in Goa to retake the island. However, the Portuguese were so weakened by the earlier clash of arms, they could only harass trade for a while. On hearing of the Company's victory at Hormuz, it became clear that James I of England strongly disapproved of the expedition, seeing it as putting peace with the Spanish at risk and jeopardising the match of their Infanta with his first son and heir. Not only this, but the Company's Board did not feel obliged to share their spoils either with the Crown or with the Admiralty, and the matter slid into a legal challenge until Buckingham (the King's favourite) presented the Company's representatives with the ultimatum that its ships would be the subject of a sequester for war against the Spanish were their demands not met.⁵⁷ A sum of £10,000 was settled on Buckingham and a similar amount for King James to close the matter. This wrangling and the time it took to conclude indicates the Company, not for the last time, appears to have acted on its own initiative in conducting an offensive aimed at securing major trade advantages for themselves.

According to the Company's correspondence, the Persians were likewise not entirely honest in their division of the spoils and plunder from the city. During the battle the small proceeds from the city had been shared but during the siege the main wealth had been moved to the fortification, and the Persians in their thousands took this for themselves without sharing. Moreover, the captured ships and their materiel were held back by the Persians and the English excluded from the island. To compound this, the Company had to pick up the full costs of their part in the campaign lasting three months and was given charges for provisioning their ships for their own use and for the transportation of the Portuguese garrison.⁵⁸ This lack of financial success was offset over the longer term by the benefits gained from the grant of the much coveted *Farman* which had been the key objective in the campaign in any case. Furthermore, the Company, if only belatedly, had engaged the Admiralty and Crown in their affairs and these were now aware of the financial benefits the Company could bring without the need for any risky investment. As for the Portuguese, they were to be subject to harassment by both VOC and Company ships, either separately or in concert with one another, for some time thereafter, indeed the VOC made it a particular mission to capture Portuguese settlements. The Dutch, as we shall see, capitalised on the joint English and Persian success; as immediately as news could travel at that time, they despatched forces with equal speed.

The *Farman* of Abbas I

The *Farman* forms an important part of the Company's history in Persia, holding an important place within the historiography of the relationship between the Safavids and the English. A *Farman* was a royal decree from an Islamic ruler, conferring certain rights upon an individual, community or, in this case, the Company. Previously, the English had encountered a similar system of decrees in their trade with the Ottoman Empire, where a set of 'Capitulations' were passed onto the Company by the Sultan in a document called an '*Ahdnameh*'.[59] The English had been given an *Ahdnameh* by the Ottomans in 1580,[60] while in 1618 a *Farman* was granted by the ruler of San'a in Yemen, establishing the Company in the coffee trade.[61] The Company was granted limited privileges by various regional governors in the Mughal Empire, though any grant for the whole empire was not forthcoming until 1716.[62] The *Farman* was the agreed reward directly from the Shah to the Company for their successful naval assistance in prosecuting the siege of Hormuz against the Portuguese. The *Farman* in its various iterations appears again and again in the Company's records and archives, whether as a guarantee of its rights and privileges, as a cover for its ill behaviour or as proof of its probity and long relationship to the Safavid state.[63]

Before the Company's Persian *Farman*, a treaty had already been agreed between Abbas I and the Company. This treaty, made between the Shah and Edward Monnox in 1621, was somewhat grand in its scope and concerned the military targets of the campaign. The major terms of the treaty concerned the division of the spoils of the city of Hormuz should it be taken, 'Then by the Power of God the Country of Jeroone [Hormuz] shall be possessed by the Subjects of His Majestie of Persia whatsoever monnies, Goods, treasures &c, shall bee taken and surprized from the city, castle, shipps, howses the one moyety shall bee ours and the other the English Companys.'[64] The Shah also requested that any Portuguese possessions in India that were taken be divided between himself and the Company, despite how unlikely any such acquisitions might be.[65] It is in this treaty that the Company was first granted a share of the customs at Hormuz. The agreements between the Company and the Shah for the division of spoils and the sharing of customs would lay the foundation for the Company's interaction with Persia and set the tone of the future relationship. Ferrier notes that the treaty was not the first agreement made between the Persians and the English, showing copies of some of the previous articles agreed between the Persians and both the East India Company and the Russian Company.[66] Ferrier's exploration of these agreements and the *Farman* is limited by the source material available. However, the records from the Company's consultations and letters give details about all the subsequent iterations of the *Farman* until the death of Nader Shah in 1747.

After the capture of the island, the treaty was replaced by the promised *Farman*, in which the relationship between the Company and the Shah was formalised in much more specific ways. According to the Shah Abbas' *Farman*, the Company was to assist in the administration of customs and tolls at Bandar Abbas for a share of those same revenues, at first negotiated as half the total take, but subsequently reduced to 1,000 toman, but even this was rarely realised.[67] In the 1720s and 1730s the Afghan and then resurgent Persian authorities found it necessary to renegotiate with the Company at Bandar Abbas from the original positions that had been laid down in the *Farman* issued by Shah Abbas and its subsequent renewals under Shah Safi I and Shah Soltan Husayn. These negotiations and the way in which the *Farman* was used by both sides across this period make it a living agreement referred back to and renegotiated by both parties on multiple occasions.[68]

The *Farman* of Abbas I included the right for English merchants to trade in silk throughout Persia free of customs charges and *rahdari*.[69] This right was most important to the English at the time of the treaty as it allowed them to purchase and transport the valuable silk produce of Gilan and Mazandaran on the Caspian littoral in the North of Persia down via Qazvin, Isfahan and Shiraz to Bandar Abbas for shipment. This put them in an advantageous position when compared to their Dutch rivals, whose own agreement with the Safavid Crown required for them to buy fixed quantities of silk at fixed prices.[70] The English therefore gained materially over the long term, though not as much as they had expected initially, due to the costs of the campaign. More importantly they had achieved their legitimacy through being useful in the eyes of Abbas I and securing his interests, the patronage which would last until the end of the dynasty and beyond. Abbas I had similarly benefitted by increasing demand and competition for silk in the hope of generating greater revenue from its production, transportation and sale.

The treaty and *Farman* of Abbas I were to become the beginning of a long thread of continuity within the Company's time in Persia, with renewals of the Company's privileges becoming a feature of the accession of new rulers. These new iterations of the agreement are equally vital to our understanding of the Company's place and influence in Persia, though they too have received relatively little scholarly attention until now. In the India Office Records (IOR/G/29), there are translations of the *Farman* granted between *Shavval* 1036AH and *Muharram* 1036AH (1627–9 AD) by Shah Safi I; the renewal given by Shah Soltan Husayn in *Shavval* 1108AH (1697–8 AD), and finally those grants made by Shah Tahmasp II and Nader Shah throughout the 1730s and 1740s. After the Afghan invasion, the Company was also granted all its former privileges by the new regime with no negotiation necessary.[71] The text of these *Farmans* alters relatively little; however, the amendments that are made are indicative of important changes and trends in the Company's interests and those of the Persian government. When considering the importance of the Company to the Persian state one should note that edicts like the *Farman* normally ended with the death of the granting ruler. That the Company's *Farman* existed for over 100 years is therefore highly significant.

The renewal granted by Shah Safi I is documented and recorded in the consultations as an addendum to the original *Farman* from Abbas I, Shah Safi's direct predecessor.[72] Shah Safi's *Farman*, while granting all the previous rights enjoyed by the Company, adds a list of new ones. The Company was given ownership of their factory at Bandar Abbas, rather than only having the right to reside in the town. Another issue of ownership addressed in the *Farman* is the return of the effects of a deceased Company merchant to Bandar Abbas by the Khan of Lar.[73] This not only shows that the Company was becoming settled in Persia on a permanent footing but also shows that the Shah was sensitive to the Company's anxiety about the status of their property in his kingdom. This is again addressed by an undertaking from the Shah to right any wrongs done to the Company through remuneration for goods lost or the retrieval of them, as well as a promise to punish anyone attempting to defraud the Company.[74] Shah Safi, unlike Shah Abbas, also removed all *Rahdari* from the Company, whereas previously the rate for these duties had only been reduced, though silk was specifically exempt. The *Farman* of Safi I retained previous agreements while adding permission for the Company's servants to only be prosecuted or punished according to English rather than Persian law.

Following the renewal of the *Farman* by Shah Safi I (r. 1629–42) there were no documented renewals throughout the reigns of Abbas II (r. 1642–66) and

Suleiman I (r. 1666–94). However, when Shah Soltan Husayn (r. 1694–1722) renewed the *Farman* in 1697, many of the privileges remained the same but there were added provisions for more social concerns, such as the grant that any child of an Englishman and a local woman would be given over to the care of the English.[75] These concerns reflect how settled the Company had become and that there were clearly pastoral issues that needed addressing as well as those of trade.

Farman of Shah Soltan Husayn 1697

1. Rogum for the Company's house in Shiraz wherein it is ordered that no officers in Shiraz do presume to meddle with the said house or give the English the least trouble about it but continue in the quiet possession of it.[76]
2. A rogum ordering all officers, rhadars etc. that whenever a caphila belonging to the English goes from Spahaun to Gombroon in case there is any danger in the road from rogues that the said officers shall supply the English or their servants with guards if they desire it and not suffer any damage to happen either to their goods or persons.
3. A rogum ordering the English shall have liberty to export twelve horses annually and that in case they send less one year they may transport so many more the next.
4. A rogum ordering the Vizier of Shiraz to permit the English to make drink and export what quantity of wine they please and notwithstanding among the Musselmen it is not allowed yet the English are at full liberty to do it.
5. A rogum ordering that the English are free of Rhaddarage all over the Kingdom mentioned as a present to the Chief of Isfahan.
6. A rogum ordering that all goods belonging to the English that come to Spahaun are free of *Sad-yeck and Havoy*[77] and they may bring them into their house and disperse of them without the least molestation.
7. A copy of a rogum ordering the English twelve jareebs of ground in what part of Gombroon they please and that no officers presume to molest or hinder them on this score.
8. A rogum ordering all governors, viziers, *Darughas*[78] and other officials all over the dominions of Persia for this reason that there is a perfect harmony between the King of England and me and the English are my Guest and whenever they have business with the aforesaid officers that they do not refuse but do them justice and not ask any the least gratuity for such services of them.

9. A rogum ordering the *Shahbandar* and his officers to treat the English and merchants civilly that they may promote and increase the trade of Gombroon and I have likewise ordered another *Shahbandar* and directed him to do as the English desire and the English may be assured of my favour and make the merchants content that they shall likewise receive the same and that afterwards nobody shall treat them ill that they may trade and make the port flourish.
10. A rogum ordering the English their house in Spahaun and that the *Meerob* (Amir-i Ab) or Head of the Waterways does not prevent the water coming to their garden.
11. A rogum ordering that nobody presume to force the Chief or his servants to sell goods to them and if the English Chief etc. sell any goods that he or they shall receive ready money for them and if any presume to act contrary to this order, they shall be severely punished.
12. A rogum ordering that one house belonging to the Linguist be free of the *Jizya*[79] and all duties and assessments.
13. A rogum ordering that six banians and a broker be free of *Jizya* and all Duty and assessments.
14. A rogum ordering that the English be treated with respect all over the dominions and that no Khans or officers presume to use any the least force nor ask anything from them or injure them on any account or manner whatever, but assist them about their affairs.
15. A rogum ordering that whereas the English Banians in Gombroon and Spahaun have nothing of their own and what is in their hands belongs to the Company, nobody presume to force or take anything from them and if any person owes them anything he shall pay it back again.
16. A rogum ordering that the English are permitted to one hundred loads of silk in Gilan at the current price free of all duties whatever.
17. A rogum ordering that if the English servants commit any faults the governor or *Darughah* of such place those crimes are committed shall send them to the English to be punished and not ask anything at all of them.
18. A rogum ordering that the English are permitted to buy 2,000 maunds Kandahar of hing free of all duties (added in 1730).
19. A copy of a rogum attested by the Sheikh-ol-Eslam ordering that the English are free of customs and all manner of duties whatever.

Through the *Farman* the Company was entitled to half the customs duty for goods landed at Bandar Abbas; however, the Persians never consistently rendered what was owed. The Company often demanded payment of their share including demands for payment of arrears.[80] We will see later this was only partially successful, with the Company instead deriving revenue from a system of consulage (a duty paid by merchants for the Company's protection of their goods while abroad). The main factor where this version of the *Farman* is different, however, is the addition of clauses for the production and exportation of wine and freedom to buy and export Kerman wool. Significantly by 1680 silk is no longer listed separately by the Company, though the provision for its duty-free purchase and transportation persists within the text of the *Farman*.[81] The continued presence of the silk privileges is no longer demonstrative of the Company's aspirations, so therefore it must be evidence of Persian attempts to stimulate the trade. Throughout the seventeenth century, we see the repeated use of contracts as a formalisation of the Company's trade directly with the Shah, these often required a set quantity of English cloth, tin and silver to be presented annually in exchange for an agreed quantity of silk. As Ferrier notes, these contracts were almost never upheld, either one side or the other, or indeed both, failing to provide the amount or quality of goods that had been promised.[82] Later iterations of the *Farman* do away with these contracts, which instead provide for the general conditions of English trade, particularly the continued freedom from various customs and charges. By disposing of the contracts, both parties must have recognised the unnecessary tension they caused, leading to a more comfortable system of general privileges to smooth the way for Company commerce, while always maintaining the potential for a later return to the silk market.

The last list of privileges received by the Company comes from 1736, when Nader Shah had taken over effective control of the Persian Empire. Unlike his predecessors, Nader Shah was unwilling to allow the Company to operate as it had done for the previous century, so he attempted through a variety of means to bend the Company to his will. He did this through a variety of measures, the most notable of which was his complete withdrawal of the *Farman* in its entirety, which he then promised to reinstate only if the Company's Factors did as he wished. Nader Shah clearly saw uses for the Company in his new regime and tried to keep them pliant either through threats or the promise of his friendship. The following quote is taken from the renewal of the Company's *Farman* granted by Tahmasp II in 1736:

> And desired that I would renew the same, I that am King of Persia do order in consideration of the great service that the English have done and their friendship with me is entire and without blemish.[83]

Regardless of this cordial tone, this renewal was not all it seemed, as extra stipulations were added concerning the sale of goods, the production of which had been made a royal monopoly. Unlike the beneficent Tahmasp II, Nader Shah's approach during his own direct reign was far less gentle. Indeed, Nader Shah used the granting of the Company's individual privileges (*raqam*, rendered in English as Rogum[84]) as a means of controlling the Company and gaining tactical military support and supplies from Company ships. By manipulating the Company through the *Farman*, adding or removing individual *rogums*, Nader Shah was demonstrating the importance of these privileges to the Company. Reciprocally this indicates how careful the Company was to try and keep naval support at arm's length to trade and how important projecting naval power was to the Shah. Ogborn has suggested that the use of the written word was a significant tool in the European mastery of Asia, but as Nader Shah's tactical use of the *Farman* demonstrates, this was evidently a double-edged sword.[85]

The *Farman* and its terms are a continual feature in the events of the period, often providing the justification or impetus for the actions of the Company's Factors and Agents in the Gulf. It should not be overlooked, however, that the *Farman* was a Persian document, granted to the Company, rather than a mutual treaty, and that its clauses dictate the behaviour of the Company and its interaction with the Persian state. The terms of the *Farman* show that the Persians, whether the Shah or local officials, were dictating the relationship with the Company, while the Company itself could only make requests on the privileges granted to it. Despite this the *Farman* provided the Company with the stability to operate over a huge territory profitably with only a handful of merchants and agents, while maintaining relationships with the third most powerful regime in the region. The Company tried and failed to gain similar agreements in India, China and Japan until the Company's *Farman* with the Mughal Empire in 1717. The Company's relationship with Persia, unlike with the Mughals, was maintained through the person of the Shah as enshrined in the Company's *Farman*. This meant that the Company had a direct link to the highest authority in Persia. In Mughal India, China and Japan, no such high-level connection could be procured, with either regional terms being negotiated or none at all.[86] The Company was able through the *Farman* to access all the potential markets, goods and wealth of Persia and while this may not have been at the same scale as the fabulous riches of India, it was nonetheless politically and economically attractive and expedient.

The eighteenth century

The eighteenth century, whether long or short, was a period of definitive change for the Company and for Persia. Britain's role in the world changed dramatically, taking centre stage as the first global superpower. The Dutch had come under constant and ever-increasing pressure on the European mainland from Louis XIV of France, with support from the Stuart Kings Charles II and then James II. While the French and their allies were never able to deal a decisive blow, the pressure took its toll on the economic and military strength of the Dutch Republic. William's accession to the thrones of England, Ireland and Scotland through the Glorious Revolution of 1688 brought some succour to the Dutch by making a friend of a former foe, yet this was not sufficient to reinvigorate the Republic to its former glory. Indeed, despite William's constant subordination of his new kingdom's resources to Dutch interests, the Republic's gains were modest. On the other hand, England and Scotland were united by the Act of Union of 1707, Ireland was pacified by the Treaty of Limerick in 1691 and France's navy was defeated at Barfleur the following year. This left Britain secure from French invasion, politically unified, at least ostensibly, and in possession of a burgeoning empire in North America. The Company throughout this time had suffered from the political and financial instability in England and Europe, as well as firm competition from the Dutch, but by 1700, their fortunes had rapidly been buoyed up by relative economic and political prosperity at home. The Company received a renewed Charter in 1693 from King William and Queen Mary, further boosting confidence in the Company and its trade for the coming century.

One of the major changes that increased the importance of Persia in the Company's trade came with the stipulation in the Company's charter of 1693 that it was now positively required to export £100,000 of English goods annually, particularly woollen cloth. This meant that Persia, one of the few areas where this English cloth was in demand, was of renewed interest to the Company, not only as an area of commercial growth but now also as an outlet for its politically mandated cloth exports. Meanwhile, as we have seen, the Company received a renewal of its *Farman* from Shah Soltan Husayn in 1697, further precipitating the Company's renewed activity there. Elsewhere, the Company's gaze had shifted westwards from the Spice Islands, firmly under Dutch control, to the Coromandel Coast of India, where cotton cloth, widely in demand throughout both Europe and Asia, was produced. The early eighteenth century also saw a major change in the Company's fortunes with the amalgamation of the 'New' and 'Old' East India Companies in 1708. This brought an end to competition within London itself and generated a huge increase in the Company's profitability. The Company's servants could seemingly afford to look forward with optimism on its second century.

The Safavid Empire, on the other hand, suffered from continued economic difficulty caused by the expatriation of bullion, civil unrest and a series of less than competent rulers. In the decades from 1700 to 1750, with which this book is concerned, the Safavid Empire ceased to be the dynamic state that Abbas I had formed and ruled. The final collapse of the Safavid Empire was the result of the rapid expansion of a dispute between a local governor and Afghan tribes into a full-blown rebellion. What followed was a series of civil struggles between the Afghan occupiers, Safavid loyalists and other foreign and domestic interests. The Ottomans and Russians both occupied Persian provinces, while Baluchi raiders attacked towns and settlements along the Gulf littoral, including Bandar Abbas. The Sultanate of Muscat, which had become a major power after the Yarubid Dynasty expelled the Portuguese from Oman in 1650 and then went on to capture former Portuguese possessions in East Africa, had become a significant naval power in the Gulf. It would take until 1729 for a Safavid claimant to be restored to the throne. Tahmasp II (r. 1729–32) and his infant son, Abbas III (b.1732, d.1740) were under the sway of Tahmasp's leading general, Tahmasp Qoli Beg, who is better known by his regnal title, Nader Shah. He dispensed with the fiction of Safavid rule in 1736 and assumed the throne until his murder in 1747.

Nader Shah's reign (1736–47) represents the most dynamic period in the Anglo-Persian relationship since 1622 and was built upon the recognition of the Company's demonstrated potential as a military partner and a means by which Persian commerce and diplomacy could be transacted and stimulated. Nader Shah took advantage of civil unrest in Oman to launch an invasion of the Arab Shore (the area facing Iran across the Gulf), briefly capturing the region before an insurrection by the Al-Busaid clan pushed the Persians out again in 1749. The Omanis would maintain themselves as a major power in the Gulf well into the nineteenth century, until the British abolition of the slave trade began to undermine their lucrative transportation of East African slaves to the Gulf region and Persia. Indeed, by this point, British nominal control of maritime affairs in the region was fait accompli and has long been used as an example of the concept of 'informal empire'.

It has long been considered that the first half of the eighteenth century was a period of relatively little importance in understanding the history of the

Company. John Keay asserts that the period between 1710 and 1740, with the exception of the receipt of the Mughal *Farman* from Farrukhsiyar in 1716, was 'a glassy wave of unruffled tideway [which] invites no frantic recourse to the records'. Yet these decades are only fallow when viewed from the perspective of India, and even then with significant caveats, where trade continued, though little else of consequence seems to have occurred. In other parts of the world the Company inhabited, a series of military and trading defeats – such as at Bantam, where the Company lost its trading rights after the area was taken by the Dutch in 1683; at Mergui, where Thai forces defeated two Company expeditions; and not to mention the embarrassing events of Child's War in India – forced upon it a period of retrenchment rather than an aggressive policy of expansion. During this same period, Persia was anything but 'unruffled'. Instead, the Company had to carefully manoeuvre through significant political changes, foreign invasions and regime change to maintain its standing in Persia and the Gulf. Why then, given such complexity and political risk, did the Company expend time, effort and funds on maintaining a presence there? This is one of the key questions this book will attempt to answer, one that has been long overlooked due to the almost exclusive interest of scholars on events in India.

The chapters of this book will show the complex story of how and why the Company maintained its presence in Persia; from the commercial concerns engendered by the need to sell large quantities of cloth, to the day-to-day struggles and uncertainties attached to serving in Bandar Abbas. The constant fears of losing the *Farman* led the Company's servants to take extraordinary risks in order to maintain their rights and privileges, engaging in open warfare with Arab pirates and selling fully armed and equipped ships to a nascent Persian navy. The Company's servants negotiated the complex social etiquette of their host culture, becoming part of the broad networks of Persian courtly sociability and adopting styles of address, gift-giving and consumption. The Company, both in Persia and elsewhere, relied upon the cooperation of non-European workers and employees, who were paid lavishly in coin and in kind for their services; the stories of these individuals have remained particularly opaque, even while historians have come to appreciate their almost complete ubiquity. By exploring the Persian factory in detail, this book will open up fresh avenues of research and a new appreciation for the Company's presence far from London, Bombay or Calcutta, while also shining a clearer light on Persia's place in the history of the Company and the Indian Ocean.

Figure 2 Gamron 1710 (Bandar Abbas). Von Peter Schenk, Amsterdam 1710. Photo by Historic Maps/ullstein bild via Getty Images.

1

Life in the Company's Persian factory

Histories of the East India Company tend to overlook the harsh conditions and social difficulties experienced by the Company's servants. However, there is a wealth of detail available through the factory's records which concern the lived experience of the Company's servants, whether it takes the form of descriptions of the town of Bandar Abbas and the factory or accounts of personal disagreements. The importance of these facets of human experience has yet to be fully integrated into the history of the Company or other institutions. The factory was a small community, composed of a variety of different ethnicities including Hindu and Muslim Indians, Eurasians, Persians, Arabs, Armenians and Englishmen.[1] Despite being largely administrative and official in scope, the letters and consultations written for the Gulf Factory also contain very interesting insights into the personal lives of the men serving in the Company's factory. These include not only their commercial transactions and business but also the process by which their wills were executed and their estates disbursed, their marriages, liaisons and disagreements. By studying these issues in the small Company community in Persia, it is possible to build up an appreciation of the attitudes and perceptions concerning sexuality, interracial marriage and legal jurisdiction in the wider 'Company-State' growing in India and beyond. As Stern has argued successfully, the Company modelled its cities in India on an idealised vision of successful plantations or colonies.[2] This was all well and good where the Company was founding new settlements or had reasonably unfettered control over the territory in question, but this simply could not be the case in a place like Bandar Abbas where neither of these were true. This chapter will therefore consider some of the challenges faced by the Persian factories and the efforts made both centrally and locally to overcome them.

Bandar Abbas never comes out as the ideal place to find oneself in the service of the Company.

A sailors adage of the time had it that *only an inch of deal stands between Gombroon and Hell*. 'You cannot get excited about Gombroon', wrote James Douglas, the Bombay Historian.³

This small but significant corner of the Indian Ocean's trade, then, was not the destination many of the young men in the Company's service would have hoped to be posted to. It had a significant saving grace in being a major point of transhipment, giving greater opportunities for the transaction of private trade, should one survive. Indeed, the descriptions of the town and its environs were far from complimentary, even when one takes into account contemporary views of Bombay, Madras and Calcutta.⁴ Despite this, the Company felt it worthwhile and necessary to deploy resources and personnel to keep a presence in the town in order to maintain its ongoing business in Persia.

Willem Floor has described the Gulf region as 'hot, humid and unpleasant … while winters were mild, although at times cold enough to require warm clothes'.⁵ Floor also notes the miniscule average rainfall and limited arable zone in the port's hinterland which was available and suitable to support the local population. The monsoon winds which were so integral to the importance of the Gulf as a centre of trade and exchange, while providing some relief from the oppressive weather, equally held their own dangers. Often these winds blew up into gales which rendered many of the ports and roadsteads on both the north and south littorals unsafe as docks and berths, especially for the small local boats used for ferrying goods to shore from ocean-going ships. The lack of any shelter for either ocean-going ships or local boats made the basic task of bringing cargo ashore hazardous at best due to the unpredictable strength of the prevailing winds.

Bandar Abbas, which lies on the northern coast, has the double advantages of being one of the safer, more sheltered ports in the area and had access to sources of fresh water. The port faced southward towards the islands of Qeshm and Hormuz, the two linchpins of trade and shipping in that part of the Gulf, which also sheltered the town from the worst of the wind from the mouth of Gulf to the Southeast. Qeshm offered a rare source of fresh water, an anchorage at Basaidu, at its north-western extremity and a beach at Laft suitable for the vital task of careening, the process of beaching a ship deliberately to clean the hull. (This is now likely part of the Hara Protected Area of mangrove forests.) Hormuz, though much reduced in importance after 1622, still retained a garrison and fortress equipped with heavy artillery to protect the entrance to the sheltered anchorages between the mainland, Qeshm, Hormuz and Larak, though trade now flowed directly onto the mainland through Bandar Abbas. The presence of Europeans at Bandar Abbas was a mark of the transition in importance from the island of Hormuz to the mainland port city, as the European Companies represented a major export market for Persian goods. In addition to its favourable geographical location, other positive factors, according to Cornelis le Bruyn, a Dutch traveller and artist, included that Bandar Abbas was blessed with an abundance of *gamberi*, a variety of prawns or crayfish, plenty of date palms which, in addition to fruit, provided a staple building material. Le Bruyn also described the architectural features of *badgir*, a wind catcher providing a natural cooling system for houses and public buildings.[6] In order to avoid the hottest parts of the day, local people were in the habit of taking a *siesta* in the heat of the afternoon, then carrying on their business in the relative cool of the evening.[7]

Prior to departing Bandar Abbas, Le Bruyn took note of the large European graveyard 'filled with lofty tombs and covered domes'.[8] He stated that the reader should not be surprised by the great number of graves blaming 'unhealthy air', 'excessive heats' and 'burning fevers, which are there more common than in any other place, and frequently prove fatal in the space of twenty-four hours'.[9] Le Bruyn's account supports other reports concerning Bandar Abbas, characterising the port and its environs as deadly due to heat and disease, this before even mentioning the equally unhealthy winter damp, or the 'unwholesome' water. Whether it was Winter or Summer, Bandar Abbas and the wider Gulf appeared to have something unpleasant to offer merchants and travellers. Throughout the records of the East India Company in Persia there are instances where the Company's servants complained about the heat and bad water, as well as the infrequent but heavy rains which made any work impossible, the high winds that threatened to destroy ships while tearing apart the small local craft used to shuttle goods between the sea-going ships in the road and the port itself. If all of this were not enough, there is a record of a plague of locusts in 1738 and an earthquake in 1747.[10] Bandar Abbas' punishing environment ranked above the Company's other factories in terms of dangers, worse even than the infamous Bencoolen in Sumatra, a port built on a fetid disease-ridden swamp, or the tiny, mid-Atlantic island of St. Helena. Both of these other settlements were renowned for high rates of mortality and emotional hardships rarely falling short of misery. Appreciating these physical difficulties and the anxieties which accompanied them makes it easier to understand how particular events unfolded, or gives fresh insight into individuals and their decisions.

In the descriptions of the port and town at Bandar Abbas, one of the recurrent themes is the ever-present reality of disease. Bandar Abbas had a deserved reputation as regards its lethal effects upon the health of those whose misfortune it was to be posted there. Tim Blanning describes the relationship between the people of seventeenth- and eighteenth-century Europe and disease: 'When mourners gathered around an English graveside to hear the clergyman intoning the words of the Book of Common Prayer of 1662 "in the midst of life we are in death" – they knew it to be true.'[11] In Europe, the average life expectancy fluctuated between thirty years of age to the mid-forties, depending on factors such as social class, region and wealth. In the service of the East India Company in Bombay, most young men could expect to live only three years from their arrival in Asia.[12] Given that the Company tended to only employ servants who were at least eighteen, this gave an unenviable life expectancy of just twenty-one. The situation in Bandar Abbas is shown to have been yet more stark when one considers that men would return to Bombay in order to recover their health.[13] A damning indictment if ever there was one. This is particularly remarkable given contemporary accounts of Bombay's climate, with its 'raines and pestilence' was preferable, indeed a relief, from the conditions on the Gulf Coast.[14]

The considerable problems and tensions that sickness and death caused to the Factory's residents are most starkly seen after an outbreak of plague that swept across the *Garmsirat* in July 1723 not long after the Afghan invasion of Persia. This plague, which is noted as having presented as a 'bilious fever', killed all the Company's servants within two weeks – John Larkin, the surgeon, Edmund Wright, John Frost and Styleman Gostlin, leaving Henry Fowler and John Hill to execute the wills of the deceased and run the factory.[15] Neither of these remaining men were covenanted servants of the Company and were described in a later letter as 'young men of little experience with no dependency on us so that we cannot give them any orders'.[16] Along with the Company's covenanted servants, the factory's garrison was also left leaderless, the Ensign, Sergeant and Corporal all succumbing to the same sickness. The fever struck quickly, with none of the sufferers surviving longer than twelve days after the first report of symptoms.

The human tragedy of so many deaths in a very small community and in such a short time must have been shocking and goes some way to explain why shortly afterwards, Henry Fowler ordered the bombardment of the town after the murder of two of the Company's guards who had insulted some locals while drunk. Fowler failed to come to amicable terms with the *Shahbandar*, Mirza Zahed Ali, instead ordering the *Britannia* to attack the town, resulting in the factory being put to siege.[17] Fowler's decision, after an official investigation, caused him to be recalled to Bombay to answer for it and for the large cost to the

Company in gifts given to placate the Persians, after the timely arrival of Robert Newlin.[18] Newlin's tenure as Agent was to prove short lived, as he succumbed to the same illness as his predecessors within weeks of his arrival. The extreme fragility of life in the Persian Factory is quite evident from this, not to mention that Persia had just been invaded by the Afghans and the Company's more senior servants were all under siege in Isfahan, unable to influence events. The direct attack on the city ordered by Fowler seems to be proof of a snap of temper on his part, caused by the stress of his situation, his youth and potential fear of both the plague and unidentified local threats, rather than a rational decision. It is important, therefore, to consider how specific conditions experienced at Bandar Abbas, the death, disease, temperature, led to a distinct psychological impact upon those experiencing it, leading to extreme emotional outbreaks of rage, madness or irrational hostility. Such a behavioural break could have far-reaching effects upon the Company's relationship with both local authorities and the Persian government and the Company's servant's relationships with one another. In the case of Fowler, grief, illness, heat, maybe a little drunkenness led to a significant political incident with the Persians, which was only reconciled with significant financial cost.

Securing supplies of fresh water was a constant source of anxiety for Europeans and non-Europeans alike. The inhabitants of the Gulf region and Iranian plateau had since ancient times devised various ways to mitigate this, including the building and maintenance of underground channels, wells and cisterns for year-round supply and storage. However, this in turn could cause other issues, the most notable of which was the proliferation of bacteria and parasites in untreated, stagnant water used both for personal and agricultural purposes. In one instance, the crew of the *Fort St. George Galley* returned from an uneventful cruise around the Gulf, 'being very sick and their legs filled with worms'.[19] This almost certainly means that they were infected with *Dracunculus medinensis* or 'Guinea-worm', the symptoms of which include sickness, severe pain and vomiting, with the worms eventually extruding from the lower legs (often through ulcerations which opened up in the presence of water) to disseminate their eggs.[20] The presence of this parasite in the ship's water, supplied at Bandar Abbas or Qeshm, makes it certain that the supplies for the factory and the town were also similarly infected. The problems of maintaining a supply of clean water were by no means new to the eighteenth century, and the inhabitants of the Iranian plateau had developed a number of inventive ways of guaranteeing access to it. Both cities and arable land were supplied by the *qanat* system, a network of underground tunnels which carried water down from mountains and highlands, acting as subterranean aqueducts. The Safavid capital at Isfahan had undergone a significant process of urban planning and improvement during the reign of Abbas I which had placed a particular emphasis on the availability of clean water. This had involved not only the repair and extension of irrigation systems surrounding the city but also an ambitious project to combine the headwaters of the Zayandeh Rud and Kuhrang rivers. The connection of these two rivers, it was hoped, would provide enough volume to meet all the city's needs, an idea first mooted by Tahmasp I, Abbas I's grandfather. Unfortunately for Abbas I, neither he, nor his grandfather, nor his grandson, Abbas II, had access to the necessary expertise to bring the project to fruition, a feat which was only achieved in the twentieth century.[21] The Company was very careful to ensure access to fresh water at their house and garden in urban Isfahan, just as much as at Bandar Abbas. The water supply for the Isfahan house was guaranteed by the *Farman*, a stipulation the Company was careful to get renewed.[22] The factory even had a budget set aside for the maintenance of the *qanat* each year.[23] An acute awareness of the dilatory conditions at Bandar Abbas was not unique or particular to European visitors either. On a campaign against Muscat, the Persian commanders decided not to leave their army waiting at Bandar Abbas but instead moved them westward down the coast to Kung. It was explained that they preferred to use this much smaller port as many of their troops had died at Bandar Abbas of unknown illnesses while waiting to be shipped across the Gulf. Judging by the presence of waterborne parasites as well as the other 'dangers and distresses' to be found around the town, this decision would seem exceedingly wise.

The Agents and factors had various mechanisms by which they could mitigate the unpleasant conditions of the town and its environs. To escape the heat, sickness and bad water, Company servants were often dispatched inland to higher ground, at the Company's expense, to recover from illness. In 1732 George Pack, who held the lowest rank in the Company's merchant hierarchy as a Writer, requested to serve in Isfahan, high on the Iranian Plateau, rather than Bandar Abbas, in order to preserve his health.[24] At the other end of the hierarchy in Persia, William Cockell, who served as Agent from Sunday 4 March 1733 until his health drove him to retire in February 1736, spent a great deal of his time as Agent absent from the factory. Several months of severe ill health necessitated him to take long trips to the Persian interior, nearly reaching Kerman, between 13 April and 27 November 1734. During this time, he continued to send and receive letters concerning the business of the factory, but this was hardly a substitute for his actual presence. Cockell took another trip for his health from

April 1736 until he was summoned to return to the coast in July for an official visit by the *Beglerbegi* of Fars, Mohammed Taqi Khan.[25] Owing to continued illness, including another trip away from Bandar Abbas, Cockell was ordered by the Council at Bombay to hand over control of the factory in November 1736 to John Geekie, who had previously acted as the Company's Resident in Isfahan and as Agent before Cockell.[26] Cockell soon after retired as Agent on the grounds of continued ill-health and departed for Bombay.[27] Despite the Agent's absence, business continued to be conducted by the other members of the factory's Council, composed of the Company servants in Bandar Abbas above the rank of Factor.[28] The acumen and local knowledge of the members of the Council would have been supplemented by the experience of John Geekie, both in running an establishment and dealing with Persian bureaucracy, having done so at Isfahan as Resident for some years. The only occasion in which these absences are recorded to have caused concern was when the *Beglerbegi* visited Bandar Abbas, where the Agent's presence was essential for propriety's sake. This shows the robustness of the Company's organisational structure and ability to cover and account for changes and losses in personnel, as well as a clearer understanding of the importance of leaves of absence for rest and recuperation.

The Company's servants were not reimbursed for their work, however diligent, with high wages. Miles Ogborn has shown convincingly that the Company's salaries were merely nominal and that the Company's servants were instead expected to make their fortunes in other ways: 'private trade has been understood as the main incentive that kept the Company servants loyal'.[29] Between 1729 and 1749, the only adjustment in the salary of Company officials in the Persian Gulf was measured in the Company-mandated exchange rate between the rupee and the Persian shahi, which went from eight to ten per rupee.[30] This was in response to the long-term debasement of the Persian silver coinage, exacerbated by the Afghan invasion and subsequent civil and external conflicts. The low pay received by the Company's employees was instead significantly augmented by a variety of allowances and expenses. These included the Company Table, a communal space where any member of the Company or visiting European might eat and drink, including European or Persian wines and arak from Goa. Travel on Company business was also covered for Company servants, including, as previously mentioned, journeys undertaken for health reasons. Within the factory, they were also provided with rooms and apartments.

The Company's Table at Bandar Abbas was well stocked, as reported in a breakdown of the expenses compiled in December 1734 in an attempt to extract an increased allowance from the presidency at Bombay.[31] It reports that the butler of the factory spent roughly 1,000 shahis per month, the equivalent of two-and-a-half-years pay for a Company Writer, on 'petty expenses for fowls, greens, butter, eggs, fish and &c' as well as mutton.[32] The table expenses also include ghee, sugar, water for the Company's garden, rice, Shiraz wine, candles, 'breadflower', barley, European liquors and Goan arak.[33] The factory kept its own flock of sheep for mutton, as well as 'hogs, ducks, pidgeons [sic], fowls'[34] for whom a supply of barley was kept by. The keeping of pigs was relatively commonplace among the Armenian and Georgian population of Persia at this time, including nominally Muslim members of the nobility.[35] That the Company's servants were also permitted to do so, while being allowed to produce and export alcohol, need not therefore be surprising. As there were only nine Company servants employed at the factory at the time this list was made, it is clear that their needs were well provided for, far in excess of what they could have afforded on their own meagre wages. Indeed, even at busy times, the volume and variety of food supplied would have been a conspicuous display both to the Company's servants and to their guests.

The English Factory at the time of Alexander Hamilton's visit in the 1670s was described as follows:

> formerly a caravan seraw and built after the best manner ... It bears St. George his Banner at one Corner, as do the Dutch and French their Flags, between whose Factories it is seated; Ours was the Emperor's Gift, both theirs purchased; the first Beautified and Strengthened with good Stone Building; all the rest, but the Caun's, being most of Mud and Stone, the usual Materials for Building in this Town, without either Lime or Mortar.[36]

In the new factory, completed in February 1745, there were ten sets of two-room apartments and two with three rooms, reserved for the Agent and his second in command.[37] This provided each Company merchant with a suite of rooms for their personal use free of charge. Sadly, the description of the factory does not give an impression of its layout; however, the sizes of some of the rooms are provided. The factory was dominated by a large hall 30' by 64', a further two large rooms of 30' by 24', ten sets of two-room apartments and two further apartments with three rooms for the Agent and his Second. The Secretary had a separate office and there were three 'dispensers', presumably small rooms for the collection or delivery of wares or collections of payments to the factory and its merchants. The factory was served by its own kitchen, stabling for twenty horses and a battery of eight guns protected by a cut stone wall and warehousing space for 2,000 tonnes.[38] The factory was a relatively large compound, especially when considering the temporary nature of most buildings in the town itself, with a footprint of around 3,000 square feet for the main building with a further warehouse building, large enough to contain roughly four ships' worth of goods. The inclusion of the large battery of guns speaks to the factory's perceived vulnerability and need to provide an imposing face to the Company's presence in the city, though without knowing in which direction these guns faced, it is difficult to know whom they felt a need to impress. The factory was destroyed in 1759 by a French fleet led by the Comte d'Estaing, so despite these defences, the Company was unable to fend off an attack by a European rival.[39]

The Factory was far more than a physical space and was instead a largely self-contained society of its own, but unlike wider society, one particular aspect was missing: women. The European community in Persia, being officially solely male, faced an ongoing tension common to transplanted communities, namely the propriety of female, or indeed other male, companionship. William Dalrymple in his work *White Mughals* gives a fascinating view of the relationships enjoyed by the Company's servants in the subcontinent, where Muslim and Hindu women, who had much greater latitude in their actions than did the women of Iran, sought marriage to Englishmen.[40] The source Dalrymple uses, the *Kitab Tuhfat al-'Alam*, was written by the Persian noble Abdul Latif Shushtari in 1802. Suffice it to say that Shushtari had little truck with the concept of Muslim women who 'take every imaginable liberty', particularly in their willingness to marry European merchants.[41] The female and male worlds in Iran were separated and any social interaction between the sexes was highly limited and regulated by families and wider societal norms, making it yet harder for the Company's servants to meet and interact with women on a social basis. There are a few notable earlier examples of English merchants having romantic relationships, such as Thomas Coddrington who gained the disfavour of his colleagues by marrying an Armenian woman. For this he was expelled, though only briefly, from the Factory and the Company's service. The attitudes of Shushtari were clearly shared by at least some English merchants, though as we shall see, this did not preclude the transaction of personal relationships.

The records for Bandar Abbas in the early eighteenth century contain only two cases of the Factors' relationships with local women. William Cordeux, the Company's Factor in Kerman, had manumitted a slave girl called Manna with whom he was engaged in a relationship formal enough to be recognised by his peers in the factory. It may be presumed that they were not married, judging by the description of her as his 'girl' rather than his wife and a lack of any other evidence of either a religious or legal union.⁴² What is made clear from existing records is that she was set to inherit substantially from Cordeux's estate after his murder and that she was not a Muslim. We know both of these statements to be true due to attempts by the Khan of Kerman, following Cordeux's death, to force her into converting, thereby making her new wealth liable to seizure by the Persian authorities.⁴³ In this case, Manna was protected and kept in the care of the Company's replacement for Cordeux at Kerman, Nathaniel Whitwell, who refused to heed any demands from the Khan on her person. The relative wealth she inherited can also be surmised from the lengths to which the Khan went to secure it for himself, even going so far as to petition Nader Shah for his own direct intervention in the matter.

> Yesterday by a shotter express from Mr. Whitwell at Carmania received a letter of the 13th Instant adviseing a choppar was sent thither by Thomas Caun [Nader Shah] to demand Mr. Cordeux's girl or to take 500 tomaunds.

This demand is made yet more interesting by the Khan's insistence that Whitwell pay him to guarantee Manna's freedom while the Khan also held the other suspects of Cordeux's murder in custody, access to whom he denied until he was reimbursed for what he represented were his efforts on the Company's behalf. We will see in the next chapter how Whitwell and his superiors at Bandar Abbas dealt with Khan and his prisoners. Shortly after the receipt of the Shah's demands, Manna, along with her inheritance, was spirited away by Whitwell to Bandar Abbas and on to Bombay 'to be proceeded against', concerning various demands on Cordeux's estate.⁴⁴ But Manna was not brought under the Company's protection by Whitwell purely philanthropically nor to execute her and the late Cordeux's financial affairs, as he and the other English merchants believed her to be party to Cordeux's murder.⁴⁵

The second noteworthy case concerns the will of Ursula Euston, a Jewish woman with family in the Gulf port of Kung, the widow of William Euston, the former Agent at Bandar Abbas. Edmund Wright, the new Agent who replaced William, was appointed as the executor of her estate and disbursed 300 toman to her husband's sisters in England, anything remaining after her other legacies was bequeathed to her Jewish family at Bandar Kung.⁴⁶ The Eustons' wills are particularly interesting, as they represent one of exceedingly few references to the presence of Jews in the Company's diaries, consultations and letters. Jews in both Persia and England did not always enjoy the legal and social freedoms of their countrymen, between 1290 and 1655, Jews were officially expelled from England. In Persia, Jews were subject to perennial demands for conversion, notably under

Shah Abbas II. That being said, Jews were prominent members of the mercantile communities of the Safavid realm, making their relative absence from the Company's records yet more puzzling. In the territories of the East India Company, tolerance towards the Jewish community was more entrenched, presiding as it did, over a heterogeneous society including Muslims, Jews, Hindus, Roman Catholics, Armenians and many others.[47] Whether the Company's wide-reaching toleration would have spread to a Jewish Agent controlling one of their factories is unclear; however, the intermarriage of local women to Englishmen was widespread in India. Indeed, Robert Shirley, one of the first Englishmen to visit Safavid Persia, was married to an Orthodox Circassian noblewoman, re-christened Teresia. As with the *White Mughals* of India, the Company's factory in Persia was a place of intercommunal and interreligious marriage and therefore close interaction.

In the same letter that reports the death of Ursula Euston, there is also the following passage, concerning Charles Savage and a Persian nobleman, named Lutf Ali Khan:

> he has rendered himself unworthy of the service by his former Wickedness and late Elopement as the Agent advises from the factory to the House of Loof Ally Caun [Lutf Ali Khan] one of the most notorious offenders in that unnatural and infamous vice that lives under heaven.[48]

While this passage does not explicitly accuse Charles Savage and Lutf Ali Khan of homosexuality, illegal in Britain under the Buggery Act of 1563, the meaning behind the statements certainly seems clear. On discovery of their relationship, Savage fled the factory for Lutf Ali Khan's home. Unlike in eighteenth-century Britain, Persia at this time had a rather different historical view of same-sex relations; indeed, a rich poetic and literary history celebrating such relationships exists in the Persianate World, quite different to anything experienced in Europe, at least since antiquity. However, it is quite evident that Savage's relationship was deemed in breach of the Company's rules and thus rendered him unfit for further service; he was forced to return to the factory and was thereafter sent back to Bombay. It is unclear how the two men met, or what the exact nature of their relationship was; however, from the use of the term 'elopement', it seems clear that their affection was mutual and that Savage saw in Lutf Ali an opportunity to escape the opprobrium of his countrymen. Neither the fate of Savage nor the future of Lutf Ali Khan is recorded in the Company's records; however, the existence of their relationship speaks to a greater closeness in communal terms between the Company's servants and local notables, which goes beyond merely official or mercantile business. The lives of the factors were clearly filled with a range of discomforts and frustrations, though there were some quite considerable benefits to Company service, particularly in the Persian Factory, that mitigated them.

The relationship between the Company's servants and alcohol has a long, complicated history wherever in which they found themselves. This was no less true for the first Company voyages to the islands of Indonesia where they indulged heavily, 'disordering themselves with drinke and whores', as it was for the merchants who took up their posts in Bandar Abbas.[49] Persia was no exception to the conspicuous consumption of alcohol, whether wine produced at the vineyards of Shiraz or shipped from the Rhineland, or arak distilled in Goa. There were repeated reports, particularly those in 1617 and 1672 which decried the dangers of 'toddy, rack and women'.[50] Nominally illegal in Muslim Persia, wine has a long and colourful history in Iran not least in the area around Shiraz, though the connection between the region and the grape variety is disputed.[51]

Persia is documented as a major source of wine consumed in Bombay, where it was shipped in quantity when available. The Company not only had the *Farman's* stipulations granting them permission to produce and export wine but maintained their own vineyard and vintner in Shiraz for this purpose. In July 1727, a caravan of 220 pack animals carried 280 chests of wine and 100 chests of rose water to Bandar Abbas from Shiraz.[52] In 1728, another shipment 'an hundred Chests of eight Flasks ea[ch]' was dispatched to Bombay on the Company's account 'to supply for their immediate want', the previous year's vintage having proven sour.[53] There was also mention of the expected arrival of another caravan bearing wine and the desire that should it arrive before the departure of the ship carrying the original stock, another 50–100 chests might be added to the shipment. This constant flow of wine, and consistent demands for even more, between India and Persia is demonstrative of two notable facts: firstly, the mass production of wine points towards an existing habit and market for its consumption both in Persia and the subcontinent, and secondly, Europeans saw the potential to fulfil their own needs in addition to the commercial opportunities inherent in servicing the existing market. By the beginning of the nineteenth century, Persian wines had been largely replaced by the importation of Madeira wine, which began to be preferred as a European export cargo for outgoing Company ships, the island of Madeira being ideally placed on the Southward route to the Cape.[54] Any wine that was found to be sour at Bombay was distilled into brandy and distributed to the Company's soldiers stationed there.[55] When, as in 1729, no wine was produced at the Company's vineyard at Shiraz, 50 chests were acquired from other areas for the use of the factory in Bandar Abbas.[56]

Despite being destroyed by the Afghans in December 1729, with the loss of 7,000 toman of stock, the vineyard at Shiraz was retained by the Company, with the vintner sending news to Bandar Abbas periodically concerning the state of the economy of Shiraz and news about the political changes undertaken by the new Afghan rulers. The Afghans had previously halted production of wine by their invasion in 1722 but, by 1726 a new vintage was being prepared, though at 'a much greater price than was accustomed to be paid'.[57] It took until 1732 before Bombay requested another shipment from Persia and, from then on, these requests became routine. For example, in 1740, 200 chests were purchased at 200 shahis per chest, 140 of which were charged to the Company's cash, presumably to be sent on to Bombay, the other 60 therefore were retained for the factory.[58] Considering the small number of Company servants, nine in 1734,[59] at Bandar Abbas, the presence of between 480 and 600 flasks of wine, not to mention other alcohol that might have been imported, borders on alarming, especially considering the shortage of water and the much maligned climate. Shiraz wine was far from the only tipple enjoyed by the servants, with mentions in the accounts of considerable purchases of Goan arak and European wines. In addition to this provision by the Company, there was also a Dutch 'punch house' in Bandar Abbas.[60] The presence of this European drinking establishment again leads one to consider a social environment between the Company's servants and the other inhabitants of the town of which the official sources do not speak but provides a compelling image nonetheless.

At least some of this stock of alcohol was used to keep the guards stationed at the factory in good spirits; indeed, sometimes it was their spirits which compelled the Company servants to provide them with it. In 1727, on noticing the soldiers had an extra ration of punch distributed, William Cordeux accused his rival and the factory's Agent, William Henry Draper, of attempting to bribe the guards to 'make them continue firm to his side' during a dispute.[61] The two sergeants of the guard, Sharp and Boyden, protested, saying that the men were provided an extra ration when they went to Church of a Sunday, by way of encouragement. They went on to say that Cordeux would not have noticed anything amiss had Robert Iles, one of the privates, not been 'in liquor' after a visit to the punch house. Sharp and Boyden ended by saying only nine men in the factory were permitted punch, presumably from the Company's stock, so any consumption of it could only be licit, rather than an attempt at bribing them for their loyalty. So along with poor water, dazzling heat, intermittent plague and occasionally hostile locals, life at Bandar Abbas can add hangovers to its list of attractive qualities, or perhaps it could be said that one was a result of the others.

This is mirrored elsewhere, for example, in the Company's Indian settlements, taxation of the arak supply was a contributing factor to the Keigwin Revolt in 1683; so clearly the free flow of spirits was a particularly prized privilege.[62]

While alcohol flowed freely, other pastimes were strictly forbidden by the Company's Court of Directors. Most notorious was 'the prohibition on gamming [sic]', which was enforced at the factory from November 1728.[63] This was not the first attempt by the Company to stamp out this particular social ill, the edict of 1728 coming a century after another, similar order directed at Persia in 1629, when huge debts had been incurred between bored factors. Not only was this newest decree ordered to be read out publicly by the factory secretary, but it was likewise expected to be 'affix[ed] in a publick place'.[64] The prohibition was unsurprisingly again ignored, as proven by the scandalous behaviour of two of the Company's guards who manufactured a panic in 1732, orchestrated to pay off gambling debts they had accrued. The two men, taking advantage of the constant and occasionally realised threat of Afghan and Baluchi raids on the town 'fired off their musquets and running in at the Gates told everybody they mett that the Ophgoons were entering'.[65] As the civilians fled in panic, the two soldiers began looting local houses and were only disturbed when Mir Haidar, the local Persian commander at the town's fort, led his men to challenge the supposed Afghan threat. This event somewhat damaged the Company's reputation with Mir Haidar, who angrily delivered the men back into the Company's care for punishment. While the scale in this instance was limited to just two men, it does not require a great deal of imagination to perceive the difficulties encountered elsewhere in the Company's purview. Bombay or Madras had populations and garrisons of hundreds of European and native soldiers, sailors, merchants and clerks and a proportional risk of ill behaviour, brawling or cheating at cards or dice.

The Company's Directors may have been unwilling to countenance the rolling of dice or card playing, but, along with food and alcohol, they provided for their servants in other ways. While on his convalescence in the interior of the Iranian plateau in 1736, William Cockell was accompanied by the factory's surgeon, Dr. Patrick Oliphant. The presence of a doctor at the Persian factory is remarkable considering the small population for them to serve within its confines. In the seventeenth century, the Company's Directors had not thought it worth the expense to furnish the Persian Factory with its own physician. The expectation was that the only way for their servants to survive the fevers and ailments of Persia or India was to adopt local habits around eating, or use of local remedies, in the belief that only these could be efficacious. By contrast, in the eighteenth century, doctors enjoyed the second highest salary of any European at the factory,[66] as evidence of their perceived centrality to the Company's community. While Dr. Oliphant was away attending William Cockell, another physician Dr. Russell was retained at the factory from a passing ship, enjoying a salary of 3,000 shahis, nearly equal to the annual salary of a Senior Merchant or the cost of supplying the Company's Table for three months. The expense of keeping such men might appear to have been prohibitive, especially in an organisation where thrift and profit were to be striven for. The Company surgeons, being limited in the medicines and procedures available, supported the Company's officers in more practical ways to preserve their well-being. It is documented that the surgeon in 1729 was responsible for stocking the factory's communal Table, as part of his role in looking after the health needs of the residents.[67] This was perhaps spurred by a report by two Company surgeons, Bennett and Bird, in 1672–3, who blamed many of the illnesses and afflictions of the merchants on an overabundance of drink.[68] The surgeons' remit stretched beyond caring for the living, as they were also responsible for providing reports and post mortems in cases of suspicious deaths in the factory. This included passing judgements on the causes of death, as occurred on the death of Laurence de Romade, one of the Company's 'Topaz'[69] guards who was killed in a duel by another member of the garrison, Francis Pereira. The two men had quarrelled and chosen to fight out their disagreement on the beach away from the factory with sticks, rather than deadly weapons. Unfortunately for de Romade, this was not enough to preserve his life, as he collapsed after being struck several times by Pereira. The surgeon, John Hardcastle, was ordered to examine the body, reporting that de Romade had died from a haemorrhage in his head, caused by two hard strikes just below his left ear.[70] Here we see a different aspect to the role of the doctor, not just as a physician for the living but also as an investigator and expert. Equally, the diversification of the role played by doctors and other medical professionals went through a process of distinct transformation in the later seventeenth century, perhaps best exemplified by the report of Bennett and Bird. The Company was investing in the presence and availability of medical care, while additionally using the expertise of these individuals to monitor and assess diet and habits within the Company's factories. A surgeon was therefore not just a medical expert but also an administrator, secretary and could take advantage of private commercial opportunities in their own right. In the small, rather hazardous world of the Persian Factory, this was no small responsibility.

It is clear that the Company's governors and councils went to great efforts and considerable expense in maintaining the good health of its people in their factories, making provision for Bombay, Madras and St. Helena to be subject to planning laws emplaced in England after the Great Fire of London in 1666 and a further fire in 1671. The Company also outlawed practices such as fertilising trees and plantations with dried fish remains, known as 'buckshawing', saying that the practice caused 'a corrupting [of] the air with a noisome [sic] smell'.[71] This smell, it was believed, caused illness among the population at Bombay, which the Company feared more than any gain in crop yield they might derive from the practice. Stern argues that the Company, where it had the authority to do so, was active in maintaining the health and well-being of their servants. This included legislating on the upkeep of water supplies and methods to avoid miasma (a mist or 'bad air' that carried pestilence), believed well into the nineteenth century to cause disease. In the case of the Persian Factory, where the Company was not in control of planning, the provision of a doctor for the small communities at Bandar Abbas and another for even smaller Basra was in keeping with a wider trend.

Even in a small community like the Persian Factory, there were diverse social and societal pressures and influences exerted on its inhabitants. While the Company's Directors and higher officials could do little about the unpleasant conditions of the town, the lot of the factors and merchants in Company service was improved through services such as free medical care (efficacy notwithstanding) and supplies of good food and drink.

2

Governance, information management, reporting, communication and control

When considering how the Company operated in Persia it is important to accept that the Company's system of governance had a major part to play in the success and longevity of its trade. The Company more generally had a relatively simple structure for the most part, with all factories having a council and a Chief merchant or Agent presiding over it. Clearly this success started and ended with the character and quality of the individuals governing the Company at every level and location. As the previous chapter shows, the living conditions and experiences of the Company's servants could be severely affected by disease, climate and the success or failure of personal relationships. Given the terrible conditions encountered by the Company's servants in Persia, the need for an organisational structure that was both robust and flexible was plain to see. In Persia, unlike Madras, Surat or Bombay, there was little to no redundancy of personnel. If a member of the council fell ill, which as the last chapter shows was a common occurrence, died or was otherwise unable to fulfil his duties, there was often no immediate replacement. Instead, new Company servants would have to be sent from another settlement, or another contingency would have to be found, either of which could take several weeks or months to communicate and resolve. The management of the Company's business in factories like that in the Persian Gulf was therefore rather fragile on the surface, relying on a small number of individuals. That being said, the Company had a variety of tools and approaches it used to mitigate these problems, including oaths and bonds, co-opting local frameworks, hierarchies and collective responsibility.

The Company gave their employees contracts of employment setting down the principles, interests and the standards of behaviour expected of them. The assignments of senior offices such as Agents came with extensive powers of delegated authority to allow local negotiations at the highest levels, without the need for escalation beyond the factory itself. This removed potential frustrations that could have destroyed local confidence or paralysed progress through the elapsed time between communications. The need for local resilience and flexibility within the wider systems of the Company is clearly shown in Persia, where the Agents and merchants had to negotiate with local governors and merchants on a regular basis, with more infrequent contacts with viziers and shahs. These powers of authority, freedom of local decision making and action, however, were kept in check by detailed reporting, record keeping and a system of accounting and audit with recourse to forensic analysis where required. The factory's records show regular, periodic and formulaic reports on the detailed aspects of trade volumes, values and the costs of sales including factory subsistence, construction and upkeep of a garden, taxes, tolls and Persian exactions. There were also Company 'lines in the sand', standing orders, which were enforced by penalties severe enough to discourage breach and, when thought to be infracted, were vigorously verified regardless of distance, time or cost. The Company process worked by rules, expectations of behaviour and the fear of social censure and loss of family honour. The Board of the Company may have been risking investor's capital, but their subordinates were risking their personal fortunes and indeed their lives in the Company's service. This culture of high risk and potentially high reward made the Company's direct management of its factors difficult, for example, in the relaxation of restrictions on private trade due to the inadequacy of any method of oversight for this personal business. That being said, this chapter will consider some of the ways in which the Persian factors managed the Company's affairs, and their own.

The ability to make a considerable personal fortune was one of the major attractions to the Company's service in general, with service in Persia being seen as a particularly good prospect for this pursuit. With the Company's blessing and support all employees and officers could conduct individual private enterprise; however, due to the Company's monopoly, these individuals were inextricably reliant on the Company for access to these opportunities. The benefits of this could be immense, as individual merchants were able to amass vast private fortunes in their own rights, while also overseeing the Company's business transactions. By permitting private trade, unlike the VOC, which jealously guarded its privileges, even from its own employees, the Company was able to effectively bind its servants to itself, not just by oaths or contracts but by their own desire for wealth. This freedom had not initially been extended to the Company's servants, who had, like their Dutch counterparts, been banned from transacting trade on their own accounts. The change in policy was a recognition of a variety of factors, the first of which was a seemingly constant circumvention of the Company's ban. In the face of constant disobedience and the seemingly endless measures that merchants found to turn a profit, the Company raised the ban and even adopted some of the more creative mechanisms, particularly 'colouring' which will be explored further in Chapter 3.

The Bandar Abbas factory lay on one of the major communication routes between London and India, which ran up the Gulf to Basra, then onward north through the Ottoman Empire to Aleppo and from there to England via the Mediterranean. While technically under the direct jurisdictional control of the President and Council in Bombay, there was little that these officials could do to directly control the activities of the Persian factors. Due to the distances involved and the seasonal changes in wind direction and strength, Bandar Abbas was anywhere between one and three months away from Bombay and the oversight of the Company's officials there. The Agents and merchants in Persia therefore enjoyed a particular freedom from any immediate interventions by Bombay. Such autonomy was necessary due to the relative remoteness of the factory in certain times of the year from the Company's other settlement and was accentuated further by the need for the Agents in Persia to deal directly with the bureaucratic and diplomatic apparatus of the Safavid Empire in real time. As there were also no formal diplomatic ties between the English Crown and Persia, except through the Agent, the holders of this post enjoyed a latitude of action that could not be replicated elsewhere within the Company's purview.

The significance of Persia as a destination for the Company's trade necessitated representation that could respond more or less immediately to shifts in the local political or economic balance. Earlier attempts by Presidents at Surat, most notably under William Fremlin in 1638, and the Company's Directors in London in 1640–1, to close the house in Isfahan in preference for an official presence solely at Bandar Abbas had always met with failure. This was due in part to the centrality of Isfahan in the commercial life of Persia's trade networks as well as its political importance as the capital. The need for the Agent to be present at the Persian court lapsed only with the dissolution of the Safavid monarchy in 1722, at which point the Company's servants did indeed retrench to the coast. Throughout the seventeenth century, the ability for the Agents to intervene directly with the Persian court was indispensable, particularly given the constant concerns about the payment of the customs share owed to the Company. With the loss of Isfahan to the Afghans and the decentring of Safavid authority thereafter, the Agents' independent status as an actor only distantly answerable to Bombay was further solidified.

The loss of Isfahan not only shifted more pressure onto the person of the Agent but likewise removed the familiar arena of interaction between the Company and the Safavid state. Isfahan was nominally the capital under the Afghans but given the constant civil unrest and mounting resistance to their rule, the new rulers of the city were rarely present. Persia had lurched from a largely centralised state to a region riven by war and multipolar authorities. The Company dealt with this loss of a safe place for cooperation and exchange creatively: by providing their garden for this purpose (Figure 3).

Figure 3 Garden gathering, 1640–50, probably Isfahan. Photo by Sepia Times/ Universal Images Group via Getty Images.

> At Afseen there are many gardens where the inhabitants of Gombroon retire to in the hot months; But the English East India Company's is the best, and best cultivated. It produces plenty of Seville Oranges, whose trees are always verdant, and bear ripe and green fruit with blossoms all at once.[1]

The Company Agents and servants clearly were very well versed in what one might call 'Customer Entertainment'. The considerable investment in the garden at Afseen and its upkeep are well documented in the factory's monthly steward's reports. The Company's garden is their most important, effective and immediate communication tool. Other communication methods available to the Company in Persia were effectively limited only to the reporting of past events or receiving general instructions, as any correspondence were subject to the tyranny of time and distance. Within Persia itself, communicating between Bandar Abbas, Isfahan, Kerman and Shiraz, the major political and commercial centres, could be a wearisome business even in ideal conditions.

After 1722, diplomacy and negotiations with any faction within Persia were often carried out at the Company's garden. Afseen may correspond to the villages of Fariyab-Eesin or Patal-Eesin which lie about eight miles north of the modern city of Bandar Abbas.[2] The garden provided a welcome escape from the town, lying at a higher, cooler altitude with running water nearby. The Company's servants believed the garden worthy of considerable expense, with a monthly upkeep of 234 shahis in March 1727,[3] when it is first mentioned in the accounts, rising to 400 shahis per month in November 1750.[4] In June 1727, the garden also underwent repairs costing 4,009 shahis, a cost that is justified by the 'handsomeness and conveniency of those apartments' and the 'frugality' with which the work had been completed.[5] The use of the word 'apartment' would suggest that the garden also had some manner of living space, rather than simply being an outside or transient area. Philip Stern discusses briefly the importance of gardens in Bombay and other Company settlements in India, which, unlike Afseen, existed in urban spaces and were primarily for the use of the inhabitants of the Company's cities.[6] Despite this difference, the emulation of the practice, distinctly Persian in origin, is noteworthy. Further to this we find that the Persian tradition of gardening was exported to India by the Company, with a request for two gardeners to be sent over from Persia to Bombay in 1704, while others were employed to tend an herb garden and orchards at Isfahan.[7] These gardeners were paid handsomely for their work, receiving 180 rupees per year, considerably more than a Company Writer. The Company's investment in the garden and the adoption of the practice in India is indicative of how effective these spaces were as places for relaxation and negotiation.

Afseen was predominantly occupied by visiting dignitaries, who regularly made requests to stay at the garden while en route to or from Bandar Abbas, Kerman, Isfahan or Shiraz. Its position on this main highway made it convenient and desirable as a stopping place, as did its proximity to Bandar Abbas, while not being close enough to share its unhealthy reputation. In 1740, the Governor (*Sultan*) of Bandar Abbas requested the use of the garden so that he might 'take the waters' there.[8] This implies that Afseen had a natural spring, which considering the shortage of fresh water in the region would have further increased the garden's attraction. Unfortunately for the Company's servants, the only recorded time they attempted to use the garden for their own recreation was in March 1734, when they were ambushed by bandits and forced to ride back to the factory.[9] As Hamilton mentions in his description of the site though, they at least got the benefit of the fruit grown in the garden.[10]

The garden functioned primarily as a place to entertain Persian officials and was consciously chosen as an arena for negotiation commensurate with local custom. The Dutch similarly had a garden at Naban, though again it is unclear where this might have been located precisely, it is possibly a reference to Noband, a town near Minab, east from Bandar Abbas. The fact that both the Company and the Dutch maintained a garden is proof that they appreciated the very important place of gardens in Persian architecture and sociability. By mimicking this tradition, the Company gained a diplomatic advantage by hosting their guests and interlocutors in a familiar setting. The garden maintained at Isfahan was specifically guaranteed its water supply in the *Farman*, as well as at the house the Company used and maintained there.[11] The garden had another use in providing seeds for the various settlements in India.[12] How the hot, dry climate of the Gulf littoral was seen as a suitable place to supply seeds provides an insight into how rich the horticultural value of these gardens may have been. The desirable garden was, unfortunately, also very vulnerable, its enviable position at a remove from the town meant that when threatened, it was too far away to be saved. The village and garden were both occupied by Afghan forces in 1731, who did relatively little other than steal the silver plate and equipment for the well.[13] The Baluchis in 1733, on the other hand, appear to have wrecked the place after a short time using it as a base for raiding caravans. After both of these incidents, however, the garden was repaired and brought back into use in relatively short order.[14]

Despite these incursions and the devastation caused by a swarm of locusts in April 1738,[15] the Bandar Abbas factors retained the use of the garden and maintained it to entertain themselves and their guests in local style. Though the Company's officials viewed themselves as foreign to Persia and maintained their cultural and religious identities, they equally assimilated Persian customs regarding hospitality. This was in part a conscious effort to fit in with the culture of their hosts; it is sensible to assume that the adoption of some aspects of Persian sociability was merely in recognition of how they improved the lot of the factors during their leisure time.

The adoption of the Persian garden by the Company as a space for recreation in India and of political exchange and a diplomatic meeting place in Persia was accompanied by other habits, such as the presentation of guests with gifts, as well as the consumption of coffee and smoking of *qalyan*. The first specific mention of the consumption of coffee in the factory is in 1739, in relation to the visit of a Persian official, who took coffee with the Agent while trying to extract a 'gift' from him.[16] After this meeting, several later encounters with Persian officials and VOC servants took place over coffee and, in one case, *qalyan*.[17] Rudi

Matthee suggests that Persians adopted the combination of coffee and tobacco more quickly and wholeheartedly than anyone else,[18] while Jean Chardin in his travels found coffee houses throughout the Safavid domain from Isfahan and Qazvin to Tabriz and Nakhichevan. Given that the size of the Company's coffee trade, transacted at Mocha, was measured in hundreds of tonnes annually, it is probably safe to assume that the factors were already familiar with the beverage before these meetings.[19] The combination of coffee and tobacco would likewise have been familiar, though the factors were happy to adopt local methods of consuming both stimulants; there is a note in the Company's warehouse stock from 1726, mentioning two spare 'glasses' for *qalyan*, so the pipes were evidently in fairly constant use.[20] Matthee mentions that one Persian name for tobacco was *inglis-tanbaku* (English tobacco), hinting at its original source before cultivation of the plant within Persia took off.[21] The importation of coffee was a European preserve; interestingly, the majority of ships carrying it to Persia and Basra appear to have been French, who grew their own beans on Mauritius.[22] The trade in these exotic substances and their use is indicative not only of an exchange of goods but also of the construction of habits of consumption and leisure, developed and shared in the interaction of Persians and Europeans.[23] Company officials went to great lengths and expense to lavishly entertain their interlocutors and ensure that their guests saw facilities like the Company's garden as a preferable place to go to relax, exchange information and do business. This ready flow of information was all the more necessary in the light of the huge impediments to communication between Persia and the wider hierarchy of the Company beyond the Gulf.

The Company's Directors in London had long come to accept the futility of micromanagement of their Indian subordinates through a process of attrition, but there remained a tension between India and Persia that took longer to settle. Accepting that the Persian Agent was almost invariably forced to act on initiative, rather than waiting for instruction, only added to this tension. Steensgaard characterises this problem as an inconsistency of expectation: 'There was too great a distance between reality as pictured by the Council of State and the reality in which their local representatives found themselves.'[24] The governance of the Company in Persia overcame what were fragile, insecure, agonisingly slow and unreliable communications through the principle of trust and devolved responsibility. To fully appreciate how the structure of government was determined by an acceptance of these facts, it is necessary to look in some depth at what was possible in terms of communications and how these shaped governance, communication and reporting. We will also see that the Company's

Persian factors were well versed in their superiors' expectations regarding information gathering and the passing on of news.

The East India Company's administration was based on a system of committees and councils presiding over often weakly defined and mutable areas. In the early days of Company expansion, the Presidency at Bantam founded in 1603 on Java had primacy over all other factories, from those nearby on the Spice Islands to more distant Surat and Hormuz. As Bantam lay at the eastern extremity of the Company's sphere of operations, it quickly became clear that using it as an administrative hub was inefficient. After the factory at Bantam was abandoned in favour of the (questionably) healthier climes of India, authority over the Persian factories fell, along with operations to the Red Sea and the West Coast of India, to the Bombay Presidency and Council. Although significantly closer than Bantam, Bombay's communications with Bandar Abbas were still subject to the same problems of the seasonal weather and availability of shipping. These issues of communication had a profound impact on the way in which the Company could negotiate with the Shahs either directly or through their representatives. The distance and time taken to shuttle messages, gifts and envoys to and fro necessitated the recognition of the Agents as the holders of almost complete delegated authority with whom Persian merchants and officials could deal with on a quotidian basis. This system took some time to perfect, as this chapter will show. The Company was relieved of the expensive and time-consuming need to send large, well-manned and well-laden embassies. The Company's Agent and Resident having the de facto status of consul, envoy and ambassador significantly affected the way in which the Agents were perceived by the Persians and lent certain expectations to the image they projected. This position led as we have seen to the further adoption of certain Persian customs such as the ostentatious use of chinaware to serve coffee or the use of a cool, well-maintained garden where the Agent might entertain visiting dignitaries, drink yet more coffee and smoke *qalyan*.[25]

While the Agent could act with great autonomy, there remained the overarching authority both of the President and Council in Bombay and the Court of Directors in London. Despite being at a great distance and severely restricted in their ability to intervene with the running of the factory on a timely basis, the Court of Directors retained overall control. This meant that their orders and advice, delivered to the Council at Bandar Abbas, carried significant weight and had to be taken seriously. This is notably true when considering the way in which the Agents in Persia could deal with piracy, especially that carried out by Muscati and other Arab ships. This issue was particularly stark when the Company's interests in Persia created an ever more strained situation with the

Imams of Muscat and the *Huwala* Arabs. Directives from further up the hierarchy prevented hostile action being taken against Arab groups who carried out trade with the Company in India, or who could threaten their maritime traffic.[26] The problem of piracy was one which the Company found itself constantly exposed to throughout its operations in the Indian Ocean; it was therefore unsurprising that the Directors and Presidents approached it with wide-ranging directives, rather than allowing complete autonomy to their servants on the ground. These direct orders disallowed the Agent from using his direct authority to challenge Muscati pirates and others, even when their activity was having a direct and damaging effect on the Company's business in the Gulf. As we will see presently, disagreements on this subject led to serious schisms within the Company's Council.

Communications by sea around the Gulf were largely the preserve of the European trading companies. As with naval power, the Safavids and their successors lagged significantly behind the Europeans in this arena, being reliant upon Arab shipping traffic to send correspondence internationally when the need arose. Where the Safavids were able to ignore or delegate maritime concerns, whether to the Portuguese, other Europeans or local powers, the Europeans themselves could not. Indeed, they were reliant upon access to the sea lanes of the Indian Ocean to stay connected to their masters in Bombay, Batavia, London or Amsterdam. Letters and packets sent abroad were often transported aboard whatever ship was willing to take them and was going in the right direction. This meant that Dutch, French, Indian or Arab ships would often carry Company letters and vice versa. Sea travel, and therefore also the delivery of mail by sea, was fraught with danger, perhaps even more so than by land. As on land, travel by sea carried the additional risks of brigandage, whether by Arab pirates in the Gulf, 'Sanganians' from Kutch or the threat of attack by 'The Angrias', a naval clan of Marathas. The seizure of ships by pirates or brigands presented the added danger of letters captured on board giving away the positions of other vessels that might be vulnerable, as was feared when the *Adventure Grab* was taken while carrying letters on board which detailed the dates of departure and ladings of other Company and local vessels which could be used to intercept them.[27] Ships foundered relatively often, sometimes without known reason, though storms and the violent gales of the Gulf were responsible in some instances.[28] Such incidents, while representing a tragic loss of human life, could also have serious repercussions on the delivery of important letters, papers and packets between Persia, India and Europe, thus threatening the management of the Company and its trade.

The major meteorological threat in the Gulf was the monsoon, upon which all trade in the region depended, but which effectively made all traffic to and from the region one-way for half the year. Should the timing of a letter's dispatch be poorly judged, it could languish undelivered for many months. To avoid some of these complications, mail for England from India was often sent via the Gulf; from Bombay or Surat via Bandar Abbas to Basra, then overland to Baghdad, Aleppo and finally back onto a ship at Iskenderun, on the Mediterranean coast to be carried back to England. This route took over six months and relied on the cooperation of transportation both in the Gulf, across at least four Ottoman provinces, and then a further voyage from the Eastern Mediterranean. Some letters were also sent by a route overland from Basra to Livorno in Italy through Anatolia and the Balkans, then onward by sea.[29]

The time it took to send and receive letters necessitated that correspondence be gathered and sent in packets, the problem with this being that correspondence sent in this manner, if taken and read en route, revealed much about the Company's business. Such a danger was unavoidable due to the delays between conveyances and the further associated delays in receiving any sort of reply. Letters sent to London were therefore much more formulaic than letters between the Persian factories or between Persia and India. Letters for London were divided into sections: news, goods from Europe, goods for Europe, general trade (which included events in Persia and their effects upon the Company's dealings), buildings and revenues, then personnel. These letters are by far the longest in the Company's books and included events from several months. Even so, they are often no more than 15 pages long and while quite detailed, represent only a fraction of the corresponding time in the factory's consultation books, which were sent to Bombay on a roughly annual basis.

Both seaborne and overland options remained slow and risky methods of sending and receiving post that would change little before the arrival of steam shipping and later the telegraph in the nineteenth century. In the eighteenth century communication was reliant on horses, camels and couriers, rowed galleys and sailing ships, as it had been for millennia. It was slow, inefficient and, at best, vague and unreliable in terms of expected dates of delivery. Limitations of time and the need to copy letters and consultations by hand meant that communication with India from Persia, while relatively fast by the standards of the day, had to be condensed in packets which might cover more than a year's worth of Company business and accounts. These reports were then likely packed together in Bombay to be sent back to England with the Company's other 'advices' from its various factories and stations. This brevity was compounded by the fact that any clarification would have to wait for a passage around the Cape of Good Hope and then favourable winds to the Persian Gulf. Why it was that post from England came around the Cape but letters from the East were sent via the Gulf is ambiguous, perhaps due to a belief that keeping these letters in the hands of Company servants was more dependable. The fact that letters were sent by this route goes some way to cementing the importance of the Company's factories in Persia as a hub for communications. The Gulf would continue to be pivotal in this regard until the construction of the Suez Canal, when the telegraphic cable system running through southern Persia was replaced with an underwater line through the Canal and the Red Sea.

Persia had gone through something of a transportation revolution under Abbas I, who instituted systems of highway security, *rahdar*, as well as regular way stations (caravanserais) which provided water and shelter for caravans and travellers. Despite these improvements, by 1722, travel within Persia was neither a particularly fast nor safe business; thereafter it was worse due to the collapse of centralised authority.[30] The Company's trade continued to rely on caravans of pack animals to take their goods to market, while being equally reliant on such conveyances to deliver fresh supplies of ready money from other parts of the empire. These caravans, referred to in the English sources as 'caphilas' or variations thereof from the Persian *qafileh*, were considered by the Company's servants to be a barometer for the health of the Persian economy as a whole. In good times, the caravans would be large, rich and regular, travelling long distances untroubled by banditry and extortion. In bad times, the opposite characteristics were noticed, with long delays between the arrival of caravans, which arrived only from neighbouring cities and regions with little coin to spend.[31]

The routes of the caravans seem to have remained relatively unchanged throughout the period, with routes beginning in Mashhad, running south to Kerman and, from there, southwest to Bandar Abbas via Sirjan.[32] Caravans from this region were major purchasers of the Company's woollen goods, with sales of 40,000 rupees recorded, no doubt owing to the harsher winters that prevailed in the highlands of Khorasan and Kerman.[33] While the Company's consultations give no detail of how long it took the caravans to reach Kerman from Mashhad, the regular transportation of wool and copper from Kerman to Bandar Abbas gives us a clearer impression. The timings given are not exact, but journeys of a month between Bandar Abbas and Kerman seem to have been typical, while large delays were sometimes suffered because of a lack of pack animals caused by the frequent military campaigns of the turbulent eighteenth century.[34]

Bandar Abbas was also served by a route from the city of Isfahan through Shiraz, though this one is less well documented in the Company's records, probably due to the placement of Company staff in both of these cities at varying times. It appears that caravans from Isfahan would travel southward, stopping at Shiraz, the capital of the province of Fars, then continue southeast via Lar to Bandar Abbas. These caravans could be vast. In 1727, one consisted of 220 camels carrying a supply of wine and rose water, led by the Company's linguist.[35] It is unclear how typical a size this was, nor what a normal range would be. However, even if this represented a particularly large example, the logistics necessary and expense involved would have been prodigious. Caravans were also provided with guards, either from the Persian authorities or hired by the merchants, including the Company. The Company's privileges include a command for local officials to supply the Company's caravans with guards, should they request them. While this was a useful gesture, it demonstrates an underlying fear that caravans were vulnerable and in need of armed escort. When the Persian authorities were unable or unwilling to provide escorts, the Company, on occasion, would organise their own large and well-defended caravans, presumably offering to extend their protection to local merchants.[36] After the turmoil created from the initial shock of the Afghan invasion of 1722, caravan routes seem to have taken around five years to recover back to a predictable pattern; the Company records show that it took until 1727 for the first to arrive from either Khorasan or Isfahan; this was not only a boon to the Company's trade but was also noted with joy by the merchants to be carrying fresh fruits.[37] Caravans were exceptionally vulnerable due to their size and relatively lumbering pace and, despite being guarded, were often picked off by raiding Afghans, Baluchis or local bandits after the collapse of Safavid authority. The caravans, even after the re-establishment of some centralised power structures under Nader Shah, were therefore entirely unsuitable for the transportation of the Company's mail. Similarly, the dangers posed by raiders who predated in ever-increasing numbers on the caravans, guards or no, meant that the loss of goods on the road became a much greater risk. The breakdown of security on Persia's roadways at this time was a sad end to what had been a notable feature of travel accounts in the Safavid Empire where the presence of the rahdars and the protection they afforded were praised most highly, particularly by Thevenot and Tavernier.[38]

The dismantling of central state authority over the roads and ways of the Safavid domain had a dilatory effect on large-scale transportation, but as we have seen caravans were never the preferred method of sending and receiving mail. This role was fulfilled by individual messengers. There were three different sorts of messenger available in Persia during this period: the 'cossid' (*qasid*), the shotter (*shatir*) or the choppar (*chappar*).³⁹ Despite the dangers inherent in any kind of travel in Persia during the troubled time after 1722, all these services were available. The first two were readily available, either chartered privately or permanently employed by the European Companies, local merchants or Persian officials, while the last group were couriers for the Shah and his officials. Shotters seem to have formed the largest or most commonly used corps of messengers, with the Banians, Company and Dutch retaining their own, rather than relying on general availability. Despite working for one or the other of these groups, the shotters could carry letters from other organisations, as well as their employers. Throughout the period, the Company vacillated between employing its own shotters and using those in the pay of the VOC, or local Persian and Banian merchants. This was pursued as a money-saving measure by the Company, whereby it avoided paying to maintain its own messengers and could instead simply pay for individual messages to be carried at need. By 1729 it was decided that the employment of the Company's own messengers was a necessary expense as it removed any time spent waiting for a conveyance to be available, as well as being cheaper and more secure. A Company shotter was paid 70 shahis per month for his services, nearly twice the earnings of a Company Writer and there were between six and twelve in the Company's pay at any time.⁴⁰ It seems to have taken a shotter roughly seven to ten days from Bandar Abbas to reach Kerman, or more than two weeks to reach Isfahan, so while they were slower than the choppars, they still represented a rapid service.

'Cossids' appear much less frequently in the Company's records and no information is given about how much they were paid. Unusually among the messengers, cossids appear to have been used to carry messages longer distances, being mentioned travelling only to Isfahan and Kerman, while also accompanying other messengers on shorter missions, presumably as protection.⁴¹ Cossids seem also to have been paid according to time limits, rather than at a flat rate or salary; one entry in 1746 shows a cossid being ordered to deliver a letter from Bandar Abbas to Kerman within eight days,⁴² an exceptional request considering this is a distance of around 400 miles even as the crow flies. A cossid was employed to accompany a shotter from Bandar Abbas to Kerman during a period of increased activity among the robber bands on the roads, again pointing to a role as a guard or replacement.⁴³

Choppars were not private messengers for hire but official riders for the Shah and his noblemen. Choppars were paid by the recipient not the sender, unless the letter was for the Shah, in which case the sender was made to pay for the service.⁴⁴ Choppars were richly reimbursed for their trouble, receiving 4 to 20 toman depending on the message they carried and from whom the letter was sent. An example of this is found when a choppar sent by Persian court officials delivered a letter from Isfahan and received 4 toman for the service, while a choppar who delivered khalats (robes of honour) to the Company's Agent was rewarded with 20 toman.[45] Choppars seem to have also carried out minor administrative functions, rather than acting solely as messengers, showing the social status of their position. Choppars had the right to carry arms and were identifiable through a uniform; though the Company's sources are silent on what this may have been, it's possible that they were instead noticeable from their rich dress or the caparison of their mounts. They also had the right to take riding animals wherever they required them, either from peasants or other travellers.[46] In previous centuries, horses would have been changed at way stations (*Chappar-Khaneh*), but during our period, these institutions had been allowed largely to lapse, except for a brief attempt by Nader Shah to reinvigorate them in the 1740s.[47] Choppars were therefore by far the fastest means of communication, being able to ride between 70 and 100 miles a day.[48] In one rare instance, a choppar is reported to have reached Isfahan in seven days from Bandar Abbas, though this was extraordinary. Most reports suggest instead that ten to fourteen days was necessary for that particular journey.[49]

In ideal conditions, where the roads were properly guarded and maintained, movement and communication around Persia was relatively fast, but such circumstances were rare. During the period of this study, the roads were not administered to their potential by any means and suffered the predations of Afghan, Baluchi and Arab raiders, as well as groups of local bandits. These represented a significant danger to the messengers who travelled between towns and cities, necessitating, as has been mentioned, the escorting of messengers by other men. Interestingly, even when messengers were captured and threatened, the letters they carried were afforded rather more respect. One report in 1740 suggests that a shotter's life was spared by Arab rebels when they were told he carried mail for the Company. He was not killed on the proviso that he carried a letter back to the VOC and the Company, asking them not to interfere with their uprising.[50] Furthermore, the Arab rebels made a point to say that they had not read the Company's letters, despite capturing the messenger. There appears to have been an understanding that mail was inviolate, meaning that Dutch messengers carrying Company letters would not read them and vice versa. This was partly reliant on trust but was backed by the surety that should one party read the letters of another, their own would not be safe the next time they used a foreign conveyance. This did not mean that precautions were not taken, including the omission of previous correspondence in order to avoid giving context to the present letter.[51] Some letters appear to have been purposefully left behind, with one instance in 1724 of Ottoman messengers delivering official correspondence from the Pasha of Baghdad, while the Company's letters, sent by the same messengers, were mysteriously missing.[52] During times of war, letters and packets would be purposefully seized, as was the case with French mail found aboard a Dutch ship which was examined and forwarded to Bombay in 1748 during the War of the Austrian Succession.[53]

Communication by land in Persia would appear to have been comparable, if not preferable, with contemporary European means of sending and receiving mail, even given the major drawbacks explored above. The major road networks of Europe, such as the Turnpike system in Great Britain, would not begin to emerge until the end of the eighteenth century, with travel before this appearing, if anything, considerably slower there than in Persia, not to mention more expensive.[54] There was quite evidently a thriving market for messengers around Bandar Abbas, whether employed by one of the European companies, the Banians, Persian nobles and merchants or those despatched by the Shah or his administration.

The ability to communicate with the rest of Persia was another way in which the Agent and Council at Bandar Abbas were able to exert greater or more direct control over their business than was possible from Bombay. But the structures put in place by the Company's higher echelons were nonetheless put in place in Persia as elsewhere. The Agent was not an autocrat, far from it. The factory at Bandar Abbas, like all East India Company establishments, was governed by an executive Agent with the consent and support of a board of every covenanted Company servant present above the rank of Factor.[55] This rule was followed to the letter, covenanted servants only being elevated to the board on their accession to the rank of Factor, which occurred after a period of five years serving as a Writer. After serving at least three more years as a Factor a covenanted servant became eligible to become a Junior Merchant and then after a further three years, a Senior Merchant. The Company's servants could also augment their standing and salary by serving in certain 'stations', such as Warehouse Keeper, Secretary and so on, all of which carried extra responsibility and remuneration. According to the payrolls of the factory at Bandar Abbas, there was a mixture of Writers, Factors, Junior and Senior Merchants on the payroll, as well as the Agent, and surgeon, though never amounting to more than twelve covenanted Company servants.[56] We have seen that in exceptional circumstances, uncovenanted men might be left in positions of power, as occurred during the plague that left only two young men, Fowler and Hill, in charge of the Company's business after the deaths of everyone else in a position to act. This governing body therefore excluded anyone not covenanted with the Company and the youngest, least experienced members of the factory's staff. All the covenanted servants were required to sign off each order, letter and the board's consultations. Any member of this board who withheld their signature was effectively exercising a veto, which as we shall see could lead to severe repercussions.[57]

In 1729, in the public bazaar, there was a brawl between John Fotheringham and William Draper, the Chief Factor (Agent) at Bandar Abbas. The case was referred to Bombay, though neither party was dispatched there to stand trial. The case revolved around a dispute over shipping orders written up by Draper concerning a Muscati ship. Draper had given orders that the *Bengal Galley* 'take, capture or burn' the Muscati vessel, a stance that John Fotheringham and William Cordeux, the Council Secretary, feared would cause undue animosity between the Company and the Imam of Muscat. Despite the orders being changed to suit all three men, the disagreement between them became public and acrimonious, leading Fotheringham and Cordeux to publicly declare that Draper was 'no longer our Chief'.[58] After this, Draper and Fotheringham drew swords on each other in the public bazaar and fought; Fotheringham was wounded in 'the right breast, left shoulder and hip bone' while Draper was cut 'slightly on the right cheek'.[59]

The merchant's reactions to these events show how fragile the hierarchy within the factory could be, including the relationship with the garrison. While it is evident from the testimonies from all three of the Factors that no one was fully in control of the garrison, which did not react to orders given by Draper, it equally did not succumb to any instigations against him. Eventually, the garrison agreed to support Draper, or at least uphold his position as Chief.[60] Draper ordered for Fotheringham and Cordeux to be disarmed and put in custody. Draper himself retreated to his rooms, where he had weapons 'put around his chair'.[61] Despite Draper originally ordering for Fotheringham and Cordeux to be sent to Bombay, these orders seem to have been quickly overturned as Fotheringham and Cordeux remained at Bandar Abbas.[62] The garrison was ordered to read a declaration promising to obey Draper's orders, which raises questions concerning the garrison's view of the chain of command and why they did not respond immediately to Draper's orders. Perhaps the most interesting aspect of this case is that Fotheringham and Cordeux, on being released from confinement, delivered letters of protest to Draper both against him and against the two other members of the Council, William May and Mr. Forbes, for failing to act with them to curb Draper's actions. Cordeux also accused Draper of defrauding the Company after examining the accounts and records.[63] This exceptional falling out shows how, particularly in the relative seclusion of the Persian factory, there was a need for robust structures which could mitigate personal issues. There seems little doubt that while Cordeux and Fotheringham objected professionally to Draper's behaviour, there was a level of personal animosity too. Despite their severity, these events elicited little response from Bombay; instead, Draper reasserted his position through a re-statement of the Company's rules, particularly within the Council but also with the garrison.

Events like this accentuate the need for cooperation between the Company's employees of the sort Chaudhuri calls 'Business Constitutionalism'[64] characterised further by Stern as 'a strict hierarchy and consultative government'.[65] In this way, neither party, whether the Chief Factor or two members of the Council, had complete authority to judge what was and was not a criminal act or breach of the Company's rules. Therefore, a synthetic form of 'justice' was necessary and fundamental to the factory's governance. Clearly this system worked by requiring unanimity to proceed on contentious decisions, however it was reached. This rule must have required each member to have negotiated and sold their ideas to the satisfaction of all, including the Agent, who was constrained by the veto of his Council. This disagreement demonstrates that the system, although precipitating a regrettable local incident in this instance, ultimately resulted in more sensible, negotiated and consensual outcomes which meant there was no offensive against the Muscatis in contravention of standing Company orders. While the injunction against the Muscatis was upheld on this occasion, other problems required clarification and interventions. On occasion, updates of the Company's standing orders had to be requested and lists made and amended on a regular basis on the initiative of the local Agent and Council.[66] These instances, however, were never in response to immediate problems but more general questions about day-to-day activities, such as record keeping and the allowances for certain expenses.

Above the jurisdiction of Bombay, where criminal or malpractice cases were sometimes referred, was the even more distant power of the Court of Directors in London, to whom appeals were made directly by covenanted servants on a variety of pretexts. In 1719 alone two petitions were sent to the Court of Directors in London concerning a trade dispute between two Factors and a complaint concerning a perceived breach in the rules of seniority, which dictated the position and rank of a Factor within the council of his factory.[67] It is unclear why these particular disputes were referred to London rather than Bombay in the first instance, but from the letters dispatched from Bandar Abbas between 1719 and 1727, this seems to have been common practice. The Court of Directors seems to have been used as a court of appeal for personal matters between Company servants, while day-to-day business was submitted to the Council, then to Bombay in regular, structured reports. This is most likely a reflection of the difficulty in transmitting people and paperwork for criminal cases, all the way back to England, whilst balancing the need for personal disputes to be dealt with by the highest authority.

The Agent at Bandar Abbas was responsible not only for the business of his own factory but also for the administration of the factories at Isfahan and Kerman in Persia and Basra, at the head of the Gulf, in the Ottoman Empire. The Agent held the power to recall recalcitrant Company servants, audit their books and had limited power to appoint members of the Company's staff to new positions, though this was also governed by the whims of Bombay and the Company's strict adherence to seniority, as well as the politics of the Council at Bandar Abbas. Despite this premier position in the hierarchy of the Persian factories, the Agent was limited in his ability to effectively communicate with his distant charges, the Residents, relying either on slow, risky overland transportation or on the quicker but even more mercurial shipping up the Gulf to Basra. This meant again these local officers were trusted to act on their own initiative and with delegated authority subject to later audit and scrutiny.

The Residents were the officials in charge of the Company's houses and factories in Isfahan, Basra and Kerman. Isfahan, as the Safavid capital, had long played host to Company representatives and had formerly been the seat of the Agents for Persia, who acted in the dual role of merchant and consul with the Persian Court. While the Agent was technically superior to the Resident at Isfahan, the latter had significant personal authority, being the first line of communication with the Court and therefore responsible, more than any other, for the maintenance of the Company's good standing. From the 1720s onwards, there was only an intermittent presence in the Persian capital, due to the 'distracted state' of the region, sparked by the Afghan invasion and occupation. When no Resident was present in Isfahan, responsibility for negotiations with the current ruling power in Persia reverted to the Agent at Bandar Abbas, applicable for most of the period after 1722. Kerman was likewise only sporadically served by a Resident due to the costs incurred by having a European live in the city. When no European was present in either Isfahan or Kerman, a local employee was given stewardship, something that will be considered in more depth in Chapter 5. In Isfahan, this role was carried out by the Company's linguist, who was normally an Armenian from Julfa, and in Kerman this was often left to a local Persian merchant or broker retained in the Company's service.

We have discussed earlier in this chapter how the vast distances involved in communication between the Agent, the Residents and then Bombay and ultimately London made any centralised control at any level impossible. Santhi Hejeebu has suggested that the Company's use of contracts and charters had 'little currency as an enforcement mechanism'.[68] While the arguments of Hejeebu support the idea of a 'resilience' within the Company's systems, they deny that the contractual obligations undertaken by the Company servants were the framework in which this resilience rested. However, whereas it seems reasonable to assume from a variety of recorded misdemeanours that the Company's bonds and contracts were not a suitable enough deterrent, the relative dearth of serious cases suggests these were exceptions and not the rule. Out of eighteen criminal cases listed in the Factory records between 1700 and 1750, only one-half resulted in the guilty party being sent to Bombay for trial. Considering the long period of time studied, such a small number of cases in a far-flung part of the Company's establishment would seem to suggest that the bonds and covenants sworn were actually in the main effective and the punishments of infraction a suitable deterrent. Given how tiny the European community was when compared against the population in which they lived, it also reduced the likelihood of anyone being able to misbehave without being caught.

The Company employed a relatively rigorous accounting system and the India Office Records document eighteen cases where fraud was investigated over the period 1700 to 1750, making it one of the most common misdemeanours encountered in the records. This is perhaps unsurprising given the nature of the Company's presence in Persia and the singularly avaricious goals of the Factors themselves. Three in particular are noticeable, those of Thomas Waters and John Peirson, which revolved around keeping false accounts, with a third, involving William Cordeux, also accused of false accounting discovered after his death.[69] These three cases demonstrate that there was indeed some manipulation of the Company's business for private gain through embezzlement; Cordeux, for example, had used funds entrusted to him to carry out the wool investment at Kerman for his own trade, apparently with the unfulfilled intention of paying it back. The three men listed may have merely been the only ones to get caught in the act, rather than isolated cases in a sea of otherwise sensible and law-abiding business. It is perhaps also important to note that Cordeux and Peirson were stationed in Kerman and Isfahan respectively when they committed their frauds, rather than under the noses of their colleagues and superiors at Bandar

Abbas. That they got caught under the weight of the Company's administrative machinery when their accounts were checked either at Bandar Abbas or at Bombay says a lot for the Companies' auditing and rigour of their accounting at all levels.

While Hejeebu's argument that the Company's various legal mechanisms for the prevention of illicit activity were unsuccessful seems bolstered by these examples, the power of the Company to identify irregularity, recoup losses and censure their servants for breaching what was considered proper conduct suggests this conclusion is an over-generalisation. This is supported by the great lengths to which the Company would willingly go to check whether the covenants of their servants were genuine. In one instance in 1729, Martin French, who served both as a ship's captain and as Resident in Basra, was asked to provide proof of his covenant,[70] for which purpose one of his guarantors was traced all the way to Lisbon where he was convalescing after an illness.[71] The effort and time expended in tracing the witnesses in this way would strongly suggest that such legal contracts were considered, both by the Company and its servants, to be both binding and suitably proscriptive to discourage misbehaviour. Not only this, but the Company was also both willing and able, from the example of Martin French, to track down and verify its servants' compliance with legal process at some great distance and over long periods.

As we have seen already, the Company operated a distributed model of control, giving Residents and Agents decision-making authority with the minimum direct involvement from the central organs of London and Bombay. Again, distance and slowness of communications were overriding factors making this a necessity. However, when required, decisions were channelled back up the hierarchy as a ruse to delay having to give responses to demands or to leverage negotiations. In 1736, when it came to the purchase of ships for the Shah, the Agent, John Geekie, being unsure as to how he should proceed, decided to delay negotiations with the Persians by insisting on his need to consult with his superiors in Bombay before agreeing to anything.[72] This was a protective mechanism for Geekie, who could legitimately inform Nader Shah and his agents that he lacked the necessary authority to carry out the request, thereby avoiding the ire of the Shah or censure from his superiors.

In 1734, a serious political situation developed, resulting in a major deception of the Persians precipitated by Nader Shah's preoccupation with owning his own fleet of ships, which will be explored in much greater detail in Chapter 4. The Company had long outlawed the practice of private individuals selling their own ships to the Persians, it being expressly banned by the President and Council at

Bombay. The Shah's requirements, however, led the Company's Agent to decide to publicly adopt the practice.[73] As we will see in more detail in Chapter 4, this deception was necessary to mislead the Persians about the true level of private trade in the Gulf that the Company allowed to abuse the favourable rights of the Company *Farman*. Many of the ships trading at the Company factory were in fact privately not by the Company owned, carrying the goods of private merchants and as such liable to pay full duty at the port of Bandar Abbas. By claiming to the Persian authorities that, although the Company had not been willing or able to sell its own ships, they had encouraged, or indeed facilitated, the sale of two ships owned by private individuals who were in the Gulf on charter for the Company.[74] This adroit manoeuvring served the purpose of satisfying Nader Shah, an essential political dance step, while perpetuating the appearance of the Company's control over all British shipping, and also appearing to preserve their ban on the sale of their own ships.

The Company was flexible about how business was carried out in the factory but offered no such flexibility where the Company's own finances were involved. Here there was a definitive response by the Company's local structures to recover losses caused by their servants. In 1735, Captain John Harris, who deserted his command of the *Rose Galley*, fled to the islands in the Gulf, until he was captured by the Persians, whose help the Company had enlisted to detain.[75] The case of Captain Harris differs from that of the Draper, Cordeux and Fotheringham affair; Harris was not a member of the Council, though he commanded one of the Company's ships. Harris had stolen 3,500 rupees in cash, as well as other items belonging to the Company. The theft of Company property removed the opacity from his case and automatically created the Company's clear suit against him. Harris' case is noteworthy also because of his repeated requests to be examined by the Council at Bandar Abbas and not to be tried in Bombay, even going as far as to offer to satisfy Agent Cockell and his local debtors by proposing to auction off his belongings to raise funds as quickly as possible, an idea rejected given the seriousness of his crimes. Thus sentenced to further examination in Bombay, Harris orchestrated a botched escape attempt in 1736, with the assistance of his crew, four of whom were then arrested and confined in the factory with Harris. Apparently, they were too drunk to row themselves and their erstwhile captain to safety.[76]

Dealing with recalcitrant captains and their loyal, if misguided, crews may have been a frustration unlooked for, but there were other instances where the ships used by the Company raised other issues. The shipwreck of the *Gombroon Merchant* was one such issue, as the events surrounding the ship's loss showcase how extraterritoriality was managed between the Persians and the Company particularly through the medium of the *Farman*. The *Gombroon Merchant* ran aground in March 1734,[77] and a keen interest was taken in apprehending all those members of the crew who had survived but left the wreck, many with goods and cash stolen from the ship.

> He [Agent Cockell] proposes that those in Custody and charged with this ill behaviour may be publicly and solemnly examined, the better to fix the facts on the Persons that did it, as well as to recover what is possible of the proprietors.[78]

What follows was essentially a trial of the captain and mate, Prince and Ewins. Some of these men were found in a gambling den, others had fled to Minab after having stolen various articles from the hold or belongings of the dead.[79] The Company's men were keen to secure not only the goods that had been taken but also the perpetrators of the thefts, as they were recognised to fall under English legal jurisdiction, not that of the local authorities.[80] There doesn't appear to have been any resistance to the Company's men taking charge of any of the former crew of the ship, many of whom are made to answer questions at the same time as Prince and Ewins. The cooperation shown to the Company by the *Kalantar* of Minab, who informed Agent Cockell of the presence of some of the wanted men in his town, along with their apprehension and trial is demonstrative of a mutual recognition of authority and jurisdiction. While the *Farman* specifically mandates local governors and officials to assist the Company in any way within their power, the case of the *Gombroon Merchant* is a clear example of the principles of the document being acted upon with immediacy, while showing that the Agent and Council exercised legal functions in their own right.

Lastly, it is vital to consider the status of crimes committed against the Company and its servants by Persian subjects. The Company's right to try its servants under its own law, enshrined in the *Farman*, did not have the same implications as the 'Unequal Treaties' forced upon Qing China but were instead consensual.[81] The most striking example of the *Farman's* principles and the reach of the Company's jurisdiction being tested was the murder in 1734 of William Cordeux while overseeing the wool investment at Kerman.[82] Cordeux's death was reported to Agent Cockell by Nathaniel Whitwell, who arrived shortly after the event, having been dispatched to take over the wool purchasing. Whitwell informed the Council that Cordeux was strangled by his own servants as he was a 'severe master', which one might imagine given the standards of the time was exceedingly uncomplimentary.[83] Of the four held responsible for the murder, Whitwell reported that two had escaped, while the other two had been caught and held by the Persian authorities in Kerman. Whitwell advised the Council that he could have the two men in captivity executed should they provide a small bribe to the Khan of Kerman.[84] Whitwell was ordered to keep them alive and hold them for questioning concerning the murder, but as we have already seen, the Khan had designs upon Cordeux's 'girl' Manna, who had inherited Cordeux's partially ill-gotten fortune. It was at that point that she was spirited away by the Company, while the two men in Persian custody were simply left there, Whitwell being unwilling either to pay for their execution or to give into the Khan's demands for Manna in exchange for their release.

The importance of understanding the Company's reach in terms of the Persian justice system is demonstrated in the case of the brother of the Company's Banian broker, who was accused by the *Sultan* (Governor) of Bandar Abbas of murdering a thief who had attempted to rob the brother's residence.[85] The brother and other Banians had indeed caught and held the man, but according to their testimony to Agent John Horne, they had called the *Katwal* (local constable), who had then beaten him so severely he had died. The death of a Muslim, apparently at the hands of a group of Banians, incensed the local population, leading to their arrest by the *Sultan*, Mir Mehr Ali. The Broker was subsequently also imprisoned after trying to intercede on his brother's behalf. Agent Horne responded swiftly to this news taking a very active role in defending the rights and freedoms of not only the broker's brother but all the men. Armed with the *Farman*'s various articles, Horne demanded that the men be released and money returned that had been extorted from them on their arrest. The *Sultan*, after several complaints and the threat of direct intervention by Nader Shah, eventually relented to an extent, returning half the money taken from his captives, but rendering no apology, other than to the Agent himself. While this doesn't immediately appear to be a ringing endorsement of the *Farman* as a shield against unfair treatment, the appearance is deceptive. While the *Sultan* did not do all that the Agent asked, he was not technically obliged to do any of it. The Agent might well have insisted on release and restitution for the broker himself, but certainly this did not extend to the man's brother, let alone an unspecified number of his compatriots.[86] We must therefore accept that either the *Farman* or Horne himself, whether in the guise of the Agent or personally, held considerable sway locally and even nationally, if the threat to involve the Shah was taken seriously by the *Sultan*.

The Company's attitude towards other unaffiliated Englishmen not directly in its employment was also a point of contention, especially as the *Farman* did not differentiate between Company servants and other Englishmen. This is exemplified by the case of Captain Forbes, who, in 1727, was imprisoned by the

Pasha of Basra having been accused of keeping two Muslim women as slaves aboard his ship, a crime punishable by death.[87] Forbes was spared punishment at Ottoman hands by the intervention of the Company's Resident, William May, and the English trading community, who paid collectively for his release. The letter recounting these events mentions that the Court of Directors censured their servants at Basra for paying up as they believed 'the Pasha durst not go so farr [as to execute him]'.[88] In reply, May defended the decision, explaining that it was 'the advice of all the English in the place who were unanimous for giving it'.[89] The Directors may have been in favour of saving Forbes' life had they deemed it in danger, though in this instance they evidently believed that their subordinates had showed their hand too early. Forbes was the captain of a Company ship, raising important questions about the status of various members of the Company's extended network in the region. If saving the life of a ship's captain was not a matter for the Company to concern themselves with, then where did their responsibility begin and end? It cannot have been only with the covenanted servants, as this would exclude the broker and his brother, though Forbes, despite being an employee of the Company, was not covered or was liable to be bargained away.

The letter from 25 March 1727 in which these events are recounted also provides a window onto the perceived authority which the Residents believed that they had beyond the experience of their superiors beyond the Gulf:

> and your petitioner is Humbly of [the] Opinion that all the English in Bussorah [Basra] when met together are better judges of the nature of that people and Government than any can supposed to be who were never before off the Coast of India and your petitioner is Humbly of Opinion that the Supracargoes would give their Opinions to the best of their Judgement their Interest in that respect being the same with your Honours.[90]

Unfortunately, Isaac Housaye, the Resident at Basra, was charged the 55,000 shahis for Forbes' release as a penalty for his actions. He resigned soon after this following sixteen years in the Company's service. Despite the remoteness of the Persian factories from either London or Bombay, the Company's stable systems of organisation, based upon the executive appointments by seniority of its local Residents, Agents and Councils, created a recognisable matrix of authority from which trade and diplomacy were successfully carried out over an extended period. This hierarchy was able to exercise adequate administrative, judicial and commercial control over the Company's servants, while also presenting a recognisable system with which local powers and authorities could interact, building long-lasting and trusting relationships enabling them to conduct trade while balancing local and national political interests.

The Persian factories provide an example of the relative universality of the Company's control structure and the efficacy of its accounting and auditing, even at a distance both in space and over time. This supports Ogborn's description of an intricate, if fragile, administrative system, dependent completely on trusting the small number of individuals 'on the ground' but governed by a robust system of checks and balances.[91] We should conclude that the Company's rule by contract and delegated authority, although challenged by several cases of fraud and misuse of funds, are, in fact, under the circumstances, effective enough. Misdemeanours and breeches are few, discovered, investigated and result in punishment and reparations from the individuals, no matter the distance between them and central administrations in Bombay and London. These example cases must have served as an object lesson and salutary deterrent to all the Company's officers.

The question of the governance of the Company's holdings and operations in Persia is inextricably linked with the Company's relationship with the Persians themselves. The diplomatic link that the Company forged in the joint campaign against Hormuz in 1622 not only was a useful tool for the Company itself but also provided a route for diplomatic exchanges between the Persian and English/British states. This also leads to questions concerning the separation, whether practical or nominal, between the Company's commercial ends and the diplomatic strategies of the English/British Crown. Further to this, if no such separation is to be found, or is unclear, then it is just as important to consider the overlap between Company and Crown policy, attitudes and ends.

The period between 1700 and 1747 was a time of considerable upheaval in Persia. It saw the collapse of the 200-year rule of the Safavid Dynasty, the chaotic rise and fall of the Afghans and then the puppet rule of Tahmasp II and Abbas III, leading to Nader Shah's reign. Due to this instability, diplomacy took on a renewed importance to the various would-be dynasties that came to prominence in this period. Despite this unease, diplomatic traffic with the British residing in Persia was not limited to letters exchanged with the Company's Agent and other officials. The mission of Mirza Nasser was dispatched by Shah Soltan Husayn with orders to negotiate with the President at Bombay and then to go on to England if he failed to get a desirable response.[92] Mirza Nasser was charged with carrying letters to the President and Council at Bombay in order to negotiate for Company assistance in combatting the increasing threat of Muscati piracy to Persia's southern coast.[93] This exchange had been prompted by a letter sent by Queen Anne to Shah Soltan Husayn which was delivered by the Company's

Agent, Alexander Prescott, to Persian dignitaries who were being entertained at the Company's garden at Afseen. Prescott had elected not to take the title of Ambassador when carrying out this mission until he was informed that the Persians would only recognise embassies from London, despite being happy to send and receive letters to and from Bandar Abbas and Bombay.[94] This demonstrates that the Persian Court was clearly aware of the division between the Company and the Crown; indeed, they were not only aware of it but enforced protocol on the basis of it. This followed the pattern of previous royal embassies and letters sent in the previous century; Agent Gibson, for example, had been entrusted with a similar letter from Charles I, exhorting the Shah to extend every privilege to his subjects.[95] This shows a clear separation between the experiences of the East India Company in Persia as opposed to that of the Dutch Company, who suffered under their own pretext of representing the *Stadhouder* in the Netherlands while attempting to carry out a separate diplomatic correspondence throughout Asia through the Governor-General at Batavia. Adam Clulow has shown that this deception was necessary in the early stages of trade with Asian states, especially Japan, where there was no cultural cognate with the concept of the elected States-General.[96] Matthee suggests that the Shahs and their courts were more comfortable with the concept of dealing with European monarchs and the associated pomp and gifts contingent on these missions, putting the Dutch at a similar disadvantage as elsewhere.[97] Matthee likewise argues that the VOC and Company were ill-served in their status as servants, while benefitting from being representatives of powerful states. When considered with the almost universal silence of Persian sources on European merchants and their presence at the court, one can only sympathise with Matthee's point.[98] That being said, the Company, like the VOC, clearly had access to both local and royal officials and representation throughout their tenure in Persia, both in conjunction with and separate from royal embassies.

Unlike the Dutch then, the Company could still at least point towards a sitting monarch who fitted within the Persian paradigm of kingship and therefore bestowed upon the Company's European servants a form of sovereign protection and a clearer sense of nationality. The Company was able to easily trace its activities back to a recognisable ruler in the King of England/Britain. This then made it possible for them to create a frame of reference that would be palatable to Persian concepts of rulership and sovereignty. The Company used its royal connection to its fullest extent in order to mirror the Persian conception of rulership, meaning that all their treaties and the *Farman* were based on a relationship between the Persian Shah and English/British monarch.

The *Farman* granted to the Company after the capture of Hormuz and its subsequent reissues were exemplary of this. The final renewal of the *Farman* came about after a letter was sent to Shah Soltan Husayn from Charles II just as the letters carried by Mirza Nasser were in reply to correspondence delivered from Queen Anne. The fact that Mirza Nasser was the Shah's chief merchant, rather than an appointed ambassador, is also demonstrative of the Persians' attitudes towards the Company and Crown. Essentially, if it is reasonable for the English/British monarch to send letters and petitions via merchants, it must be likewise for the Shah.

Despite the inferred royal sanction to the letters delivered to the Shahs by various Kings and Queens, the period between 1700 and 1750 did not see a widespread exchange of official embassies between the courts of Europe and Persia. The lack of any official, royally appointed embassies is symptomatic of the view held in London that the Company's Agent also acted for the Crown as a consul.[99] In this way, the need for official embassies, like the one that was originally meant to deliver Queen Anne's letters, was abrogated by the formalised position enjoyed by the Company through the *Farman* recognising them as not only Company servants but also the representative of the English/British Crown. In practice, the Agent and Council in Persia do not seem to have ever been given an official mission from the Crown, nor any orders. This suggests that the Crown was either unaware of the clause tacitly handing consular authority to the Company or was simply happy to allow the Agent and Company to run their own affairs; after all, the vast majority of the Englishmen in Persia would have been Company servants.

Despite not recognising the Company's representatives as fully fledged diplomats from a foreign, sovereign power, the Company benefitted from this relatively lowly status as it obviated the need for large, impressive and expensive retinues, gifts and baggage which would normally be a requirement of foreign embassies. This is exemplified by the mission sent to gain the Company's first *Farman* from the Mughal Empire, in this case John Surman's mission to the court of Farrukhsiyar, the gifts alone consisted of:

> 1001 gold coins, a clock set with precious stones, an unicorn's horn, a gold escritoire, a large lump of ambergris, the inevitable ewer and basin and a globe, more than six feet in diameter inlaid with gold and silver.[100]

Other embassies to the Persian court, conspicuously those sent by the Russians and Ottomans, were vast undertakings. One Russian embassy, according to the consultation books from Bandar Abbas, consisted of 125 attendants which was met by an escort of 300 mounted troops who conducted the Russians to Isfahan.[101] Two later embassies from Russia were reported to consist of 500 and as many as 3,000 men,[102] causing concern for the Russian Resident, who did not believe he could obtain passports for all of them in time.[103] Ottoman embassies were, if anything, even grander, more lavish affairs and required the Persians to give the ambassadors large gifts and allowances while they remained in Persian territory.[104] This level of expense was not unusual and mirrors the huge sums spent on embassies in this period, including the Dutch *Hofreis* to the Shogunal Court in Japan.[105] It is not unreasonable to assume then that the much less formal nature of the Company's interactions with the Persian Court was conspicuously less burdensome, time-consuming and expensive for both parties and represented a pragmatic even pleasant way of continuing a relationship which, by the end of this period, had lasted 150 years. While technically serving a dual purpose for two different masters, both as the Agent of the Company's holdings in Persia and the Crown's consul, in reality the latter responsibility was largely notional. During the period between 1700 and 1750, there was little need for official embassies to be sent from London and, in this way, emissaries' missions like the one carried out by Mirza Nasser sufficed to maintain diplomatic dialogue. While the Company's presence in the corridors of Persian power did not draw the rapt attention of Ottoman embassies, it was nonetheless consistently close at hand and served the purposes of both parties without undue expense or fanfare, though perhaps had there been more of these we would now have the advantage of a Persian view of the Company's activities.

The modest yet persistent activity of the Company's servants at the Persian court gives an insight into why Santhi Hejeebu concluded that the Company's system of administration, control and operation was weak and ineffective.[106] However, by investigating the way the Company operated in Persia, a small, remote part of the Company's operations, one can see that this was simply not the case. We have seen how the interests of the Company and state were projected abroad based on basic guiding principles, how servants of the Company were empowered to act on their own initiative, necessitated by the slowness of communication. Even the Company's Agents, imbued with a great deal of personal power, were forced to delegate significant authority in the Residents of distant cities. It had to be accepted that apology was better than permission. Control, punishment and censure could also be applied. There were notable failures that included fraud and arguments that turned to violence that were resolved within the community of the factory. It is clear that the Company deployed excellent communicators and relationship builders, able to act as ambassadors, diplomats and military advisors. The use of the Afseen Garden is testimony to their skills as relationship managers, able to put their interlocutors at ease and develop strong interpersonal bonds and friendship. The Company servants gathered intelligence and were adept in its analysis to interpret circumstances and respond in order to develop trade. This chapter gives evidence of how the Company functioned operationally and how the people working in even its farthest flung outposts were central to its success and longevity in Persia. The Company's communications were shaped by the technology of the time and the extreme distances over which it operated. The massive delays, risks and difficulties involved in communicating even with the Company's regional centre again point to the autonomy enjoyed by the Agent and factory at Bandar Abbas and the trust inherent in holding this office. Operationally the Company servants for the most part repaid the trust endowed, although on occasion their decisions are audacious.

3

Trade's increase: The Company's commerce in Persia

The previous two chapters have focussed closely on the material conditions of the Company's employees in Persia, exploring their lives and deaths, as well as the abstractions of the practices of governance, justice and diplomacy. This chapter will move on to the nature of the Company's business in the Gulf during this tumultuous period. Contrary to what might be the general expectation, the Company's trade continued throughout the Afghan interregnum, civil wars and then the upheavals caused by Nader Shah's campaigns in South Asia and Muscat. The Company's financial survival was in large part due to their willingness to diversify the goods and methods used for purchasing and selling, including accepting copper as payment, in order to benefit from a beneficial balance of arbitrage between Persia and India. We will explore the different commodities which formed the Company's commerce, from luxuries like wine and silk to wool and unprocessed copper.

Scholarly study of the 'Persia trade' has given rise to numerous debates concerning the economics of the commercial activity of the Gulf region and its place within the wider Indian Ocean and World economies. Niels Steensgaard, for example, explored the European dimension of trade in the Indian Ocean, seeing it in terms of a competition between the European Companies and local 'pedlars'.[1] Steensgaard's focus on the transition between the Portuguese dominance in the region and that of the northern European companies, however, leaves relatively little room for the agency of regional powers, let alone individual local merchants in his characterisation. Nor perhaps does he see the broader trajectory wherein the 'pedlars', rather than competing with the companies, served as a route by which the Company's servants undertook their own, private trade. Steensgaard does, however, provide a guide to how trade and commerce looked at the beginning of the Company's tenure in the Indian Ocean, allowing for an expansion of scholarly work on later periods by providing a map of gradual shifts and changes. Rudi Matthee's work 'The Politics of Trade in the Safavid Empire' explores the detail of the Safavid economy through the lens of the silk trade.[2] Matthee's work successfully covers the other side of this discourse, wherein Persian official policy affects the business of the companies, rather than only reacting to it. In order to do this, Matthee uses the example of the silk trade to demonstrate that the Safavid state was by turns actively, or inactively, involved in managing its own economy and trade quite separately from the commercial policies of European merchants.[3] By building on Matthee's example of the policing of the silk market, this chapter will show how the Persians appreciated the usefulness of the Company in stimulating competition for export goods, while also realising the potential of the Company's Indian trade as valuable arenas of experimentation in other exports. This chapter will also explore how Persian policy, especially concerning silk sales and cloth purchases from English merchants trading through Russia, was geared towards diversifying trading links and partnerships. As yet, this dimension of the silk trade and Persian commercial policy has gone unexplored. Matthee's work, though essential to this area of study, ends in 1730, a decade before the arrival of the so-called 'Russia Merchants'. By expanding the scope of Matthee's analysis, a more nuanced understanding of the Company's place in Persia's trade is presented. The expansion of the time frame of this study as opposed to others has also revealed a fascinating new insight into the relationship between the Company and their Dutch rivals. For most of the history of both these organisations, competition for the same resources gave rise to mutual antagonism. What this chapter will demonstrate is that this antipathy and competition, which limited the trade and profit of both organisations, could be overcome in the interest of mutual gain. In 1735, this culminated in an agreement between the Company and VOC to fix the price they would pay for wool, forming a European cartel in the wool markets of the Iranian Plateau.

Stephen Dale's work, highlighting the role of Indian merchants in the commercial life of Asia, also goes some way to dismiss the centrality of Europeans and their companies in the intercontinental trade networks of the early modern world.[4] This line of scholarship highlights the significant changes brought about in the Indian Ocean by the arrival of European merchants and companies, while also showing that the impact of these changes would not be felt until well into the eighteenth century. Indeed, Sanjay Subrahmanyam has even questioned how 'European' some of the trade networks that have been associated with the mercantile companies actually were.[5] This chapter will explore how the Company's trade interests sometimes intersected with those of the Persian state and how both sides used the other to achieve their aims. Through the lens of the

Company's records and the lists of privileges given to them by successive Persian regimes, we can track the policies and changes in outlook both of the Company and their Persian interlocutors.

The Company's interests in Persia sprang directly from its inability to sell its major European export, woollen cloth, in India. Unlike tropical India, Persia, with its mountains and harsher winters, was a much more likely place for the English merchants to sell profitably their European wares in exchange either for silver or other produce, which could be used to fuel the Company's interests in India.[6] The Company, led by Anthony Shirley's assurances of a good market and reception for their products, therefore began shipping its cloth to Persia in 1616. The cloth that the Company exported proved much in demand in Persia's markets, forming a major part of contracts that were signed between Abbas I and the Company. Along with Japan, it was hoped that Persia would provide the specie or goods needed to run a successful trade in India and the Spice Islands. Wool and cloth production had formed one of the largest industries in England for centuries, particularly the export of unfinished cloth to the Netherlands, where it was dyed and dressed for sale around Europe. In 1616, James I was persuaded by a London merchant to ban the export of unfinished cloth in an attempt to stimulate the English economy by building local expertise. The Cockayne Project was named after its main proponent, William Cockayne, a wealthy London merchant with interests from the Baltic to the Spice Islands. While Cockayne's idea of bringing the entire manufacturing and finishing process into English hands may have seemed financially sound, particularly as only European exports were shipped without having first been dyed and prepared for sale, he did not reckon with the staunch opposition put up by the Dutch. The planned ban on the export of unfinished cloth was met with outrage across the Channel and an ensuing trade war which led to a depression in England's premier industry. This was a boon for the Company, however, as they were now able to pay less for cloth in a depressed market, while opening up new destinations for its exportation. The Company continued to sell English cloth in Persia to reasonable profits for the remainder of the seventeenth and into the eighteenth century, despite competition from Armenian, Russia and Levant merchants bringing the same commodity into Persia from West and North.

The promise of a good sale for the Company's cloth was not the only factor that drew the Company to Persia. Silk, which was produced in the northern provinces of Gilan and Mazandaran, also held firm in the imaginations of the Company's servants.[7] The seventeenth century saw various attempts by the Company to form contracts with Shah Abbas and his successor, Shah Safi I, for cloth and silver to be exchanged directly for silk. These contracts were enshrined in the early iterations of the Company's *Farman*, but proved too much of a strain on both parties, eventually being quietly done away with. There remained a mutual interest in silk, whether a Persian desire to diversify the market from its traditional routes and buyers or occasional and brief flirtations by the Company to revivify its own ambitions for the fabric. These attempts ultimately failed and no major future attempts were successfully made to reignite the purchasing of silk by the Company after 1722.[8]

While the silk trade was not renewed, it still appears in the Company's records, but under rather different circumstances to those seen in the seventeenth century. The last exploration of the silk trade before the end of Nader Shah's reign was spurred by competition neither by the VOC nor the established Armenian merchant families but from other English merchants, who had begun to trade in Persia through Russia. These men, referred to by the Company as the 'Russia Merchants',[9] were led by John Elton and Mungo Graham and were trying to reignite the long routes dreamed of by Samuel Jenkinson during his journey through Persia and Central Asia in the 1570s. These merchants arrived in the silk producing provinces of Gilan and Mazandaran in 1741–2, where they entered into direct competition with the Company by selling consignments of English woollen cloth to Nader Shah. The Russia Merchants' interests were primarily in the purchase of Iranian silk which they planned to ship to Europe via Russia. In response to this, Agent Whitwell in Bandar Abbas ordered for musters and the prices of silk available for purchase at Isfahan and Kerman be sent to him for inspection. This was in preparation to compete with the Russia Merchants directly for silk should the need arise. However, this renewed interest in silk petered out fairly quickly, when the Russia Merchants discovered for themselves what the Company's merchants had long known; Persian silk was expensive, of variable quality and often uncertain in its supply. In addition, the Russia Merchants had faced numerous difficulties in establishing themselves, and thus no longer represented a significant threat to the Company.[10] We will return to these men in due course.

By 1700, the Company's trade was thus dominated by other, less costly commodities, most notable of which was wool from the Kerman region. The trade in Kerman wool is a useful demonstration of the Company's willingness to invest in an industry that had the potential to create a steady profit, albeit in a relatively volatile and inaccessible region. The Company maintained the wool trade during the Afghan occupation of Persia in the 1720s and sporadically through the reign of Nader Shah. Danvers Graves, one of the Company's servants and Resident at Kerman, whose story we saw at the opening of this book, was still collecting wool when Nader Shah sacked the city.[11] Graves' account shows how the Company used its connection to local dignitaries and merchants to carry on this trade, even in the face of present dangers and stark economic outlooks, let alone the city's wholesale destruction thereafter.[12] Graves' experience during the sack of Kerman lends further weight to the importance of these local links in conjunction with the overarching protections granted by centralised governments through the *Farmans*.

While wool, a bulk product with which the English had long experience, formed a major part of the Persia trade in our period, it was far from the only important commodity which the Company invested in with increasing enthusiasm. Luxury goods, particularly wine, which the Company gained permission to produce and export in its *Farman*, have never been adequately appreciated in the research on the Company's trade, let alone the economy of Shiraz and other wine producing areas. As Matthee points out, Persian wine was produced in relatively large quantities and was popular as a luxury commodity throughout the Indian Ocean.[13] The Company's records show that its ability to ship a significant volume of wine was a major advantage in terms of both trade and diplomacy. An example of the use of wine as a diplomatic *douceur* can be found in the records of the Bombay Presidency, which document an occasion when the Jesuit mission at Salsette was given a number of cases as a gift.[14] Shiraz, where the Company maintained a vineyard, was also the main centre in the production of rose water, used as a perfume and sweetener throughout Asia and Europe. Both these products, along with others such as nuts, dried fruit, cereals and livestock, suggest that the Company and private traders were active in the exploration of a variety of Persian products that could be sent for sale or use in India.[15] Clearly, from the records of the Bombay Presidency, the Company was concerned with the purchase and shipping of goods not only for simple profit but also for wider reasons, be they the comfort and leisure of its servants, their diet or wider geo-political goals requiring the presentation of expensive products as gifts. The Company's factory was therefore not maintained on the simple premise that it would be a post from which silk would be exported, nor solely as a terminus for English cloth. Instead, we can now begin to appreciate the dynamic ways in which the Company acted as a vehicle for profit through trade, a point of taxation for private shipping and merchants and as a hub of political representation to the Persian state. If the Company's sole interest in Persia had remained the purchase of silk, it would have abandoned Bandar Abbas early in the 1630s, after it became clear this trade would not flourish.

Instead, through diversification the factory was maintained by the Company as a going concern, showing that the establishment was profitable and influential in other ways, whether this was in terms of other trade goods, political and strategic importance, or for the purpose of generating cash through revenue collection and taxation and for the private trade of Company servants.

Having established that by 1722 the Company's interests were no longer served by the exportation of Persian silk, it is necessary to consider in more depth why the *Farman* continued to maintain the freedom of its trade. Abbas I had attempted to create a state monopoly for the exportation of silk in the last two decades of his reign, but this initiative lapsed under his successor, Safi I.[16] Unlike other traders, the Company was permitted under Abbas I's monopoly to purchase 100 bales of silk and transport it free of taxation to Bandar Abbas, where it could then be shipped to India or Europe.[17] Company records show that this privilege was restored by Nader Shah as a way of stimulating the silk trade anew during his reign. As the sale of silk was re-established by Nader Shah as a royal monopoly, the promotion of its sale was of direct benefit to the exchequer.[18] Attempts to woo the Dutch in a similar way are not recorded in the Company's letters and consultations, though it would be unlikely that Nader Shah would have missed the chance to further improve competition for silk by not courting Dutch interest. There are clear similarities between Nader Shah's silk policies and his co-opting of the Company to build up naval power in the Gulf discussed in the next chapter. Just as with the fleet project, the Persians were using the Company's own interests in the profit that could be derived from cooperation to achieve their ends. In the case of silk, the Shah hoped to induce the Company into purchasing and exporting his monopoly product, and anticipated, no doubt, to build further demand for it. This had the added advantage of creating competition over the silk itself both between the maritime route through the Gulf and the traditional overland route dominated by the Armenians, which ran through the Ottoman Empire.

Further evidence that Nader Shah sought to make use of European merchants to generate competition for this monopolised resource requires us to return to the Russia Merchants. Previous research on the European entry into the Iranian silk trade, which has focussed on the period before 1730, has not considered the case of the Russia Merchants who began exploring the northern route to the silk producing Caspian provinces. Stefan Troebst's work, outlining the Russian-Swedish route of trade from North-western Europe to Persia, goes some way to rectifying this gap.[19] In 1741, an exchange of correspondence between an unnamed Member of Parliament and a group of merchants took place. These merchants, according to their petition, wished to begin trading English cloth for Persian silk, but rather than pursuing this trade via the shipping route around the Cape, or through the Mediterranean, the petitioners sought to trade through Russia.[20] The rationale behind this was that Persian silk was produced in the Caspian provinces in Northern Persia; therefore, it was quicker to travel from England through the Baltic and then south through Russia, into the Caspian and then trade in these provinces directly.[21] The response from Parliament to the correspondence, the promise of the importation of raw silk cheaply through Russia, eased with a guarantee of free navigation of the Caspian,[22] is countered by the fear that the Russians, who had previously increased the duty charged on rhubarb,[23] would do likewise with silk or, worse, make it a state monopoly tradable only at St. Petersburg.[24] Equally, the response to the letter questions whether the new trade for silk was worth pursuing, when it would quite evidently interfere with the commerce of both the Levant Company and the East India Company.

Despite these obstacles, however, John Elton, a merchant with experience of the Russia trade, and a number of other merchants made the journey through Russia to the Caspian provinces of Persia.[25] They soon discovered that their intrusion was not welcomed, either by their countrymen in Bandar Abbas, or the Armenian merchants in Resht, who refused to accept their bills, or the Persian authorities, who arrested the other leading merchant, Mungo Graham.[26] Despite these setbacks, it is reported that the Russia Merchants were accepting payment in bills from their clients and purchasing silk for over 300 shahis per *mann-i Tabriz*.[27] They also secured a sale of broadcloth to Nader Shah, who was encamped at Derbent.[28] Nader Shah was evidently unconcerned about the presence of competing British merchants in his northern provinces. The response of Nader Shah is consistent with the policy he was pursuing regarding the sale of silk: the entry of the Russia Merchants into the silk trade increased competition for his monopolised resource, while their sales of English broadcloth, vital for clothing his troops, reduced the price that the Company and VOC could charge for the same product.

The expedition through Russia had a salutary effect on the Company's merchants, who immediately sprang into action, sending orders to their Factor in Kerman, as well as to their other contacts from Resht to Mashhad, to keep an eye on the activities of these interlopers. Not only this, but the Company's Agent, Nathaniel Whitwell, by now an old hand in Persia, also had 3,000 toman of broadcloth sent up for sale at Isfahan, in an attempt to flood the local market.[29] The major concern for the Company remained that the merchants coming through Russia, being British, would be able to take advantage of their trade privileges, while not being answerable to the Company hierarchy and competing with them in the same markets and trading in the same commodities.[30] The Company responded by ordering musters of silk from Isfahan, Kerman and Gilan, determined anew to get a firm grip on the silk trade to Europe.[31] This reaction seems to be less indicative of the Company's overwhelming need to control the silk trade, which was neither possible nor plausible, at least while the Armenians could control all the overland routes to Europe from Gilan. Instead, the outcome of the Russia-ward push for silk demonstrates how the Company was interested in its cloth sales remaining competitive and in retaining the integrity of its trade privileges.

For Nader Shah, the situation in this period was ideal, with a surplus of cloth which he used to clothe and pay his troops lowering its value, while demand for silk rose with competition. Even without charging customs, the potential profit for the Persian government was considerable and the manipulation of the Company's privileges to compel them to purchase silk, along with allowing extra competition in this market, proved that Nader Shah and his regime were sensitive to the ways in which they could shape and profit from the Company's presence. While we cannot corroborate this with sources from the Persian perspective, the behaviour of the Shah and his officials and merchants gives us a clear indication of their attitudes and interests. Not only was the Shah willing to offer new privileges to the established companies to further his financial aims, he was also willing to sanction and support new ventures to the same end. As such, there can be little question about the agency of the Persian state in its trade policy, especially during the more dynamic period under Nader Shah. The Bombay Presidency continued to reiterate its interest in purchasing silk for export back to Europe, with small amounts being acquired and sent to Bombay from Persia until as late as 1748, though as we have seen, these plans never came to fruition.[32] Company policy was directed loosely on this topic, with occasional requests from Bombay to Bandar Abbas for musters of silk, or an appraisal of the market. Ultimately, however, the officials in Bombay were reliant upon the judgement of the Agent and his council. At least in the case of Whitwell, they could be sure of his long experience in the country, as well as the practicalities of local trade. The Company's interest in the silk trade never became more than exploratory in this period, any silk having been acquired either in payment of a shipment of broadcloth or in place of cash when the Safavid government was unable to cover the Company's share of the Bandar Abbas customs.[33] Unlike in previous periods, where silk had fixated the Company, in the early eighteenth century it was now the Persians who were promoting it as a valuable product for trade. In some instances silk was used as a means of payment in kind, while for Nader Shah, silk exportation was used as a source of ready income to support his military ambitions and as a way of promoting competition between foreign and domestic merchants, guaranteeing an increase in price.

The Company's exportation of Kerman wool first began as an attempt to increase the profitability of its Persia trade. As we have seen, silk simply couldn't fulfil this requirement. Kerman wool, being readily accessible from the European factories on the Gulf Coast, was viewed as a possible foil to the volatile silk supply and attempts to purchase and export it began in 1659.[34] Despite the relative proximity of the wool producing region to the Gulf factory, there were other issues that might have precluded its development. These ranged from the cost of picking, cleaning and packing the wool for transportation, and increasingly specific orders from Bombay and London concerning the maximum prices that could be paid for wool, as well as which colours were desirable in the London markets.[35] On top of these financial concerns, the Kerman region was, as we shall see shortly, ravaged by warfare and the state. Despite all these difficulties, however, the Kerman wool trade endured as a commercial interest for the Company, which used a variety of methods to secure its supply. These included making presents and loans to local officials, making substantial investments with local producers and merchants, and even making an agreement with the Dutch to fix prices. Kerman wool, or *kork*, is gathered from the soft down beneath the fleece of the species *Capra Ibex*.[36] The wool was the basis for a local weaving industry in Kerman which produced carpets and shawls.[37] In Europe and India it was used in weaving and the production of felt for hats and other garments which had previously used beaver fur.[38] Before being shipped from Bandar Abbas, the wool had to be picked, packed and then carried by caravan from Kerman and nearby villages to the coast. Kerman bore the brunt of Baluchi and Afghan incursions in the 1720s and 1730s. If this were not enough, in his constant search for revenue to support his military adventures, Nader Shah comprehensively sacked Kerman, not long before his murder in 1747.

The Company employed local merchants to carry out their wool investment. This was preferred as it reduced the costs that the Company incurred from supporting a European, who, unlike the local merchants who were only provided a salary, had to be provided a living allowance, accommodation and other expenses in line with the Company's policies that were discussed in Chapter 1. Local merchants had the added advantage of being familiar with the local market, though they also faced the increased likelihood of facing extortion from local officials and were less able to enforce the repayment of Company debts. Owing to these issues, European Company servants were dispatched to Kerman to audit the wool investment, collect outstanding debts and also, it is likely, remind the local authorities for whom the Company's agents ultimately worked. This meant that the Company developed a system which avoided the expense of maintaining a constant European presence and circumvented some of the major issues with relying on local brokers, while maintaining their expertise.[39] Working in this way saved costs, about which the Company was obsessed, while keeping a visible presence in Kerman all year round. From the outset, for the Company's trade in Kerman which was established in 1659, either Armenian or Banian merchants were dispatched to oversee the trade there. From 1729 the position was left in the hands of a father and son, 'Seawax' (Siavush) and Esfandiar.[40] Previously, the Company had employed a separate broker and wool merchant, 'Cosroe' (Khosrow) and 'Cossim' (Kasim), both of whom were dismissed having been found to be dealing dishonestly with the Company and because of repeated failures by them to provide the correct colour and weight of wool.[41]

In order to keep their agents in good standing, the Company made gifts to the local officials in Kerman, both on their accession to their post and annually on *Nowruz*, the Persian new year.[42] The Company went so far as to set a budget of 70 toman annually for the Kerman factory to buy presents or provide cash to local officials in order to keep on a good footing in the region.[43] These gifts, while meant as a gesture of goodwill between the Company and the governor or *Kalantar* of Kerman, were also used as a reminder to these officials to repay the debts they owed to the Company.[44] The exchange of gifts as well as lending money to local officials were methods of oiling the mechanisms of Persian officialdom in order to avoid any interruption of the wool trade. In cases where wool was lost or stolen on the road, sometimes abandoned by the *Charwardar* (Muleteer or camel drover) tasked with transporting the Company's goods to the coast, these connections were used as an effective means of recovering the Company's goods or gaining restitution for any losses.[45] The co-opting of local forces and officials through the exchange of cash and gifts can be likened to a form of informal insurance, whereby the Company could expect the return of their property in case of theft or protection of their people and goods throughout the region. The Company's wool merchants were employed to buy up supplies in the markets of Kerman, using their local knowledge to maximise supply and limit costs. Money was supplied to them by bills drawn by Banian brokers upon the Company who operated between the city and the coast; this avoided the risk of transporting cash overland and it also took advantage of the high exchange between silver and the copper coin commonly used around Kerman.⁴⁶ As a general rule, the Company in Persia did not provide money in advance, nor did it extend large amounts of credit, other than to its broker at Bandar Abbas. The wool trade was an exception to this rule, receiving a large annual investment. This change of approach appears to have been in imitation of the Dutch, who advanced cash to shepherds in the villages surrounding Kerman as early as 1722, putting the Company at a significant disadvantage by the time the wool was available for sale in the city's markets.⁴⁷ Matthee suggests that this practice began with the Company and was then adopted by the Dutch, who saw the English practice of forwarding money and providing gifts to local officials as a form of bribery.⁴⁸ Both companies were in effect accusing the other of underhand practices, while certainly doing the same thing at the same time. Matthee shows Dutch primary sources telling a story of English corruption, while the Company accused the Dutch of swindling them of their wool supplies. It is impossible to tell from either set of sources who first began this process, though it is clear that both companies were active in slandering each other where possible, while carrying on whatever underhand dealing they could get away with.

In 1728, to further pursue their trade, Agent Geekie dispatched William Cordeux to oversee an investment for wool, he would of course later die in this same post. In order to do this he was given an allowance of 10 toman per month and the freedom to act as he saw fit.⁴⁹ In pursuit of improving the wool supply, Cordeux was given a treasury of 100 toman in silver mahmudis and 500 Venetian sequins.⁵⁰ This outlay of cash would then later give way to the continued use of bills and shipments of English cloth which found a strong market, especially among merchants who came to Kerman from Khorasan.⁵¹ The market for cloth at Kerman was a particular spur to the Company, as the region therefore represented a consumer of the Company's major import and a vendor of a product desired in Europe. Cloth was considered valuable enough to the Company to require the oversight of a European Company servant to oversee its sale; therefore, Cordeux served a dual purpose, increasing the pace of the wool purchases while selling off the Company's cloth.⁵² Neither Cordeux nor his successors at Kerman succeeded in completely funding the wool investment through cloth sales, partly due to the huge quantities purchased annually and the difficulties in getting the cloth to the city from the coast.

Despite the expense involved in procuring wool and shipping it to Europe, the trade remained durable throughout this period. The Directors in London learned quickly how best to profit from this product, their interventions often concerned the colour of the wool to be bought, with white and red going in and out of vogue in London's markets at varying times.[53] The Company also sometimes limited the price that should be paid for the wool, after it had been cleaned and transported to the coast, but despite this limitation still insisted on a supply of 10,000 maunds in 1736.[54] For most of the period after 1700, however, orders of 50,000–60,000 maunds were common,[55] despite the political upheavals and repeated movements of armies across the region. This suggests that the Company was able to effectively co-opt local officials and forces into securing the routes to the coast and therefore the wool supply to such an extent that very large amounts of wool could be transported to the coast for shipping.

Perhaps the most interesting feature of the wool trade was the competition between the Company and the VOC. As has been seen, both companies accused the other of false dealing, bribery, corruption and the English even accused the Dutch company's Armenian *vakil* (agent) of poaching wool previously contracted for by the Company.[56] This lends some credence to Dutch accusations that the Company began the pre-payments for wool, though it does not prove that the Dutch had not been doing so first with other merchants. Certainly, the Company was guilty of furnishing local officials with cash and loans, but whether this constituted bribery is hard to establish, as this practice was common among Persians and Europeans, including the Dutch, and constituted a part of normal business around the Early Modern World. The Dutch were accused in return by the Company of unfairly flooding the markets of Kerman with silver and offering outrageous sums to secure the largest supply of wool, though again, this is hardly likely to have differed from the normal practices of the time.[57] These attempts at industrial and commercial sabotage, whether real or imagined, reveal the importance placed on the wool trade by both companies. Matthee conjectures that this was due to the continuing debasement of Persian coinage, which no longer carried enough silver to make its export worthwhile, thereby robbing the Europeans of yet another potentially worthwhile export. Wool therefore represented one of the few commodities in which the Europeans were interested in investing, providing a steady stream of revenue to Kerman, while, at least partially, satisfying the Company's need for profitable exports.[58] Despite the difficulties with cash flow, transportation, invasion and regime change, the Company maintained a steady trade in wool and copper, with shipments worth 200,000–2,000,000 shahis arriving annually in Bombay between 1728 and 1750. The exportation of goods on this scale from Persia suggests that the Company made a considerable profit, despite the adverse conditions, whether through the mass exportation of cheap copper to India or wool to the felters and hatters of Europe.

One of the contributing factors to the volume of Company wool trade came through an agreement made between the Company and the VOC in 1735. The rapprochement came about after a period of intense competition which raised the prices at which wool could be purchased to a point where both sides had to agree to cooperate or risk leaving their masters' indents unfulfilled. This took the form of a promise to pay no more than 30 shahis per maund of wool, where prices of between 60 and 75 shahis had been recorded previously.[59] As the two major competitors in the market, this ceiling forced down the price from its previous high levels. As the Company's investment in wool was reported to be three times larger than that of the Dutch, it is also evident that it was the major beneficiary.[60] This evidence shows that the Company and their Dutch rivals were willing and able to act together on a local level, without the need to refer back to Bombay or London.[61]

The agreement between the European companies was not to last long; by 1745 it had lapsed completely and all efforts to revive it failed.[62] Nonetheless, the agreement demonstrated that the European companies were willing to work together to ensure a supply of wool for sale back in Europe, despite the competition this might cause when it was sold in their home markets. Matthee suggests that the competition between the companies was by far the largest block to their success in Kerman. Had he continued his research past 1730, he would have found how accurate he was, as the mutually set price limitations allowed the Company to make orders of 50,000–60,000 maunds at low prices.[63] By agreeing to cooperate, both companies removed the barrier of each other's competition, only to have the political situation in Persia deteriorate at the same time. The agreement also showed that the companies were now more intent on profit, rather than the one-upmanship that had permeated the wool trade since it was first explored.

The trade in Kerman wool demonstrates a number of features important to the Company's position in Persia. Firstly, the Company's inability to gain a foothold in the silk trade drove them to consider other avenues to draw profit from their factories in Persia; Kerman wool provided the Company with an opportunity to do this, while also being an outlet for the Company's English cloth. Kerman also mined large quantities of copper, which was constantly in demand in India for the minting of low-value coins. The VOC likewise engaged in the exportation of copper through various means, though it did not engage in barter as the Company was willing to do.[64] The Company could therefore ship English cloth to Persia, sell it for locally mined copper which was then shipped to India where it increased in value due to arbitrage before any processing; lastly, the Company purchased wool for sale back in the markets of London.

The exportation of wool and copper provided a rare and much-needed income of silver into the economy of Kerman. Gifts and loans to the governors and officials in the city forged links of mutual assistance, while the Company could also resort to the auspices of their *Farman* should local officials prove intransigent. The Company's ability to enforce the *Farman* is shown by the disregard with which the local namat (*namad*, felt) makers were treated when they attempted to intervene in the Company's trade. Starved of raw material they demanded a supply of wool back from the Company in order for their work to continue. This request was flatly ignored by the Company, while the local Khan failed to take any action against the Europeans, to whom he was indebted.[65] While Matthee is no doubt correct that local weavers were unlikely to have consumed a large proportion of the wool supply and that European entry into the market would have spurred a surge in production, the inability of these local tradesmen to affect the Company's trade demonstrates the relative value of European business in the bazaars of Kerman.

In Shiraz, the Company found another region where a valuable trade could be transacted, as this city produced large quantities of wine and rose water, both of which were then sold around the Indian Ocean World. In 1711, Charles Lockyer, a former Company employee, published a memoir and guide to trade in the Indian Ocean. In his chapter on the trade of Persia, he mentions that three varieties of wine were available for purchase, *Ashee*, *Kishmish* and *Shyrash*.[66] Of these, the first was the most expensive at 160 shahis per chest, while the other two were 140 per chest.[67] Lockyer goes on to tell his reader that the chests consisted of 'ten bottles, each containing 5 quarts; or two carboys and two bottles; but of late they leave out two bottles, reckoning two carboys to a chest. The Carboys hold out 5 gallons, one with another'.[68] While Lockyer was not clear on where this wine was produced, *Shyrash* was a common anglicised spelling of Shiraz, while *Kishmish*, the Persian word for 'raisin', probably refers to an *Auslese* or *Spätlese*.[69] By Lockyer's reckoning, each chest of wine at 160 shahis was worth £2.6s.8d, making it almost as valuable as silk, though at a much greater weight and volume. The Company's own reports suggest that Lockyer's prices were, in fact, only about half of what was often paid for chests of wine, with prices between 200 and 300 shahis being recorded on various occasions.[70]

Alexander Hamilton, another traveller to the Gulf, lists the great benefits and quality of the wine produced at Shiraz in his travelogue of 1739:

The Armenian Christians have the privilege of making wine, most excellent in their kind, and it is a Question whether the World affords better, for they are excellent Stomachicks, and being strong, they'll bear 4 Times the Quantity of water to mix with them without being flat.[71]

In the 1670s Jean Chardin had likewise praised the quality of wine produced in Persia:

They make the best in Georgia, in Armenia, in Media, in East Hircania, at Chiras, and at Yezd, the Capital City of Carmania. The Wine of Ispahan is the Worst of all, until the nice Europeans pretended to make it, which they did about 20 years ago.[72]

Viticulture in Persia, according to Chardin, was widespread and enjoyed the favour of the Safavid Shahs and elite, both in their extensive consumption of the produce of non-Muslim vintners, as well as from the money that could be made from permitting the trade in it to continue.[73] The Company was granted permission in their *Farman* to export wine and maintain their own vineyard, which, judging by Hamilton's effusive description, must have been one of many.[74] Their house and vineyard were maintained by an Armenian, who also passed them information on the state of Persian politics and the roads to and from Shiraz. Again, this demonstrated a supportive relationship between the Company and native Armenians, including the Company lending their 'wine man' money on an individual basis, as well as providing an advance on the next year's vintage.[75] There is even a connection between the Company's vineyard and their linguist, who is said to have owned it.[76] According to Jean-Baptiste Tavernier, the Armenians of Shiraz were producing somewhere in the region of 580,000 litres of wine per year,[77] Hamilton states that around 24,000 gallons of rose water were also exported yearly from the city.[78] Tavernier documents that out of the full production of wine at Shiraz, the vineyards of European Companies accounted for around one-quarter, presumably all intended for exportation. Matthee adds that in the trading season of 1716–17, 625 cases of wine were exported on native ships in the Gulf, suggesting an extant native trade before the intervention of the companies.[79]

When the Company's house and vineyard at Shiraz was burned, 7,000 toman of stock and property was destroyed, suggesting that they stored thousands of bottles there.[80] Letters from Bombay, as well as shipping orders found in the factory records for the Gulf, show that wine was shipped in large quantities to India and was then distributed among the Company's factories and servants.[81]

We saw in the first chapter of this book how important access to wine and spirits was both to the health and well-being of the Company's servants, who consumed it on a daily basis mixed with water. Wine was also a mark of status, separating Company servants from sailors and soldiers, who were instead provided with much cheaper (not to mention much more alcoholic) arak.[82] When the wine was found to have 'gone bad', it was distilled into brandy, which was also distributed among the soldiers and sailors stationed at Bombay.[83]

Wine as well as rose water were exported not only for the use of Company servants to slake their thirst and keep their clothing smelling sweet but also to be sent as gifts and signs of goodwill. In one instance, the Father Superior of the Jesuits at Salsette was sent a supply of wine in 1704 in thanks for provisions provided to the Company at Bombay.[84] Persian rose water is mentioned by Bhawan Ruangsilp as having been provided to Phra Narai of Siam by the Dutch.[85] The purchase, exportation and then use of Persian goods as courtly gifts mark this trade as being of particular value to the Company, if not in volume, or raw profit, then as a source of prestige derived from access to such resources. The use of wine in the day-to-day life of the Company's servants also adds to its value, demonstrating the Company's generosity in providing this rare, relatively expensive beverage to their diet.

Persian wines and luxury goods represent a new way of exploring the context of trade conducted by the Company in the Indian Ocean. While the supply of these goods was somewhat sporadic, especially in the period after 1722, the Company's ability to purchase and ship wine and rose water to India for the use of its servants, not to mention as a prestigious commodity or for gifts, is indicative of the Company's attitude to Gulf trade. The ubiquity of wine in Europe and the social capital its consumption represented made the Company's ability to supply it, whether from Persia or Europe, an important part of keeping its employees happy; indeed, it was sometimes used as an incentive. In one letter, Euclid Baker, an engineer working in Bombay in 1704, was given a gift of Shiraz in thanks for his work and in the hope of further encouraging his efforts.[86] The consumption of Shiraz in India would come to be replaced by mass imports from Europe by the mid-1760s, especially from Madeira, where highly prized sweet wine was produced, with the added advantage that the island was a common stopping point for Company ships on the way to the Cape.[87]

The history of drugs and intoxicants and the expansion of European empires is inextricably linked, from the tobacco plantations of the Caribbean to the opium fields of India. The wine trade offers a differing view of this relationship.[88] This is borne out in part by the levels of exportation, amounting to around 35,000 litres a year, according to Matthee's estimate of the Company's share of production during the later Safavid period leading up to 1722.[89] At the same time, Hancock shows that in this period only about 5,000 litres of Madeira was being imported around the Cape for the Company's consumption.[90] When demand for Madeira rose in the 1760s, following the receipt of the *Divan* of Bengal, this was not only in response to the expansion of the Company's staff but also an attempt to sell more for profit.[91] Although Matthee makes mention of European exportation, the focus of his work is firmly on the Persianate and Islamic attitudes to wine consumption, not upon the European attitude towards it, nor the companies' trade in it. This section has therefore provided an added context to the history of the Company's servants' consumption of wine, the trade in it as a luxury commodity and also the economic benefit its production and exportation had to Persia.

The factory at Bandar Abbas was not just a conduit for the Company's official trade, as we saw in the previous chapters; private trade was an important facet to the lives and livelihoods of the merchants there. The Company recognised this and made various attempts to profit from it, after earlier attempts to stymie private enterprises had consistently failed. The value of the factory and its location was augmented by the Company's ability to use their position at the port to gather revenue. This could take the form of the 1,000 toman that the Company was owed annually by the Persian *Shahbandar* from the port's customs but also from the taxation of intra-Asian and European trade. In discussing the goods traded by Armenian merchants between India and Persia, Edmund Herzig gives what can be considered as the closest approximation of the shape of more general private trade in the Gulf region, including that of Company servants.[92] Herzig highlights the importance of private trade in importing Indian goods to Persia, while also showing the goods, such as dried fruits and woollen textiles, which the Armenians found it worthwhile exporting. It is not much of a stretch to imagine that anything the Armenians found worthwhile to buy and sell, the Company's servants did as well.

The East India Company's original charter granted a monopoly of all trade between England and the Indian Ocean. This included freighting cargo, cash and people from one side of the globe to the other. However, despite the best efforts of the Company to protect this monopoly, it soon proved too tempting for 'interlopers' to eat into the Company's captive markets. Part of the problem came from the Company's own servants, who worked with interlopers to improve their own private fortunes. This kept their personal transactions off the Company's books, allowing for greater personal profit and the facility to send such profit back to England away from prying eyes.⁹³ The Company's servants also bought local ships for their private use, or had them built at the local shipyards at Surat.⁹⁴ By the 1680s the Company circumnavigated this hole in their revenues by permitting their servants to trade on their own accounts, as long as this trade took place only between Asian ports.⁹⁵ By doing this, the Company was able to not only eliminate the value of interlopers to its servants but also tap into the private country trade itself.⁹⁶

In the Persian Gulf this was achieved not only through the passes issued to native shipping, discussed previously, but also through the duties levied at Gulf ports. This practice was well entrenched by the 1730s having developed through various iterations and forms, ranging from the charge of flat fees for freight and passage, to a system of charges by weight in 1640.⁹⁷ The Company also charged 1% on transactions carried out in the factory, a fee they could well expect to receive from merchants when the alternative was the 7% customs charged by the *Shahbandar*.⁹⁸ The Company's Agents insisted that all goods belonging to Europeans associated with the Company were assessed at the factory, rather than by the *Shahbandar*. Circumventing the *Shahbandar* was preferable to the Company as it removed the Persian bureaucracy from between the Company and what they saw as their share of the customs of the port. The Company was, in effect, deploying a state-like apparatus of taxation that superseded the local system. By doing this, the Company was able to set up a virtual monopoly over the shipping of Indian goods to Persia. Landing goods at the Company's factory rather than at the *Shahbandar*'s warehouse was an advantage that could be, and was, extended to Armenian and Banian merchants. The process of declaring goods falsely in this way in order to avoid taxation is known as 'colouring'. The extension of the Company's benefits to these native traders through colouring was in clear contravention of the permission given to the Company to only have control of their own goods. However, it had long been the case that the Company's merchants transacted their trade under these conditions, so extending it to local merchants was an easy means of deriving further profits.⁹⁹ Company ships coming from India were habitually unloaded at the Company's premises, no matter to whom the cargo belonged.¹⁰⁰ Unloading Indian goods at the factory gave the Company a limited monopoly over the goods being imported on their ships, whoever owned them. In doing this, they removed a level of competition from their trade in Persia by overseeing the sales of a large volume of goods, apparently all belonging to them, when in fact the Company was merely brokering sales and charging the owners a percentage. The same system was also used at Basra, where the Company charged 2%, rather than just

1% in order to support the factory there solely through this revenue.[101] Floor has shown that at Bandar Abbas, as well as Basra no doubt, the Company was in league with the local *Shahbandar* to turn a blind eye to the importation of private goods by Armenians, Indians, the Company servants and private merchants.[102] While this is certainly the case, he also suggests that the Company introduced this policy after its servants were unable to gain its full share of customs.[103] Both the *Shahbandar*'s official customs and Company 'informal' taxation were run concurrently, meaning that even if the Company was not able to collect their full share of the port's income at any given time, what they received was effectively total profit, minus the expense of presents and gifts to local officials.

Throughout both the seventeenth and eighteenth centuries, the Company struggled to ever receive the share of customs promised to them in the *Farman*.[104] Floor lists the income from the customs that the Company received, as well as an attempt to estimate the actual value of Bandar Abbas' trade for the seventeenth century.[105] He goes on to suggest that this income represented a major problem or barrier to the transaction of the Company's business and their incomes,[106] but then perhaps, paradoxically, discusses some of the alternative revenues collected by the Company in place of their official customs share. As the previous paragraph shows, the collection of consulage from Company merchants and coloured goods belonging to other merchants represented a major income stream. While it's certainly true that the Company's revenues from the customs never matched what they had been promised, their informal incomes when tallied with the payments that were forthcoming probably made up for it. From the example of private and coloured trade in the Gulf, one can see that at least part, if not the largest part, of the Company's interest in Persia and their long maintenance of a factory there sprang not from sales of cloth or certainly from the purchase of silk but from taxing the privately held wealth of Company merchants. Due to its very nature, the trade of private merchants is difficult to trace, as the Company did not take account of it in official ledgers and correspondence. However, there are signs of the level of personal wealth that could be accrued by Company servants in Persia. For example, in one instance, the Company's Agent purchased the majority of the lading of the *Fanny*.[107] As the Agent's annual income was only £150, it is evident that he had significant other means at his disposal with which he could purchase the most part of a ship's cargo. Equally, he would not have purchased the goods without the means and ability to sell it on. It seems fair to assume that the Company's directors were interested in maintaining their position in Persia, not only for the sake of their shareholders but for the pockets of their servants. The Company's servants were able to use Persia as a market for goods bought and shipped cheaply from India, such as cotton textiles and pepper, while some Persian goods, such as dried fruits, nuts and dates, found a ready sale in Bombay.

The Company's trade in Persia should not be solely viewed through the lens of European manoeuvres; the Shahs and their officials, from the *Shahbandar* or *Sultan* of Bandar Abbas to the Khan of Shiraz, had their own agendas. As previously explored in this chapter, the Persian authorities were perfectly capable of effecting policy that controlled the European companies, such as the encouragement to buy silk through reduction of specific duties. Even using European documents, it is easy to discern ways in which the Persians attempted to use the Company's trade to further their own ends. By having these mechanisms and then deploying them, it is clear that the Company acted as a commercial surrogate to the Persian state. This surrogacy was not always willingly undertaken, though it ties in clearly with the findings of previous chapters in this book, that show the Company was willing to undertake significant operations on behalf of the Shah and that both he and his officials were aware of the Company's usefulness.

This relationship is demonstrated through several examples that have already been mentioned, particularly silk, but instead of recapitulating that example, we will instead consider the seemingly innocuous commodity known as hing.[108] Hing was a recognised commodity in Asia, being used commonly as a condiment in cooking and medicine, the plant from which the substance is derived grows particularly well in dry uplands of Khorasan and Afghanistan. Nader Shah attempted to ship and sell large quantities of this product in India, along with copper, which the Company had proven to be welcome in Indian markets.[109] This evidently did not go quite as planned, as the Company later discovered that their *Farman* had been adjusted to include an article allowing the Company to transport and ship the foul-smelling herb free of any duties.[110] By changing the *Farman*, Nader Shah was evidently trying to manipulate the Company into selling hing where he had been unable to. The Company was tempted to an extent, until it was discovered that Persian officials, including Mirza Ismail, the Khan of Bandar Abbas, had secured almost all the supplies of hing and therefore the Company would be forced to pay whatever price he asked. In one case this was as high as 50 shahis in silver per maund, which can only be ranked as pure extortion.[111] While the Company and VOC did occasionally buy and ship hing,[112] the demand was not enough to meet the appetite of the ever-avaricious Shah through the *Shahbandar* of Bandar Abbas, Mirza Ismail. Failing to persuade the Company, their broker was targeted next and in 1735 was forced to buy 500 maunds, despite numerous protestations from the Agent, William Cockell.[113]

Persian attempts to stimulate trade in this way, through either preferential taxation or access to a state monopoly, demonstrates a clear awareness of the potential power of the Company to support both economic and international ambitions when managed properly. Previous attempts at embargoing the shipping of cash and bullion throughout the Safavid period had failed to prop up the Persian economy satisfactorily,[114] and agreements to supply silk in return for cash and goods failed. Nader Shah's attempts to use ships purchased from the Company to ship hing and copper to India, as well as his somewhat heavy-handed encouragement to the Company to purchase hing, are clearly to increase revenue in the short term. The Company was seen by Nader Shah as a useful vehicle for selling and transporting products he had seized from his own population. The issuing and renewal of the *Farman* was also an obvious attempt to stimulate commerce, allowing the Company to pursue their business around the empire, providing cloth for the Shah's armies while buying up cheap stocks of copper. Nader Shah was willing also to permit the entry of other British merchants, exemplified by the Russia Merchants, as this guaranteed him the cloth he wanted, while undermining the Company's monopoly on providing it.[115] Such attempts to manipulate trade in this way were relatively rare, and despite the longevity of the *Farman* given to the Company, its various provisions were only untidily upheld. Previous attempts to stimulate the Persian economy by way of European trade were made during the reign of Abbas II, by his pioneering, though largely unsuccessful, Grand Vizier, Mohammed Beg.[116] Where Mohammed Beg had failed, Nader Shah had only partially succeeded. The Company's close attention to the health of the Persian economy in this period is helpful to historians, especially considering the relative dearth of contemporary local records. Nader Shah was also clearly sensitive to the importance and potential of Europeans to support his economy, to which end he was willing to use the Company's many technological and commercial advantages. Equally, the *Farman* shows an ability and awareness of ways in which the Persians could use written agreements, so treasured by Europeans, to their own advantage, adding unasked for privileges in order to stimulate an underperforming or newly discovered trade. The success of such measures appears to have only been limited. However, this can be explained in part by the brevity of their duration, as well as the changeable control Persian officials were able to exert over the Company.

The Company factory at Bandar Abbas was not the culmination of a century-long obsession with silk, nor was it simply a warehouse for the purchase and conveyance of wool. Instead, the factory represented a nexus of Indian Ocean trade, as well as an outpost of the Company's political network. In the period after 1700, silk had ceased to function as a major attraction to international trade, though the ability of the Company to sell its cloth remained. The Company was able to collect its share of customs from the Persian government, even if the amount they received was somewhat less than they had been given to expect. This collection of cash, through taxation or political transaction, was increased by the volume of goods processed by the Company's officials, augmented by the private trade of Company servants in the Gulf and India, as well as goods carried on Company ships owned by native merchants avoiding high Persian customs duties. The Company's complicity in the 'colouring' of goods was a considerable source of revenue and income, which served to replace some not received from the Persian customs house; indeed, the circumvention of Persian systems of collection was beneficial to both the Company and the traders themselves. Instead of the laborious battle with the *Shahbandar* described by previous studies, one can see the circumvention of the official process by a tacit agreement, permitted by local officials with the aid of financial inducement.[117]

The wool trade reveals the depth of Company connections to local officials, through whom the Company was able to protect its profits through official channels, essentially insuring themselves against loss or theft. The trade to Kerman is also indicative of the major issues that could be caused by competition with the Dutch, proven most clearly by the large profits made by both sides when they reached a mutually supportive agreement. As this occurred in a period after which most studies end, its discovery adds a significant fresh dynamic to the debate over the interaction of Europeans in Persia. The Company's trade in luxury items, such as wine and rose water, is demonstrative of a keen awareness of the desirability of these products, to Company servants, other Europeans, as well as the elites of the Indian Ocean World. By holding a stock of wine, which could be used as a gift to a foreign king, or an incentive to a Company servant, the Company proved that the commodities which it bought were valuable in excess of their price in silver. Likewise, the use of rose water as a political gift, as well as a means of improving the lives of Company servants, shows a strategic approach by the Company to capitalise fully on its relationship and access to the markets of Persia, even when silk ceased to be a viable target. Throughout this period, however, the role of the Persian government in stimulating trade cannot be dismissed. Whether through the use of the Company as a surrogate exporter of goods held by Persian officials or the adjustment of the Company's *Farman* to encourage sales, the Persian authorities were aware of the commercial power wielded by the Company as well as their ability to harness this power to their own ends. As with the use of the Company to act in place of a Persian navy, or eventually as a supplier of one, and the utilisation of the Company as an extension of diplomatic networks, the Persian state capitalised on the Company's presence to further their own commercial ends.

4

A navy for hire: The continuing maritime operations of the East India Company in the Persian Gulf 1727–43

After freeing themselves of the Portuguese at Hormuz, the Persians pursued a strategy of preventing a single European power from taking control of the Persian Gulf. From 1622 and into the mid-eighteenth century, this strategy was played out by successive Persian regimes and rulers.[1] The Safavids were able to use both the Company and the VOC as enforcers of their authority, while leveraging the cooperation of both companies by playing them off one against the other. Should these attempts at maintaining a balance of European powers fail, there was always recourse to the strictures and benefits bestowed in the *Farman*. This could either take the form of enforcing the letter of the document itself, or by threatening the total withdrawal of its benefits. These interplays of balancing European interests with Persian *Realpolitik* are most clearly visible in the disputes and negotiations around naval power and shipping in the Gulf and beyond. This chapter also explores how the Company engaged with the Persians in such a way as to make their maritime and naval military capability a major bargaining tool in sustaining their long-term trading position. The fundamental basis of these interactions can clearly be seen in the historic understanding by both sides of the campaign to take Hormuz over a century earlier. There are three distinct aspects of this relationship which require historical contextualisation of their own, as each aspect, the lending of ships for military purposes, the carrying of embassies and the purchase of naval materiel, represents different issues, particularly the purchase of ships which was an innovation of the eighteenth century.

The basis of the balance of power rested on the mutual antipathy and competition between European interests in the Gulf, while also securing Persian access to commercial and diplomatic channels around the Indian Ocean. The

Dutch and English companies' mutual dislike of the Portuguese in the early seventeenth century had significantly overridden their dislike of each other which served Abbas I exceptionally well. The Dutch had the added good fortune of trading prestige goods commanding high prices from the Persians in their cargoes of spices and sugar, while the Company's goods, especially woollen cloth, though rather less glamourous, were nonetheless practical and important commodities in Persian markets. To this foundation was added the Company's ongoing interest in investing and purchasing large quantities of Persian goods including wine from Shiraz, wool and copper from Kerman. The Europeans' ability to offer transport to Persian embassies, desirable goods and guarantee some measure of security for local shipping in the Gulf made their presence a valuable asset to continued Persian political hegemony in the region.

As with many aspects of the Company's business in Persia, the *Farman* played a central role in the balance of expectations between the two parties, though in this instance the Persians were unusually reliant on Company cooperation to achieve their aims. It is clear that Persian officials at local and national levels were able to constantly exploit their partners' desire to use their ports for the trade of their goods as leverage to make these naval powers bend to their will. Using a combination of the grants of rights and the threat of their withdrawal, fines, veiled and outright threats, the Persians were able to generally get the services they required, sometimes after a good deal of resistance and negotiation. The Company's ability to measure situations and turn complex and dangerous circumstance to their advantage is equally displayed in the events this chapter will explore. In many ways the Company functioned as a fractious but valuable local ally to Persian designs and ambitions. The Company's capability is seen in their long-term success in managing their own side of the relationship through leveraging their strong diplomatic and personal networks of Persian officials, nurtured over many years. That the officials like the admiral Latif Khan, Ali Mardan Khan and especially Taqi Khan adroitly manipulated the Company can be seen in how the Company was obliged to provide ships for a Persian navy during the rule of Nader Shah. The Company was a key component in assisting this otherwise terrestrial state with a population and administrative centres hundreds of arduous miles from the sea. Most of the time Persian rulers and officials recognised that they lacked the expertise in seafaring matters, and as we shall see, whenever they attempted to interfere too deeply, things worked out badly for them.

The focus of the following discussion is on the Safavid/Persian resurgence after the Afghan invasion of 1722 and more particularly the reign of Nader

Shah (r.1736–47). The period between 1727 and 1743 provides the clearest evidence of wider trends across the relationship between the Company and the Persian state. The events that occurred across two tumultuous decades are notably important as they give an understanding of how the Company behaved and reacted when dealing with a local power from an initial position of relative advantage. The Company was deeply concerned in maintaining the safety of its ships and sailors, while also offering their services, whether in expectation of commensurate reward or to avoid the displeasure of the Shah or his officials. Equally, the Company actively avoided being used against any of their other trading partners in the Gulf, like Muscat or the Ottoman Empire.

Laurence Lockhart's article on the construction of a navy by Nader Shah has formed the basis of scholarship on this topic, but while covering the naval project in some detail it neglects to place the Company in the central position that it enjoyed during this process.[2] Two further articles by Willem Floor[3] and Michael Axworthy are mostly based on Lockhart's work.[4] Floor rests more heavily on Dutch sources, adding a new perspective to Persian activities, whereas Axworthy attempts to tie in the naval fleet project with Nader Shah's wider political and military ambitions. These scholars have viewed these events from the perspective of the internal politics of Nader Shah's regime while remaining reliant upon English and Dutch accounts for the vast majority of their data in the absence of Persian sources. All three authors treat the construction of the fleet either as a discrete event or as an extension of a policy being carried out elsewhere: in this case, Nader Shah's continued campaigns to assert his dominance over Persia and beyond. This chapter differs from the three works mentioned above and gives an in-depth analysis of the Company's role in the fleet's completion. Additionally, it considers the political and military influence this fleet would have for Persia and the ramifications on the other polities of the Gulf region and the opportunities naval supremacy locally afforded Persia more widely within the Indian Ocean.

At his coronation, Nader Shah had proclaimed his intention to 'throw reins around the necks of the rulers of Ottoman Turkey and Kandahar, but also Turkestan and India';[5] in order to achieve this, he set about major military reforms and reorganisations, including the acquisition of modern naval technology. This policy had its origins in the power vacuum and chaos caused by the Afghan invasion of 1722 and Nader Shah's subsequent campaigns to recover the territories of the now fractured Safavid Empire. The Afghan invasion was spurred by a failed attempt by Shah Soltan Husayn to put down a rebellion among the Ghilzai in Kandahar. This political misstep set off a greater rebellion among the Hotaki Afghans, who in company with other several other tribes swept westward into Persia until they took the Safavid capital city of Isfahan. Following the surrender of the city, Shah Soltan Husayn was captured by the invaders, deposed and replaced with their own candidate, Mahmud Hotaki, who in turn faced ongoing resistance from a number of quarters. The most significant threat to Mahmud's reign coalesced under the banner of Tahmasp Mirza, a surviving Safavid prince, who with the assistance of loyalist forces eventually regained power. With the help of his able general, Tahmasp Qoli Khan, Tahmasp Mirza was put on the throne after the Afghans were finally defeated in 1729, taking his regnal title, Tahmasp II. Tahmasp Qoli Khan then proceeded to supplant Shah Tahmasp II and then his infant son, Abbas III, proclaiming himself as Nader Shah in 1736, though in truth he had been the real power in Persia long before this. Nader Shah was a member of the Afshar tribe of Khorasan in the north of Persia and his rise to prominence was due to the military victories he secured against the Afghans in the service of the Safavid loyalist forces. He proved his mettle fighting the Ottoman Turks, expelling them from the western regions of Persia which they had occupied during the Afghan occupation.

By the time Nader Shah came to prominence in the chaos following the Afghan overthrow of the Safavid Dynasty, Persian rule in the Gulf Coast region, or *Garmsirat*, was nominal at best and subject to the whims of various Arab confederations, including the *Hawala*, a grouping of several Arab Sheikhdoms settled along both shores of the Persian Gulf, and the Imamate of Muscat.[6] The Arab naval powers were able to operate at will, the Omanis and *Hawala* fought each other intermittently for control over the island of Bahrain, which was still considered a Persian possession.[7] Indeed, by the end of the 1720s the Company's servants and captains no longer felt comfortable challenging Omani ships, whether to collect payments from them for passes or to stop piracy, which had become endemic.[8] It was into this dangerous mix of local competition, competing territorial claims and growing symmetry of naval strength between the Arabs and Europeans that Nader Shah began his campaign to reinstate Persian control over the Gulf.

One of the first signs of renewed Persian influence in the Gulf came as Afghan resistance to the resurgent Safavid forces began to crumble, precipitating the flight of many of their troops eastward and southward. Those that fled south found themselves hemmed in by the Gulf Coast, unable to escape the advance of their formerly supine foes. Hearing that a number of Afghans were attempting to flee by sea, Nader Shah ordered the local Arab sheikhs to deny them passage. One notable regional ruler, Sheikh Rashid of Basaidu, drove the Afghans ashore, while another Sheikh let another group slip away, having sympathised with them on the grounds of their shared Sunni religious beliefs.⁹ On 19 March 1730 the Company received a similar request to deploy what ships they had to stop any Afghans escaping, which was agreed to on the understanding that the Company had accepted some responsibility for maritime peacekeeping.¹⁰ It is important to note that, in contrast to later events, this 'request' was mentioned as such in the Company's consultation books, rather than as an order or a demand, and action was taken to gain the favour of Nader Shah and the Persian government by showing their readiness to assist in his campaign. However, the Council under Agent John Horne was becoming increasingly aware of tensions within the Safavid court, especially in the relationship between the Tahmasp and Nader. During the early period of Tahmasp II's reign it was unclear who was in control of Persia; both Tahmasp and Nader issued orders that were sometimes contradictory. Indeed, it is recorded in 19 March 1730 Company Consultation that Horne applied to Tahmasp to rescind an order issued by Nader Shah in his name.¹¹ All this was to change, however, when Nader Shah took full rein of the governance of Persia in 1732, having already strongly influenced and controlled policy during the reign of Tahmasp II and then his infant son, Abbas III, after 1729. The change was marked by Nader Shah's declaration of all previous agreements with the European companies as null and void. For the Company, this resulted in the loss of any claim to customs from Bandar Abbas and 3,000 toman owed by Shah Soltan Husayn from loans, their share of the customs of Bandar Abbas, as well as their freedom from tolls and customs.¹² This in turn meant that the renewal of centralised Persian authority suddenly threatened the Company's position due to the ostensible loss of their trade and social privileges. While previous requests for naval support had been cordial, Nader Shah's combative new approach shows an almost complete shift in the dynamics of the Company's relationship with him and with their neighbours in the Gulf.

In 1734 Nader Shah demanded the use of Company ships to blockade Arab ports only nominally under Persian suzerainty. The Company Council agreed, promising to blockade one port with the only ship they had in the Gulf at that time.¹³ No doubt this was a way of setting a limit on Nader Shah's expectations of the Company and their exposure to his displeasure should he expect better results or greater commitment. Here the use of the word 'demand' in the records is certainly deliberate and the response given by the Company, in an official letter, was intended to make their displeasure at being 'commanded' rather than 'requested' quite clear. Indeed, this change, along with the continued withdrawal and reinstatement of the Company's privileges, became a feature of the Company's interactions with Nader Shah. The Shah insisted on cooperation between the English and the Dutch, forcing both companies to agree to joint cruises, designed to reinforce his authority over the coasts and islands of the Gulf.[14] While uncouth, blunt and impolitic, Nader Shah's approach worked. Neither the English nor the Dutch were willing to risk their position within Persia with outright defiance to the Shah's orders; indeed, both sides were willing to undergo joint operations under Persian supervision in order to guarantee their ongoing position in the region.

While cooperation was insisted upon by the Shah and both the Company and VOC were obliged to humour him, they were still limited in their field of action by the rules and the scruples of their superiors in Bombay or Batavia. It is clear that the Company was obliged to accede to these demands to an extent, while being unwilling to either fully submit or act as a subject or vassal, despite their treatment as such by the increasingly mercurial Shah. Essentially, while both parties' interests aligned, the Company was willing to accede to most demands, though it was equally clear that the Agent and Council had not abandoned their superiors' interests. In particular there were concerns about maintaining good relations with Muscat, the Mughals or Ottomans and would therefore not submit to orders without question, especially where these other powers were concerned.

The inconsistencies of expectation on both sides were made clear when the *Shahbandar* of Bandar Abbas, Mirza Ismail, visited Agent Cockell on 9 May 1734, asking what the Shah could expect in service from the Company. Agent Cockell replied that the Company 'could act nothing against Bussorah [Basra], the Muscat Arabs, The Mogulls Subjects all whom Wee were in a Strict Friendship and Alliance'.[15] He added that requests to assist the Shah against his own subjects would be assented to whenever possible, though no limitation on whether these subjects recognised the Shah's authority or not were discussed. Both Cockell and Carol Koenad, the VOC Director,[16] were subsequently asked to lend ships to bring the rebellious Mohammad Khan Baluchi, a Baluchi Chief from Eastern Persia, to heel. The *Prince of Wales Galley* and a Dutch ship were dispatched to join the *Britannia* and another Dutch ship already present to carry out this order.[17] Cockell was evidently trying to make clear to the *Shahbandar*, and by extension the Shah himself, that the Company's interests were reliant on far more than its trade in Persia and the Gulf, while also trying to prove that he recognised the need for local support to maintain his employer's privileged position in Persia.

On a further occasion, the *Prince of Wales* was dispatched on a sortie under the Shah's instructions, its mission this time was to attack the Arab rebels on the island of Kish. This is a clear example of the Company complying with a Persian request in accordance with Cockell's earlier commitment to support the Shah's authority against rebels. Cockell received further orders by the Shah in 1734 to capture Sheikh Rashid of Basaidu, of which the Dutch were kept in ignorance, despite also sending a ship to the island as part of the blockade. Cockell and the Council believed that the Persians would eventually capture the Sheikh themselves, thereby mitigating any benefit the Company might come by with his capture, not to mention the goodwill they wished to accrue in order to regain their privileges, which Nader Shah had abrogated.[18] Here Cockell and the Council can be seen to play politics adroitly as they cooperated with the Shah's immediate demands, while also delaying their efforts to catch Sheikh Rashid until it was clearly to their advantage. This had become particularly important, as Nader Shah had appointed a new admiral for his nascent naval efforts in the Gulf, a noble named Latif Khan. The admiral had made early and supportive contact with the English merchants and so the Company's servants believed that by saving their wholehearted support for Latif Khan they would gain greater favour with this new contact.[19] The Company's employees were at this point looking particularly to gain an advantage over a powerful merchant at Basaidu on the island of Qeshm, named 'Hajji Tenaul', who had been interfering with their trade at that port.[20] The merchant had managed to force all commerce with the Company through his person, forbidding the other merchants to deal directly with the Company and therefore deriving significant profit.[21] The Council demanded the removal of this merchant, or the end of this practice, before they would take any action against the Arab and Baluchi rebels.[22] In this instance Cockell and the Council were trying to impress upon Latif Khan the need for reciprocal assistance, no doubt hoping by doing so they were setting the tone of their relationship with him going forward.

While this attempt to manage and set expectations with Latif Khan was well thought out and executed, the Council would be disappointed in the long run, as they had not reckoned with the persistent pressure that would be applied to Latif Khan by Nader Shah, especially through Mohammad Taqi Khan Shirazi. Taqi Khan and Nader Shah had befriended one another in 1729, when Nader Shah visited the city of Shiraz, where Taqi Khan's father was an official. Taqi Khan helped Nader Shah to understand the tax system while showing a deviousness and cunning that appealed to the latter's needs and sense of humour.[23] In 1736, Nader Shah wished to use his nascent fleet to capture the island and pearl fisheries of Bahrain. On this occasion, the Company was approached by Taqi Khan, the *Beglerbegi* (Governor) of Fars province, and Latif Khan, on orders from Nader Shah for their assistance.[24] Cockell, still Agent, but now often absent due to his health, demurred, claiming that they had no ships suitable to the task and therefore would have to request both ships and permission from Bombay before entering into any such undertaking.[25] The consultation concerning this event reveals that this was, in fact, an attempt to extract a full confirmation of their trading privileges from Taqi Khan directly, as he was in town, through confirmation of the *Farman* by him. Cockell and the Council were no doubt also concerned about damaging their relations with the Arabs by pursuing this course of action but decided that they now had little choice.[26] Cockell and his colleagues were to be disappointed as their attempt to regain their privileges on this occasion failed. Taqi Khan showing some of his guile, said that the *Farman* was a royal privilege and therefore beyond his power to renew, instead promising his good offices in obtaining a renewal later, should the Company's men apply directly to the Shah.

Taqi Khan and Latif Khan were also actively soliciting the VOC to provide ships for their campaigns in the Gulf, though the relationship between the Dutch and Persian officials was often represented as sour by the Company, even though these accounts can rarely be relied upon to accurately reflect its true nature. The VOC, like the Company, had often been asked to provide naval assistance to the Safavids. Floor posits that the presence of the VOC in the Gulf actually obviated the need for a Safavid navy, a claim that, given the general disinterest in naval matter displayed by the Shah, seems unlikely, while also ignoring the presence of the Company and its role in protecting and promoting Gulf trade.[27] It is likely that both the English and the Dutch realised that disruptions to trade in the Gulf were far more likely to hurt them, rather than the Shahs, a lesson particularly highlighted after the abortive Dutch blockade of 1645. Indeed, the relationship between the VOC and the Safavids was rather more tumultuous than that of the Company, from the VOC's failed blockade to their outright refusal to assist the Safavids materially against the Muscatis following another failed mission undertaken in the 1660s. Nor did the Dutch do much to stop attacks upon Bahrain by the Portuguese and Arabs towards the end of the Safavid period, further undermining Floor's rather idealistic claim to the VOC being the guarantors of Persia's southern border.[28] By the period of this study, the attitude of the Dutch had seemingly changed very little.

While the Dutch did help in the Gulf campaigns on occasion, they never appear to have found a comfortable balance between their own business and the demands made of them. A Dutch ship accompanied the Persian fleet that departed for the Arab Shore on 1 April 1737 carrying forces to 'assist' the Imam of Muscat against a rebellion, a thinly veiled, uninvited and unwelcome military intervention.[29] Rather than agreeing to Persian demands consistently, however, the Dutch are represented in the consultations as refusing utterly, not bothering to undergo the negotiations in which the Company often found themselves in. Again, this appears to be a continuation of the VOC's policy of over a century, where refusal was the rule rather than the exception. In one case, Taqi Khan's requests for a large Dutch ship were ignored outright, angering him to the point where even an expensive gift was not recompense enough, following a sour precedent adopted by the VOC in the previous century.[30] This is a clear manifestation of the costs that could be associated with being uncooperative with Persian demands, the avoidance of which required a nuanced diplomatic approach. Later in the campaign, Taqi Khan decided that he would go himself to the Arab Shore, not satisfied with the plunder sent back to him by Latif Khan. In order to get there, he requested the use of the *Halifax*, one of the Company's merchantmen which had called at Bandar Abbas. This was agreed to and preparations were made with the captain by the Agent, John Geekie, only for Taqi Khan to change his mind the next day and demand that instead the *Halifax* take horses and reinforcements for Latif Khan. Taqi Khan explained that he felt this was only fair as the Dutch had already made two trips themselves and so the Company should at least do likewise once.[31]

Persian demands did not always focus on large ocean-going ships but spread also to the small local lighters, known as *trankys*, that were retained by all parts of the merchant community in Bandar Abbas to carry goods from their ocean-going vessels to port. In 1737 the Persian fleet commandeered all of these boats in order to load men and horses for the occupation of Muscat.[32] This interrupted the loading of goods aboard the *Wilmington* and provision of water for the *Harwich*, both of which were delayed until the loading of the Persian fleet was completed, petitions for even a single *tranky* for this purpose being bluntly refused by both Taqi Khan and Latif Khan.[33] This event was a severe irritation to all the merchants of Bandar Abbas, European or otherwise, all of whom lost time as their ships were forced to wait in port for their lading. Similarly, it is a clear sign of where power in the port lay, certainly not in the hands of the Company's Council, nor the Dutch Director.[34] For Taqi Khan and Latif Khan, the annoyance of the merchant community was as nothing to failing the Shah, which given his temper was unsurprising.

The ban on action against the Arabs did not stop John Geekie choosing to provide the services of a ship to carry supplies to Taqi Khan during the campaign along the Arab Shore. Geekie deemed that this sort of freighting mission did not contravene their orders to not engage in hostilities with the

Arabs, with the rest of the Council likewise signing off on the orders.³⁵ There was no repetition of the struggles between Draper, Cordeux and Fotheringham in this instance, rather suggesting the tenuousness felt by the English at this time in regard to their position in Persia. The *Rose Galley* was selected to undertake such a mission, with her captain, Henry Venfield, being issued strict instructions to avoid liaising with other ships in Persian service. This was to avoid the ship being seized by the Persians themselves, but was also an attempt to protect the Company's relationship with the Omanis, many of whom had taken to their ships to resist the Persian invasion. On delivering his charge, consisting of some supplies and reinforcements, Venfield was told he should stay no more than three or four days off the coast of Muscat.³⁶ Another passenger, an Armenian merchant named Khawaja 'Sohawk', was also to be taken with them, though Captain Venfield was instructed to leave him behind if he did not return to the ship within the time allotted in his instructions.³⁷ Venfield was expressly forbidden from taking any hostile action against the Arabs under any circumstance.³⁸ Despite these orders and precautions, the ship was significantly delayed. Captain Venfield wrote in explanation that Taqi Khan delayed him numerous times, spuriously claiming that he wished to return with the ship to Bandar Abbas, but never making a certain move to board her.³⁹ Further requests on the *Rose Galley* were delayed by news of an Arab fleet cruising the Gulf and putting a stop to any shipping between Bandar Abbas and the Arab Shore, highlighting the tenuous situation for traders during the campaign.⁴⁰ This danger was highlighted when the *Rose Galley* was captured by the Arab fleet and threatened with dire consequences should they be caught supplying the Persian army again. Captain Venfield was taken prisoner by the Arabs as an insurance for the good behaviour of his crew.⁴¹ The crew thereafter refused to carry anything for the Persians to the Arab Shore under any circumstances, causing a minor incident between the Geekie and Taqi Khan, who desired the use of the galley to again carry supplies.⁴² The limitations placed upon the Company's servants in Persia were manifold, not only did they have to avoid the ire of local officials but also negotiate competing demands, alliances and the readiness of their naval personnel to take risks outside of their usual duties. There were obviously limits to the risks that the Company's servants would take themselves and the clear demonstration of a threat, such as the incident with the *Rose Galley*, was enough to give them pause. Assistance to the Persians in their naval experiment was therefore not to be pursued at any cost even though it represented a useful means of garnering favour with both the local officials, Latif Khan and Taqi Khan, and by extension the Shah himself.

Avoiding providing assistance to the Persian campaigns in the Gulf became a cat-and-mouse game for the European companies and local merchants alike. The refusal of the *Rose Galley*'s crew to undertake any further journeys in support of the campaign on the Arab Shore precipitated yet more, rather than fewer demands.[43] The *Bombay Grab*, a native ship flying Company colours, was requested to go to 'Julfar' (Ras Al-Khayma) to resupply the Persian army there. The Company originally did not consent to sending the ship, perhaps concerned by the possibility of repeating the incident with the *Rose Galley*, but the *Noqudah* (*Nakhoda*, Captain) of the ship was willing to let his ship go while he sold his goods ashore.[44] Unfortunately for the captain a proportion of his goods were sequestered for use by the Persian expeditionary force and not paid for, despite the service his ship was providing.[45] When a similar request was made to transport grain along the Persian Coast after the ship's return, the captain agreed only after being offered suitable compensation for his previous losses and the presence of a European on board his ship, in the hope this might prove some security against the Arabs patrolling the seas.[46] Like the Company's ships, the captain was able to negotiate for better terms after agreeing to provide the services required of him. This latitude was based on the clear needs of the Persian expedition, who could not afford either to wait for another ship to arrive or rely on the good ordinances of the VOC.

The Company had to balance the demands made upon it for ships with the competing interests of their trade at Muscat and Basra, as well as the danger of aggravating Persian officials, on whom the continuance of their trade relied. The Company's servants were willing to lend their ships for the transportation of goods and attacks against recalcitrant subjects of the Shah, even when this risked reprisals from the Muscatis, by taking soldiers and supplies to support the Persian invasion of the Arab Shore. There are obvious similarities between these events and the Hormuz campaign, as yet again the Company was providing a Persian regime with naval assistance to fulfil its territorial and military ambitions, though Nader Shah and Taqi Khan seem to have rather lacked the acumen of Abbas I and his subordinates Allah Verdi Khan and Imam Qoli Khan. These services do not represent the only role the Company played in extending Persian power over the Gulf; indeed, the Company would help the Persians in extending their influence much further afield. The Company was asked by the Persians not only to carry out these military missions but also to carry their embassies abroad to facilitate Persian diplomacy.

The Safavids had long appreciated the facility of using European ships and intermediaries to further their diplomatic and commercial policies. In 1598 a band of adventurers from England led by two brothers, Anthony and Robert Shirley, had journeyed to Persia from Italy in the hope of making their fortunes. They were encouraged by the Venetian authorities who hoped that the presence of these Englishmen would destabilise the growing Iberian control over Asian trade. The arrival in Persia of the Shirleys and their companions was greeted with an audience with Abbas I and led to Anthony Shirley being dispatched on an ambassadorial mission back to Europe in 1599. This sadly ended in failure when Anthony and his Persian counterpart, Hussein Ali Beg, came to blows in Rome, where their ill-fated partnership ended. Robert Shirley remained in Persia for some years, reportedly helping Shah Abbas to train his army and reform his artillery along European lines. He married a Circassian chieftain's daughter who accompanied him on his own mission to Europe in 1608, the objective of which was to create an alliance against the Ottoman Turks. Shah Abbas hoped to tempt European powers into such an agreement with the promise of trade rights and access in Persia.[47] Robert and his embassy visited the courts of the Polish-Lithuanian Commonwealth, the Holy Roman Empire, Florence, Milan, Spain and Rome, where he was received and showered with gifts and titles but no treaty emerged. Robert eventually returned to Persia on an East India Company ship via Surat in 1615,[48] perhaps signalling most poignantly the reach and presence of the Company in the Indian Ocean, even at this early stage. On a second trip back to Europe, Robert met with another Persian ambassador named Naqd Ali Beg, who tore up his credentials and struck him, declaring he was a fraud, continuing Shirley's run of poor relations with Persian dignitaries. Naqd Ali had been brought to England aboard the East Indiaman *Star*, again seeking an alliance against the Ottomans.[49] Wright points out that the Company promoted the cause of Naqd Ali, providing him with accommodation and financial support throughout his time in England, representing him beneficially at court. The English Court paid for the return of Naqd Ali to Persia after his perhaps inevitable and irrevocable break with Shirley.[50]

The Shirley brothers' embassies were exceptionally significant, despite the breakdown of their stated objectives as they precipitated return embassies to Persia from Poland-Lithuania, Sweden and the Duchy of Holstein. Though all ended in failure, the attempts made to secure a trade in silk via Astrakhan and to form military as well as commercial alliances against the Ottomans show a willingness on both sides to engage constructively with the other.[51] This early engagement with Europe, despite the lack of any firm results, demonstrates an awareness of Persia within European courts its importance as a regional actor, if not a global one. This awareness was reciprocal, Abbas I was clearly aware of the growing significance and importance of the European balances of power and the potential these had to directly affect the powers on Persia's borders; war between the Poles or Swedes and Russia left Persia significant latitude in the Caucasus, while any attack on the Ottoman Empire from the West was a potential opening for Persian ambitions in Iraq. While these links persisted, the death of Abbas I also signalled the end of regular exchanges of embassies between Persia and the courts of Europe. His successor Shah Safi neglected trade interests, during which time the Dutch became the pre-eminent maritime exporter of Persian silk, the main commodity of interest to Europeans. The Company would not enjoy such good standing in Persia until the conclusion of the English Civil War and Restoration, after which stability at home permitted for resurgence abroad.

The relationship fostered by the Company with Naqd Ali Beg and the presence of the Shirleys, Catholic missionaries from France and Iberia, the Company's factors and then Dutch merchants too, made Europeans a constant presence in the Safavid Empire. The fostering of good relationships, including the exchange of embassies, no doubt eased and framed the arrival of the Company and the cooperation with Abbas I and his subjects during the Hormuz campaign. It also created an historic precedent of Anglo-Persian diplomatic assistance, which the Company, as we shall see, exploited in the early eighteenth century. The transportation of embassies on behalf of the Persians was another way in which the Company engaged with their hosts; fulfilling these requests was a useful way for the Company to gain prestige and favour. For the Safavids, the presence of the Company as a willing carrier for their embassies opened new possibilities for contacts with other powers throughout Asia and even Europe, as shown by the voyage to Siam and the embassies carried to India and Europe.[52] Nader Shah continued to use the facility provided by the Company, which followed on from the habits established with the dispatch of the Shirley brothers back to Europe. Persia's most frequent diplomatic exchanges remained with Russia, the Ottomans and Mughals, the latter two of which, as Muslim empires, shared a common tradition of diplomatic exchange centred around political events, such as the deaths of incumbent rulers and the coronations of their successors. These exchanges were so ingrained within the fabric of shared courtly life that a complaint was made by Abbas I after it was realised that the death of his predecessor, Tahmasp I, in 1576 had gone unremarked by the Mughal Emperor Akbar.[53] According to Subrahmanyam, before the arrival of the Northern European companies in the Gulf, Persian embassies had to travel to India via Kandahar, a region disputed by the two empires, or gain Portuguese approval to travel via the Gulf.[54] The arrival of the Company therefore facilitated communications between India and Persia via the Gulf, by providing transport for Persian embassies. In contrast, the Portuguese had been deliberately obstructive and refused the transit of Persian emissaries through the Gulf at will. As well as this, the Company facilitated faster and more secure communication with the Mughals, with whom contact had been reduced either by the great distance and risk of the overland route or by Portuguese interference in the Gulf. The presence of the Northern Europeans on the Gulf littoral therefore allowed for speedier communication with European powers, permitting the dispatch of embassies to England, France and the Netherlands, as well as greater freedom of navigation after the severe curtailing of Portuguese power. Nader Shah's use of the Company and its ships as a vector for international diplomacy was a continuation of these previous policies, benefitting from a long history of cooperation.

In 1730 Nader Shah demanded that the Company provide shipping for an embassy to the Mughal Court at Delhi. This embassy was led by Ali Mardan Khan, the *Ishik-Aghasi Bashi* (Chief Mace-Bearer, an honorific title in the Persian Court). This demand was transmitted by the Company's Armenian broker, who incidentally was beaten by the Shah's guard and forced to pay 40 toman before being permitted to carry his message.[55] This was intended as a message to the broker's employers that neither they nor their servants were untouchable under the new regime. Ali Mardan Khan was initially sent away by the Company's Agent, John Horne, being informed that 'the monsoon is as far sett in that should either the Vesells of which We have but two stay above ten days they would not only Endanger the loss of their Passage but of the Lives of every Man on board'.[56] It transpired that the two 'Vessells', the *Severn* and *Edward*, were both privately owned and had little space between decks and therefore were unsuitable for the transportation of passengers, let alone horses. This situation can hardly have been improved by the captain of the *Severn* point blank refusing to carry the embassy in any case.[57] This led Ali Mardan Khan to request the same service from the Dutch, who at first refused, then offered a sloop to carry the ambassador with a few horses and attendants as far as Sind.[58] How helpful this was is a matter for debate, as this would take the embassy only two-thirds of the way to Bombay in terms of distance and leave its members stranded on a particularly inhospitable shore far from either home or their intended destination. Regardless, the Dutch then withdrew that offer the next day, earning the ire of the ambassador.[59] The following Monday, after the intercession of various local officials, the Dutch repeated the offer to lend the sloop to carry Ali Mardan Khan with thirty attendants and fifteen horses.[60]

The Persians, deeming the Dutch sloop much too small, this time themselves refused it. Ali Mardan Khan then returned to the Company and requested use of the recently returned *Britannia*.

Despite the previous reasoning of monsoon and its dangers, Horne, thinking it only proper to provide this ship in order to keep up with Dutch pretences and with an eye to supporting the Company's ongoing negotiations in Isfahan over the reinstatement of the *Farman*, acquiesced.[61] The offer of the *Britannia* was greeted by Ali Mardan Khan, as well as Mir Mehr Ali, then *Sultan* of Bandar Abbas, with much pleasure especially as it had been made 'without recourse to frivolous excuses as was practiced by the Dutch'.[62] The Company also managed to retain the use of a small ship on the pretext that it would prove enough of a threat to ward off attacks on Bandar Abbas by Baluchi tribesmen, who had been scouring the region, as had Arab pirates who had been raiding along the coast.[63] The Baluchis and Arabs had both seen the defeat of the Safavids as a prime opportunity to assert their own independence and take control of the territories of their former overlords. The Baluchis in particular launched several raids along the Gulf Coast, twice attacking Bandar Abbas itself. The presence of European ships with their rows of artillery at the port was deterrence enough for the most part, as the Baluchi tribesmen lacked artillery of their own. It is therefore perhaps unsurprising that after a short while, the Ambassador decided to use only the Dutch sloop after all, the threat of Baluchi and Arab aggression being impressed upon him as enough reason to keep the *Britannia* at Bandar Abbas.[64]

By this stage in the story both the Dutch and the Company can be seen to fence and trade among each other and with the Persian officials involved in the dispute. Their key contacts in Bandar Abbas mediating for the state is an interesting detail that makes the story even more informative: Their intercession displays both their loyalty to the state and trust in their ability to negotiate with the European companies on equitable terms. For the Company this exchange had the dual advantage of discrediting the Dutch in the eyes of the local governor and ambassador, as well as showing a willingness on the part of the Company to transport the embassy and defend the city from the Baluchi and Arab threats. The Persian perception of the Company willingly offering this service was calculated to assist the ongoing negotiations for the restoration of the Company's privileges, then taking place in Isfahan. Given the personality of Nader Shah this was a game for high stakes.

The next mention of this event comes when the Dutch sloop which carried the Ambassador was reported to have returned to Bandar Abbas on 31 May

1730 having met with bad weather on the way to India. This, the Company's council smugly recorded, was further proof of the Company's honesty and probity concerning the weather and safety of sailing. The Dutch ship had first called at Muscat, where the embassy was provisioned and civilly treated, but the ambassador then insisted on returning to Bandar Abbas, being 'very much terrified' by the heavy weather they encountered.[65] The rest of his party bound for India on another ship had been lost on the first night of the voyage and had not been seen or heard of since.[66] While the ambassador was clearly ignorant of sailing conditions and the true danger he may have been in, the Company's servants believed, and encouraged the Persian officials in Bandar Abbas to believe, that the Dutch had deliberately stoked his fears. The ambassador himself later suggested as much, representing to the English how 'the Dutch had bafled him in making an Excuse to go to Muscat and Sell their sugar and afterwards would proceed no further, but had frightened him into a Consent of coming back hither'.[67] He went on to explain that he would represent poor treatment of him by the VOC to the Persian Court, but in the meantime requested the use of a ship to carry out his original journey, no longer wishing to have anything to do with the Dutch.[68]

Ali Mardan Khan would not be deterred long however, no doubt spurred to attempt the journey a second time due to his own fears of returning to court having not carried out his commission. In order to do so, he turned back to the Company. Ali Mardan Khan told Agent Horne that he believed it had been customary since the campaign to capture Hormuz for the Company's ships to carry diplomatic missions from Persia, hinting that were this no longer the case, it could lead to trouble and reprisal.[69] Though the Company's English servants did not believe that the Ambassador would harm them, given the treatment of their Armenian broker, who Nader Shah had had beaten and fined, they carried some concern for their native staff, fearing their broker and linguist might suffer in their stead. Coupled with this they were still negotiating to retain their privileges in the *Farman*.[70] Not to be cowed, Horne replied that he did not see that he or his masters were under any obligation to carry Persian embassies, but they would be happy to lend a ship for this purpose 'out of gratitude and Return were always ready to Shew our attachment to their majestys and out of Friendship and Respect complyd with their request'.[71] While the ambassador certainly had the authority to requisition the Company's ships outright, that he never took this step is indicative of the perceived power dynamic between the Company and Persian officials, even of high rank. As we have seen, the Company's Agent was enrolled into many aspects of Persian sociability both locally in Bandar Abbas and beyond. That being said, anything from a veiled threat to the suggestion of violence against the Company's native servants was taken seriously by the Agent and Council. The *Britannia* was therefore set aside for the purpose, though the ambassador was informed that they would need to provide a smaller ship to accompany her, the coast not being safe for a larger ship to approach without being beached or wrecked in the process. As well as this, transportation for the entourage, horses and baggage of the embassy would also need to be paid for by the embassy itself.[72] Although the account does not report when the embassy left, the *Britannia* returned safely to Bandar Abbas on 14 December 1730, having last called at Bombay, so clearly Ali Mardan Khan made it safely there.[73]

Regardless of the power of retaliation that could have been raised against it, Horne and his colleagues continued to negotiate for their own interests and that of the Company. It seems clear that while Persian officials of any rank did not view the Europeans as their subjects per se, they expected to be accommodated in their requests despite this. Interestingly, the ambassador's suggestion that the Company had traditionally carried Persian missions in this way shows a level of familiarity with the Company's history in Persia, as well as a belief that either 'tradition' or the *Farman* obliged the Company to provide service. This further suggests that Persian officials viewed the Company as a sort of irksome lesser ally, who, while being allowed to trade and self-govern, was expected also to serve when requested to do so, owing to their reliance on Persian royal favour to maintain their position. This does not show a relationship of vassalage, where the Persians would have expected a regular tribute, nor subject status, making them liable to taxation. This event is also emblematic of the Persians' expectation of the Company's and other Europeans' naval assistance, having a pedigree dating back to the Shirleys' embassies and the capture of Hormuz. The actions of the Company facilitated the Persians to engage with politics on a global stage, sending and receiving embassies from Europe, as well as from their neighbours in Ottoman Turkey and the Mughal Empire.

The embassy of Ali Mardan Khan was not the last dispatched to India by Nader Shah. In 1732, a second ambassador, Mahmud Ali Beg, was appointed to the Mughal Court. The Company's merchants were again solicited for help in transporting the embassy to India. Again, this was presented in the Company's consultations as an order, rather than a request. Nevertheless, Agent Cockell complied immediately, promising to provide passage, but only for the person of the ambassador, on their next ship bound for India, further demonstrating that acquiescence came with a setting of expectations.[74] Mahmud Ali Beg boarded the *Britannia* in November 1732 shortly after it returned, presumably with the last ambassador, Ali Mardan Khan, on the completion of his voyage detailed above.[75] Mahmud Ali Beg also took with him a Dutch ship, used to transport part of his equipage and entourage, the rest being taken on smaller, local vessels.[76] Mahmud Ali Beg's embassy even went as far as summoning Company shipping from the Gulf to Sind to carry them back to Persia in 1734 after the completion of their mission.[77] This summons came to nothing as the ambassador was reported dead the following January when a 'Moorish' ship came to Bandar Abbas and refused to transport his body or effects back to Persia without explicit orders from the Court, though these were received later.[78] Owing to the death of Mahmud Ali Beg, two agents, Safi Khan Beg and Mahmud Siah Beg, were appointed by Nader Shah to travel to India and recover the body and effects of the late ambassador. They demanded shipping from the Company but were firmly told that the monsoon had ended and that it would be impossible to take them.[79] The Company was again pressed three days later, but this time the two agents suggested a ruse. This was to send the agents out on a ship for a couple of days and then return with a story of bad weather in order to placate Nader Shah and avoid the journey, somewhat like the Dutch had attempted some years earlier with Ali Mardan Khan.[80] Agent Cockell and the Council refused to take part, believing this to be an attempt to entrap them, instead saying that a ship would be made available to them when the season permitted passage to India.[81] It is hard to say whether this is evidence of the probity of the Company's servants or simply that they had become wary of being tricked by the Persian agents, thereby betraying their complicity in misleading the Shah about their ability to travel during the monsoon. Given the danger of incurring the Shah's wrath and the existence of plenty of detractors, not least the Dutch, who would inform of such a deceit, the Company clearly was not to be taken in by such a dangerous game, especially after the disfavour experienced by the Dutch after the expedition to Muscat.

In July of the same year, the Company's servants made good on their promised assistance to transport the agents, but pointed out that they would be unable to transport the elephants, which the late ambassador had been presented with, back to Persia. These, it was explained, required open topped lighters, rather than the small decks of the Company's merchantmen.[82] While the Company's servants were busy making preparations, the Persian agents were having trouble from another quarter. The Dutch failed yet again to provide any ships despite a promise to do so, while no local ships could be found for the horses and elephants. This was reportedly because Ali Mardan Khan, on his return from India, had beaten the Indian *Noqudahs* of these smaller ships and confiscated what he had paid them for their previous services. These native captains refused to take on the embassy's suite at Sind and thus the Dutch were tasked with supplying local shipping from the Gulf to go to India and back to collect the stranded embassy.[83] The refusal of the Indian captains to take the Persian agents shows an independence of action that marred Persian attempts to rule the Gulf's peoples directly. Indeed, the English, despite their many protestations and delays, appear to have been the least prickly group with whom the agents could do business. The embassy's agents finally departed on the *Rose Galley* on the night of 15 September 1735.[84] The agents were not to return by this ship though, despite it returning to Bandar Abbas a month later. It is reported that the two agents had so mistreated the crew of the *Rose Galley* that her captain, John Harris, in consultation with his principal officers, Henry Venfield (who would, as we've seen, later become captain) and Samuel Hough, had left both Safi Khan Beg and Mahmud Siah Beg in India.[85] The captain explained to the Company's officials that this decision had been taken due to the poor treatment suffered by the crew of their ship at the hands of the two agents and therefore, to avoid further insult and any resultant trouble, they had been left in India to make their own way back. The Company's servants may have been amenable to Persian demands, threats and other behaviour, but clearly their own captains and sailors shared the uncompromising attitude of the local captains. The main issues appear to have been the unwillingness of the Persian agents to part with their horses, which the *Rose Galley* could not carry itself, and the failure of Safi Khan Beg and Mahmud Siah Beg to provide the ship with wood and water for the ship's upkeep while it was docked at Surat.[86]

The perceived status of the Company in the eyes of the Persian agents is a useful detail in considering the wider image of the Company held by the higher echelons of the Persian ruling class. It also goes to show how precarious the actual authority of the Company's employees on land must have been and how good their operational level relationships were to cushion them from potential harm. The actions of Captain Harris and his crew brought considerable trouble to the Company, which was forced to placate the irate agents by paying 19,320 shahis to Safi Khan Beg to cover the transport costs to return him to Persia. In return, both Persian agents signed a letter declaring themselves well satisfied with the Company's services to them.[87] As well as this expense, Latif Khan, the Persian admiral, also had to be placated after Captain Harris nearly had him thrown overboard, being saved only by the intervention of the ship's mate. It is not mentioned why Latif Khan had gone aboard in the first place, but the conduct of Captain Harris was explained thus by Agent Cockell: 'our seafaring men's behaviour was generally as boisterous as the Element they must deal with and that we ourselves when we went a voyage were seldom pleased with the Captain's deportment'.[88] This seems to have satisfied Latif Khan, who also promised to represent the Company's services well to his superiors. This again demonstrates the ability of the Company's men to turn difficult and potentially explosive situations to their advantage. The use of letters to solidify the Company's reputation with Safi Khan Beg, Mahmud Siah Beg and Latif Khan speaks to a shared value and recognition of written agreements as proof of friendship and probity. Indeed, these letters were sent to the Shah as part of a packet including requests for the recognition of their privileges which were, in fact, enshrined in the *Farman* two years later, after a further request for their assistance in supporting Nader Shah's diplomatic efforts in India.[89]

In 1736, Nader Shah ordered that his third ambassador, Mirza Mohsen, be transported by the Company and Dutch to the court of the Mughal Emperor. As well as this passenger, the sister and family of Sa'adat Khan, a Mughal Vizier, were also to be taken with him.[90] By 1736, the Persians already had a nascent fleet of their own, a process that will be explored later in this chapter, but instead of utilising their own vessels, the Company was again solicited for help. As previously, the Agent agreed to carry the requested passengers on their journey. The passengers were charged 1,800 rupees for the use of the *Robert Galley*, which happened to be privately owned and only chartered by the Company. No doubt the Company's servants hoped that providing this service to the family of a Mughal courtier would assist their activities in the Mughal domains as well as in Persia. The transportation of the Persian embassies, agents and visiting guests clearly shows the Agent's willingness to create fresh and influential contact to turn to his advantage where he could. The ability of the Company's men in Persia to manipulate Dutch failures to their advantage as well as navigating around the potentially damaging conduct of the ships' companies and captains shows a nuanced understanding of their circumstances. This in turn goes on to highlight the balancing act that continued with the Persian government and Nader Shah, eventually culminating in the receipt of favourable references from local officials and enough security to allow the Company to charge for the transportation of the embassy of 1736.

A major shift in policy came in May 1734 when Nader Shah dispatched Latif Khan to the Gulf with 'orders to purchase shipping of the Europeans at Gombroon'.[91] This request was impossible for the Company's Agents or their Dutch counterparts to fulfil. The representatives of the two companies met shortly after the demands were made and agreed that they were both unable to satisfy such a request, as they were not the direct owners of any of the ships used by their organisations in the region. The Company gave a polite but firm refusal, offering to organise the construction of ships in Surat for the Persians as an alternative, should they so wish it. Despite the shipwrights of Surat being rightly famed for their skill and the quality of the vessels they produced, Latif Khan was reluctant to accept this offer, insisting that he wished to purchase ships he had seen passing through the Gulf already.[92]

Both the Company and the VOC councils were keen to provide assistance to Latif Khan in the hope of gaining him as a useful ally and advocate for their interests at court, a policy that we have seen bore fruit time and again.[93] They perceived that by giving the Shah ships of his own, both their companies were at risk of being of no further use as allies, instead being expelled from Persia, the Gulf and potentially the Western Indian Ocean. Agent Cockell responded independently from the Dutch by petitioning Latif Khan directly, requesting that he stopped offering to purchase passing ships and instead accept the Company's mediation in ordering new ones from Surat.[94] Despite this offer of mediation, Cockell and the Council still believed that they lacked the authority or resources to make good on their promises, sending to Bombay for clarification and instructions.[95]

Agent Cockell then set about trying to fulfil Latif Khan's requests in other ways, which included purchasing ships from local rulers and merchants on the admiral's behalf. Lockhart, in his article on these events, suggests that Latif Khan had bought two ships from Sheikh Rashid,[96] when in fact the Company had captured them and handed them over to him, with the Sheikh deriving no advantage whatsoever.[97] This ascribes a much more active role to the Company in the formation of the Persian fleet than Lockhart had favoured them, indeed it shows them positively enabling it. It seems that the Company was at something of an impasse concerning the Persian desire to build a naval force. It was willing to enable the creation of a Persian fleet, which would remove the European monopoly on naval strength in the region and thereby damage one of the few bargaining chips they had concerning their rights and privileges in Persia. This concern was not as important to the Company as removing their current obligation to provide ships to the Persians when they needed them, suggesting that the Company's attitude to the use of their ships as military tools had shifted. This shift may well be attributed to the reality that Muscat was already growing in strength at seas to the point that the Company could not foresee a sensible way of containing them. The attitude may have been informed by the fact that much of the shipping travelling in and out of the Gulf was only chartered by the Company from private owners, thus enjoying its protection, while not being subject to or beholden to fulfil any orders contrary to their contract. The *Britannia*, for example, was a Company ship and was therefore under the command of the Agent when present in the Gulf, hence its repeated use by the Company's servants for missions to blockade ports and collect tolls and passes.

While the use of privately owned ships had been deemed the easiest and most profitable medium for carrying the Company's goods around the Indian Ocean, it was quickly understood to be a major issue in the Company's strategy of controlling Persian access to naval vessels and supplies. Two privately owned ships, the *Ruparell* and the *Patna*, were sold by their captains to the Persians in 1734.[98] This represented a real concern, as the Company was now being threatened with the loss of its chance to profit financially or politically from Persian ship purchases. The Captain of the *Patna*, Thomas Weddell, died shortly after making the sale to Latif Khan at Bushehr, the harbour chosen as the home base of the Persian fleet, having sent his personal effects on from there with a dinghy that brought news of the sales to Bandar Abbas.[99] The Council's response to this was to severely censure Richard Cook, the captain and owner of the *Ruparell*, whose behaviour, along with his deceased colleague, was colourfully described as 'Scurrilous'. In order to attempt to take advantage of this turn of events, Agent Cockell decided to privately lead Latif Khan to believe that the ships had been sold to him 'by our connivance' hoping that if he could convince the Persian admiral of this, he could 'make a meritt of it'.[100] This event, reported to the Bombay Presidency by a letter sent on 3 December, elicited a speedy response ordering Cockell to enforce a positive ban on the sale of ships to the Persians by any but the Company.[101] The Council at Bombay hoped that by banning any further private sales, they could assist and reinforce Cockell's deception, allowing Latif Khan to believe that the only avenue to fulfilling his duties lay with the Company.

In May 1736 Agent Geekie was informed that the ship *Northumberland*, under the command of Robert Mylne who also acted as joint supercargo with Eustace Peacock, had been sold to the Persians, despite such a sale being banned by the Company's express orders in December 1734.[102] Lockhart and Axworthy suggest that this ship was seized by the Persians,[103] who then paid off Mylne for his duplicity in the seizure. According to the Company's records however, Mylne was indeed paid 500 toman for his part in the sale of the ship; he was also tasked with bringing more ships to Bushehr on the promise of 5,000 toman more. Mylne's story, recounted by Lockhart and Axworthy, was dismissed by the Company's servants as a muddled fantasy. It seems very unlikely that Mylne, against the orders of the Company and the *Northumberland's* owners, sailed to Bushehr, the home port of the Persian fleet, in order to simply sell his cargo and be on his way. This rather pulls at the bounds of credulity, not to mention being dismissed out of hand by the Agent and Council at the time.[104] The attempt by Latif Khan to again purchase a private ship shows that the Company's plans to limit the sale of ships to their own benefit were slipping. The high prices offered by the admiral, as well as the desire of private merchants and captains to make a good profit, legally or otherwise, were enough to render the Company's deterrents only partly successful.

The sale of shipping by private individuals was of particular concern to the Company as it threatened their position in Persia by making their refusal to do likewise themselves seem antagonistic and disruptive at best. The other issue for the Agent and Council was that these sales ate into their ability to organise and make a profit from the sale of ships built in India and then delivered under the Company's auspices, not to mention the potential disruption to future voyages. In response to these growing pressures, the Council at Bombay and the staff of the Bandar Abbas factory began planning their own campaign to capture this hugely profitable market. The first instance of a Company brokered sale was that of the *Cowan* in 1736. The Company arranged for the privately owned ship to be sailed to the Gulf for sale under their colours, arriving on 19 November 1736.[105] After the arrival of the *Cowan* and its exchange, which was accompanied by much fanfare and the firing of salutes from the Persian fleet, the fort at Bandar Abbas, the Company factory and all the ships in the road,[106] the Persians immediately requested that another ship should be delivered to them on like terms. The Dutch failed to take part in the salutes fired at the handover of the *Cowan*, earning the displeasure of the Persians yet further, after they had continually failed to supply any assistance to the fleet building project. This is an apt demonstration of how the Company, despite original refusals, had acted in order to preserve good relations with the Persians and make money doing it. The success of this strategy can be seen in the fanfare made on receipt of the *Cowan*.

Seeing how well received the *Cowan* was, the Company happily agreed to deliver a second ship, having made somewhere in the region of 200% profit from the 8,000 toman sale of the *Cowan*, according to an envious Dutch source.[107] The *Cowan* was later renamed the *Fath-i Shah* in a ceremony in which yet further salutes were fired, including this time by the Dutch.[108] Despite several mentions in the secondary material by Lockhart of a second ship being delivered with the *Cowan*, the Company's records contain no such detail. They show that the *Cowan* arrived in company with the *Robert Galley*, though this ship later departed carrying Mirza Mohsen, the Persian ambassador and the sister of the Mughal grandee Sa'adat Khan. The *Robert Galley* was eventually sold to the Persians, but not until 1742 and that by the connivance of the already troublesome Eustace Peacock, who deliberately travelled up to Shiraz in order to offer the ship directly to Taqi Khan, who had ultimate oversight of the fleet project. Peacock sold the *Robert Galley* for 1,000 toman but was then forced to give back 150 toman to Taqi Khan as a gift when Peacock arrived to collect his reward at Shiraz.[109]

Two more ships, the *Mary* and the *Pembroke*, were delivered to the Persians at Bandar Abbas, with naval stores, in 1742 at a cost of 186,251 rupees or around 9,312 toman.[110] Originally, the Company at Surat had purchased three ships for the Persians, but the third had been damaged before departure and therefore had not arrived with the other two. The Council at Bombay insisted that these costs be covered by ordering that the council at Bandar Abbas attempt to get the Persians to pay for the third ship anyway.[111] The Agent and council found this order impossible to fulfil, the Persians having bought several European ships already and deemed the wily Taqi Khan unlikely to be duped.[112] Instead, Agent Whitwell made sure to get a receipt and subsequent payment for the two ships delivered, thus putting an end to the issue as speedily as he thought possible.[113] The actions of Whitwell, though less than scrupulous, were somewhat better than the plan suggested by the Council at Bombay. The Agent succeeded in gaining political capital from a potentially awkward and dangerous situation, balancing the advantage of a quick, risky profit while accruing the goodwill of Taqi Khan. In many ways, the impetus behind the sale of ships mirrored that for the policy of loaning them for missions and embassies: The good will of local Persian officials, and by extension the Shah or at least intercession with him, allowed the Company to continue to transact its trade without interference. The provision of ships in this way is unique to the East India Company's operations in Persia. While arms sales by Europeans to Asian states were far from uncommon, the direct sale of powerful ships was not a feature of this trade apart from in this instance.[114] This is perhaps the clearest demonstration of the value attached to Persia by the Company, both politically and commercially, even to the exclusion of good relations with the Ottomans and Omanis.

When the *Mary* and *Pembroke* were delivered to the Persian fleet, they were accompanied by a fresh issue; that of crewing the Persians' rapidly expanding fleet adequately. Up to this point, the fleet had been manned by Gulf Arabs, whose loyalty to the Shah in his campaigns against their fellow Arabs and Sunni co-religionists could hardly be counted upon. Indeed, mutinies severely damaged the fighting ability of the Persian fleet on numerous occasions. This affected the Company directly when the Council were informed by Taqi Khan that he had decided that the Indian and European crewmen already serving on the ships would behave better, not to mention more loyally, than his current Arab crews. On getting wind of this, Agent Whitwell dispatched their Armenian linguist with the ships in order to foil any attempt by Taqi Khan to detain the crews and, if necessary, to bribe him to secure their return.[115] The crews did end up staying on with the Persians for two months but insisted on full pay from their erstwhile masters and retaining their own officers. These officers argued fiercely with Taqi Khan over whether the Persian or Company colours should be flown over the ships while the Company's officers and crews remained aboard.[116] When the *Beglerbegi* insisted on flying the Persian ensign, the crews refused to serve any longer than the two months they had been contracted for, despite being threatened severely by the irate governor.[117] This event rather aptly shows a weakness shared by both the Company and the Persians. On the one hand, Taqi Khan could compel the Company to provide the crews by threatening the disfavour at Court and the personal ire of key local officials, not least himself; however, once the crews had been secured, there was no way of guaranteeing that they would accept direction from their new employers. While the Company's servants felt the need to submit to Persian demands, they could not, or perhaps would not, say the same for the ships' crews.

An unexpected advantage to the Persians in the presence of Europeans was the potential to use deserters as military experts. This had originally been prohibited in the agreements made during the Hormuz campaign over a century before, though as Nader Shah had dissolved the terms of the *Farman*, at least when it suited him, this prohibition was no longer in force. Most notable among these renegades was Captain Richard Cook, who had sold his ship, the *Ruparell*, to Latif Khan in 1734. He was reported thereafter to have been providing advice and assistance to the Persian fleet at Bushehr, unknowingly mimicking the former careers of the Shirley brothers a century earlier.[118] As well as Cook, other European deserters appear to have made their way into Persian service, including men who deserted the *Harwich*, stealing the ship's boat in the process.[119] It is unclear why these men fled to the Persian fleet, though promise of higher pay and freedom from their officers may well have spurred them on in their defection. Unfortunately for them, the Persian fleet was plagued by poor pay and terrible conditions, which led to regular mutinies by the Arab crews, so it is unlikely that they derived much enjoyment from their new employment.

The *Mary* and *Pembroke* were officially handed over to the Persians on 28 May 1742, despite the *Mary* being in need of daily pumping, due to leaks in her hull, and the *Pembroke* lacking appropriate rigging.[120] It is suggested that just taking ownership of the vessels gained Taqi Khan enough political capital with Nader Shah that he concerned himself relatively little with the state of the ships themselves, assuming correctly that the Shah would never see them himself. The Company's servants suspected that he was deriving significant financial benefit from the transaction and was therefore less concerned with the quality of the merchandise than he might have been.[121] Despite these major issues, Taqi Khan requested two further ships agreeing to pay an advance of 20,000 rupees in order to secure them.[122] He also requested the service of sailors from Company ships but was frustrated again in this ambition.[123] The lack of concern over the state of the ships by Taqi Khan would suggest that the Company took some licence over which ships they purchased, no doubt with an eye to a large profit, while this profiteering on their part was ignored by the equally avaricious Taqi Khan. This again demonstrates the nuanced approach and understanding adopted by the Company's men in Persia. In this case, the balance struck was highly beneficial to the Company, who turned a significant profit on the sale of ships to the Persians, while also earning the gratitude of Taqi Khan, who magnified himself in the eyes of the Shah.

By 1742 there was significant evidence of both Latif Khan and Taqi Khan actively seeking out ships from other sources. These included other Company ships operating in Sind, which was now part of Nader Shah's possessions in India, as well as Arab and Indian ships. These were either purchased in India, extorted from the Arab Sheikhs of the Gulf, or received as gifts from the Imam of Muscat. On one occasion in 1743, the Persians seized eight ships from Sind which were then used to carry men, horses and 50,000 toman of treasure from that place to Bandar Abbas.[124] In the same year, during the campaign on the Arab shore against Muscat, it is reported that a 'large ship from Muscatt of about nine hundred tons and mounts 50 guns'[125] arrived at Bandar Abbas after being handed over by the Muscatis to the Persian forces. The ship was sent on to the Persian arsenal and dock at Laft, a port on the north coast of Qeshm, where she was hauled ashore and her hull was cleaned.[126] This demonstrates a shift in the power relations of the Gulf region, the Persians now being able to flex their own naval muscle in such a way that they could capture and maintain ships from the Muscatis, who had previously exercised almost untrammelled control of the Gulf's shipping, save only that of the Europeans.

While the naval project saw many successes, it was plagued by mutinies over pay and conditions, which were shockingly poor. In 1740, the Arab crews of the fleet rose up, killing the then admiral, Mir Ali Khan, along with any officers who resisted them. They then took all the ships they could from the anchorage at Laft. The Company blamed this mutiny on a lack of pay and supplies, adding that in any event, the Persian fleet was now lost without the Arabs to sail it, even if any ships were left to them.[127] In order to put down this revolt, Taqi Khan was forced to ask for the loan of English and Dutch ships, a painful return to a custom he perhaps hoped had been left behind for good. As no English ships were present in the port at the time, the Dutch were requested to provide two that they had available locally.[128] The Dutch felt compelled to order their ships to assist in the destruction of the rebellious fleet, fearing that leaving the angry and ill-treated Arab crews would lead to wholesale destruction and the collapse of trade in the region, not to mention the backlash from Taqi Khan that a refusal might bring.[129] The Company eventually assisted against the rebels by providing a *tranky* crewed with some of their factory guards and a gunner, who, if the Company report is to be believed, put up a much greater resistance to the Arabs than did either the Dutch or the Persian ships, both being accused of taking flight at the sight of the enemy.[130]

A final way in which the Company was involved in supporting Persian naval expansion in the Gulf was the provision of naval stores and supplies, as well as, on one occasion, personnel to assist in the construction of ships at Laft under the supervision of a Fleming named 'Porterie'.[131] The first major instance of this is recorded in 1735, after the Persian fleet was defeated at Basra. Latif Khan asked the Company to provide him with a supply of tin, iron shot and gunpowder, all of which he promised to pay for.[132] Despite not having the quantity he requested, Agent Cockell offered him a considerable supply of 500 maunds of tin, 2,000 round shot and 10 barrels of powder. It is to be wondered how the Company's factory would have such a quantity of shot and powder in the first place, making it seem likely that this would not have been solely for the factory's use, even though it had a battery of guns for defence. Clearly the factory's stores for passing ships included far more than fresh water and provisions of food and medicine. There are no records of military supplies being sold to passing merchants, or even to the Persian government outside of their direct demands, adding an intriguing layer to the presence of copious and expensive munitions and hardware in the factory. This seems, therefore, to be evidence either of a clandestine trade in military hardware with the Persians by the Company, which does not appear on their books, or a private trade was being carried out by someone in such materiel, though if this were the case there would have been some recourse to the owners before it was given over to Latif Khan. Such requests were made occasionally to the Company and Dutch throughout the period of the Persian naval experiment; these were sometimes made with promise of payment, or as gifts. This evidence, along with the sale of ships to the Persians, solidifies the Company's role as an arms trader in the Gulf.

The purchasing of ships and gifts of stores to the Persian fleet by the East India Company provides an interesting case, showing both a great level of military involvement in the Gulf region as well as revealing a further layer to the political balance that needed to be struck to ensure the Company's trade. On the one hand, it seems obvious that the Company would benefit from the profits they could turn on brokering the ship's sales, while on the other, it would damage any claim to naval supremacy they had in the Gulf. Presumably this would permanently put a stop to any claim they might have to collect money for passes from ships bound to or from India and subject them to whatever customs regime was put in place, aside from the *Farman*'s stipulations. There were other benefits to the Company in supplying ships; they would be seen to be assisting the Shah in his desire for a fleet, as well as building an effective force to keep piracy and threats by Arab shipping to the sea lanes. This would alleviate the Company from the need to do so themselves, as they had in the past; the presence of a Persian fleet would also allow them to relinquish any responsibility for troublesome requests to transport embassies, troops and supplies for Nader Shah. This intimate involvement also carried risks of gaining the Shah's displeasure should his expectations not be met, requiring the Company to not only placate him but also keep local officials, such as Taqi Khan and Latif Khan, firmly in the Company's camp in order to advocate on their behalf at Court.

The presence of the East India Company at Bandar Abbas allowed the Persians to engage more fully in international diplomacy, providing the Shahs with a useful means of transporting their diplomatic missions to the far corners of Eurasia. While serving this purpose, the Company's ships and crews were made available to the Persians as a navy for hire, taking part in operations against the Arab and Afghan rebels in the wake of the Safavid loyalist victories inland as well as carrying supplies during the invasions of the Arab Shore. The Company also became an arms supplier, brokering the sales of fighting vessels and stores for the Persian navy from India, at a premium, of course. These services show the extreme lengths to which the Company was willing to go in order to maintain good relations with the Persians, while also turning a steady profit and keeping their treasured privileges intact. Despite this, relations between the Company and Persia were not stable, requiring a delicate balancing act of differing expectations and interests with influences ranging from the ever-changeable mood of the Shah to the machinations of the VOC. The Persians did not simply dominate a quiescent Company, the employees of which played a constant game of cat and mouse with Persian officials in order to limit their exposure to displeasure while operating at a minimal cost to their Honourable Masters. They were able to do this by trading and negotiating on the desirable asset of their powerful and threatening naval forces, the Persians' desire for which allowed them to deal from a position of strength that belied their numbers. From this also came a difficult question regarding the status of Company ships and crews being used by the Persians, it not being clear to either side where or to whom loyalty should ultimately lie, nor to what extent such loyalty and service could be relied upon.

In terms of the wider implications of this period, the Company's provision to Persia of naval support was an important feature of the preservation of the Company's *Farman*. Indeed, the Company was only able to keep its trading privileges through the reign of Nader Shah by acquiescing to his demands for naval assistance. Despite this uncertainty, however, the Company was able to negotiate with the local officials in order to provide necessary services, while not unduly hampering business. The swift thinking and action of the factory's Agents, Cockell, Geekie and Whitwell, with the assistance of the councils gives yet more credence to the importance of the Persian factory as a place of delegated authority away from the Indian Presidencies. The autonomy of these Agents, as well as the clear assistance given to Nader Shah in his desire to create a fleet, make it clear that the Persian Gulf factory was far from the quiet quid pro quo of India. The Gulf in the first half of the eighteenth century was a politically unstable region, in which the Company maintained a steady presence and commerce.

Historiographically, these exchanges raise a number of interesting points of tension. While Sharman's hypothesis of the company as an 'empire of the weak' is seductive, especially when considering the seemingly constant need for the Company's servants to bow to the will of Nader Shah and his representatives, the story is clearly more complex.[133] While the Company was acquiescent, it also negotiated beneficial positions economically and politically through its service. The Company was further coerced by the fear that it would lose its privileges and security guaranteed through the *Farman*, though service to officials, whether the ambassadors dispatched to India or Latif Khan and their subsequent support, mitigated that particular risk. The Presidency at Bombay didn't mind the idea of a strong Persian navy, especially when that navy could only be acquired through the Company at great expense. Such a force could counterbalance the growing threat and assertiveness of Oman and could therefore help to further secure the Company's trade. For the Persians, the presence of the Company was the only route by which naval technology and stores could be easily acquired. The Dutch were inflexible and proved, at least with some English interference, to be unreliable even when carrying out seemingly simple missions and tasks, and so the Company was left as the sole avenue through which Nader Shah could achieve his naval ambitions in the Gulf.

5

Brokers, Khwajas and country Christians: The Company's employment of non-Europeans in Persia

The arrival of European companies in the Indian Ocean was far from the discovery of a previously inert or backward region; it was instead the arrival of another competitor in a complex trade network that had functioned and developed for centuries. It is no surprise that this vibrant and flourishing commercial web should have had its own entrenched and sophisticated trading and financial groups predating European expansion into Asia. Not only was the Company obliged to trade with these groups, but it was essential to conducting business to employ these local experts to ensure optimal trading and good communication, especially with Persian officials. This chapter investigates these intermediaries including issues of culture, race, religion, language and legal jurisdiction impacting Company communications.

The Banians, a mixed community of traders and bankers, represented one of these groups. The Banians originated in India and traded and settled throughout Southeast Asia and the Gulf, from Persia to Astrakhan. The other major group, the Armenians, originated in the Southern Caucasus and from there built trading and familial networks throughout the Ottoman Empire, Persia, India, Russia and Europe, with members of the community settling as far away as Lvov and Venice. The interaction between the East India Company and these groups has been the subject of some scholarly attention. The Armenian community has been researched, thoroughly through the work of Edmund Herzig and Vahé Baladouni. Their research informs our understanding of the relations between the East India Company and the Armenians. Baladouni's work with Margaret Makepeace on sources concerning Armenians in the British Library's India Office Records is a valuable resource for historians considering the intercourse between the Armenians and European traders.[1] Herzig's work has also made a number of Armenian sources accessible, as well as providing a detailed analysis of the Armenian's dominant role in the silk trade. Ferrier's work analyses the Anglo-Armenian relationship in the *longue durée*. This chapter considers the important role in the Company's commercial network played by the Armenian community. Through an understanding of the extensive trading life of the Armenians we can construct a much clearer view of Indian Ocean trade and how it was transacted in terms of financing, commodity trading and transport and distribution.

Sebouh Aslanian has also made a significant advance in tracking the historical trajectory of the Armenians' development into both a 'service gentry' in Persia and a trade diaspora elsewhere.[2] Aslanian's work helps to define the world of Armenian commerce from both an institutional and personal level. Most helpful to this study is his description of the collapse of the Julfan trading community in Isfahan. Aslanian also discusses the migration of Julfan Armenians to India via the Persian Gulf after 1722. Aslanian only recognises in detail the centrality of the Company to these events after their 1688 treaty with the 'Armenian Nation', which is more fully considered later in this chapter.[3] More importantly, Aslanian credits the Company with supporting the relocation of Armenian trading families from Persia to Europe and India, specifically Madras and Calcutta.[4] The two main scholarly sources which inform upon the Company and the Armenians during the period covered by this book do not address the specific relationship between the Company's Armenian employees and the Company's *Farman*. Before analysing this further, it is important to establish what both Aslanian and Ferrier bring to the understanding of this feature at a broader level.

The works of Aslanian and Ferrier inform our understanding of the Company's key relationship with the Armenians, with Aslanian studying the Armenians as a whole and Ferrier delivering an overview of the Armenians' interaction with the Company at a high level. Whereas Aslanian studies the Armenians as an international trading community, Ferrier delivers a broad review of the Armenians and the origins of the Company's relationship with them. Ferrier actively considers the interactions between the Company and the Armenian community in the seventeenth and eighteenth centuries, giving a wide survey of the interactions between the two groups. But Ferrier does not concentrate on the personal relations between the Company and its Armenian employees, nor on the conduct of the linguists. Ferrier states clearly that he believes that the Company was completely reliant on the Armenians to carry on their trade in Persia.[5] His case for this is based largely on the cooperation of Armenian merchants in the Company's trade, as well as giving the Company access to Armenian ready cash for trade in Persia. While these arguments are compelling, they do not consider that the Company had traded in Persia for eighty years before the period from which Ferrier draws his sources. Indeed, Ferrier's sources come from a period which saw very specific circumstances in Europe, the most consequential of which was the ongoing war through the 1690s between England and France. Masashi Haneda has briefly considered the role played by the Armenian linguists in the Bandar Abbas factory, listing the duties of the role, though not exploring the deeper connection between the Company and the wider Armenian community.[6] Both Ferrier and James Mather relate to how the Company–Armenian relationship could be much less than cordial, suffering from mistrust and rumours of distrustful conduct.[7] Apart from Mather's brief comments on Persian discrimination against the Armenians, there is little mention in the secondary literature about whether the Armenians, as a Christian community, were treated as Europeans or Asians and how these distinctions may have affected the Company's treatment of them.

Baladouni and Makepeace's collection of documents referring to the Armenians from the India Office Records sheds some light on the regard in which the English/British held the Armenians, revealing how this disposition changed over time. The earliest documents, from 1619 and into the 1620s, give an impression of the Armenians as a litigious and high-handed class of merchants determined to make difficulties for the Company, while protecting their own considerable fortunes.[8] However, by 1695, the Company was actively encouraging its Persian Factors to take any and all advice from the Armenian merchants with whom they did business, including on how best to frame the Company's privileges from the Shah.[9] The Company's officials seem to have classed the Armenians as distinct from the 'black' Indians or Asiatic Persians and Turks and while they receive much opprobrium for their hard dealing the Company seemed obliged to work closely with them. The Armenian and Banian experience of trade and commerce in the Indian Ocean, as well as their ubiquity as merchants throughout the region, reveals to researchers why they were of such use to the European companies. They provided valuable services and expertise, while also allowing access to financial backing and methods of cash transfer otherwise unavailable to European merchants. While providing these services, this research shows that the Banians also form the basis of the Company's' clientele for the inter-Asian country trade. Stephen Dale's *Indian Merchants and the Eurasian Trade, 1600–1750* addresses a specific Banian community in Astrakhan on which this book draws as an analogue for this diverse community the Company encountered.[10] There is also mention of Persians who were taken into the Company's employ, as well as the many Indian and Arab sailors, soldiers, *hammals* (porters) and teamsters who carried out vital services for them. In many ways, the great diversity within the Company's employees and the essential functions that were performed by non-Europeans would suggest a Company that was far less English than has previously been imagined. Armenian linguists would have been the recognisable face of the Company in many of its encounters, while sepoy soldiers guarded the gate to the factory and a Banian broker provided ready cash to oil the wheels of commerce.

The Armenians had been a fixture of trade in the Indian Ocean from the fifteenth century, building networks of kinship and commercial ties from Persia to Poland and East as far as the Philippines. It was due to this expansive network that the East India Company found the Armenians to be useful partners and associates in their various dealings with native dynasties and markets. The Armenians, on the other hand, found it equitable to align with the Company in order to take advantage of their large, fast and well-armed ships, which were already serving the trade routes important to the Armenians. The Armenians represented one of the richest communities in the region, drawing favourable comparisons with the wealthiest merchants of London and Amsterdam.[11] From 1604, Shah Abbas I, creating 'scorched' earth on his borders, had forcibly relocated the Armenians from the Caucasus to the new Safavid capital at Isfahan. The Armenians were given their own city quarter, which they named 'New Julfa' after one of their former commercial centres following their forced migration to Isfahan after 1604.[12] This relocation was a ploy by Abbas the Great to harness the trading networks of the Armenians to enrich his new capital, while also denying his Ottoman rivals access to the same. Not all Armenians were merchants; many involved in the production of silk were not relocated to Julfa, instead they were sent to use their own skills in Gilan and Mazandaran in the silk industry Shah Abbas was attempting to promote.

For the Company, the overwhelming control the Armenian merchants had over the silk trade made them attractive partners. The Armenians enjoyed an almost monopolistic trading connection with Russia and Anatolia, while the Company's trade with India offered fresh opportunities without threatening these established concerns. There was no lasting credible threat to the Armenians' control of the silk trade through Russia or the Ottoman Empire from the European companies; therefore, both communities by 1688 had learned to derive benefit from the expertise of the other.[13] The symbiotic relationship enjoyed by the Company and their Armenian partners is evidenced by the regular use by Armenian merchants of Company ships, to transport either goods or cash between Persia and India. By 1700, these links were well established and led not only to commercial relationships but also to the employment of various Armenians by the European Company as brokers, translators and *Vakils* (Agents, subsidiaries). These roles demonstrated that Armenians were given positions of very great importance, sensitivity and gravity as they not only communicated on behalf of the Company in their presence as translators but also acted on their behalf at a distance.

Contained in the India Office Records is a letter dated 20 June 1723 from Persia to the Court of directors which outlined the commercial relationship between the Company and Armenian families.[14] This closeness was true not only in Persia but also in India where in 1716, Khwaja Sarhad, an Armenian merchant, was made second in command during John Surman's mission to obtain a *Farman* for the Company from the Mughal Emperor Farrukhsiyar.[15] While the trust demonstrated by the Company towards its Armenian employees seems considerable, the Armenians themselves put an equal level of trust in the Company, relying on the good offices of Company servants to disburse their wills and ship cargoes of gold, pearl and other valuables to and from India. Such relationships, while essentially contractual in nature, appear to have exceeded purely mercantile bounds by becoming personal attachments. Matthee observes that this process had served the Armenians well when integrating into Persian society after the trauma of the forced migration to Isfahan.[16] Matthee also describes the Armenians as having become a 'service gentry' within Safavid society, having taken advantage of privileges granted to them by Abbas the Great, as well as familial ties with the silk producing regions of Gilan and Mazandaran.[17]

The Armenians benefitted significantly from the good offices of Shah Abbas I who conferred considerable privileges upon the Julfan Armenians who had been re-settled in Isfahan in 1613, far in excess of those enjoyed by the majority of the population.[18] Shah Abbas' policies to enrich trade therefore assisted both the Armenians, who were given the chance to reinstate themselves at the centre of the silk trade under the Shah's personal protection, and also the Company, which would take full advantage of the Shah's wishes for commercial stimulation while solidifying their place in Persia. The close and mutually beneficial relationship created between the Company and the Armenians may therefore be attributed to the recognition by both groups of the advantages that could be derived from supporting one another in what had proven a very vulnerable and formative period. Ferrier suggests that this relationship was favoured by Shah Abbas I as a way of diverting the silk trade away from his Ottoman rivals, thus weakening them by robbing their treasury of customs and taxation drawn from the sales of silk.[19] It is clear that Shah Abbas deliberately retained the traditional control over the whole of the supply of Persian silk and controlled the buy price. Abbas I used the Armenians in an attempt to boost production and efficiency. In addition, he used the Armenians and the Company to divert trade away from the Ottomans through Hormuz, by sea, a decision he reversed in time. Abbas I left neither the Armenians nor the Company with any other choice than to work with each other. Rather than dictate this partnership, Shah Abbas I allowed them to work things out for themselves over time. As evidence that the Company's relationship with the Armenians had become close, by 1688 the Armenians were given permission by the Company not only to trade within the Company's networks but also to reside in any of the Company's 'cities Garrisons or Towns in India and to buy, sell and purchase Land or Houses and be capable of all Civil Offices and preferments in the same manner as if they were Englishmen born'.[20]

This agreement was negotiated in London with Khwaja Panous Callendar, who lived there until his death in 1696.[21] It is interesting to consider that the agreement was made on behalf of the 'Armenian Nation' by a single merchant, whose family was one of the most influential of the Julfan community. There is no clear definition from the language of the treaty to suggest the scope of the Armenian community covered by this agreement. Baladouni suggests that the 'Armenian Nation' was comprised of the wealthy trading families of New Julfa as well as the Armenian clergy.[22] While this definition does not seem unreasonable, as these two castes represented the most visible and influential sections of Armenian society, it does not take into account any Armenian not living in Julfa, excluding the population in the Caucasus, Gilan or those already living in India. It is also unclear as to the mandate Callendar had to make this agreement on behalf of the 'Armenian Nation', if indeed he had any authority at all. Panous is described as 'an Armenian of eminency and an inhabitant of Ispahan',[23] but any other credentials go unwritten by the Company in the minutes of the negotiation and announcement of the treaty. The negotiation of an agreement this comprehensive is demonstrative of the closeness between the Company and the Armenian trading diaspora. This agreement cemented the relationship and from this point the Bandar Abbas factory becomes the central hub for Armenian, and joint Armenian and Company trade in the Gulf. This relationship also encouraged the already active private trade carried out between the Armenians and Company employees. In support of this Herzig notes that a seventeenth-century Armenian merchant called Hovhannes Ter-Davt'yan lent to Europeans in India a number of private individual notes of exchange.[24]

The support of the Armenian Callendar family with their Armenian merchants in London continued through their assistance of the Company in advising them on the proper varieties and colours of cloth to sell in Persia. Additionally, in Persia, the Factors were encouraged to seek the assistance of the Armenian community.[25] The above agreement also encouraged the Persian Factors to initiate a programme whereby their servants would reside in Isfahan with the Callendar family in order to learn 'the Persian and Armenian languages and arithmetics'.[26] Finally, the agreement with the Armenians and the renewal of the Company's charter in 1693 led to the two parties entering into a series of negotiations on joint ventures. These included a plan to cooperate with the Callendar family to buy up silk previously consigned to the Dutch. The Company promised to take a third of the total, taking advantage of a shortage of silk coming via the Mediterranean, but this plan was met with coldness or outright hostility from the Callendar family. This was presumably due to the huge potential costs involved and the reliance on the Armenians' expertise in pricing and selling the silk appropriately.[27] While the hoped-for cooperation never came to pass, in 1691, the Company was able to sell large quantities of their cloth in Isfahan with the help of their Armenian linguist Da'ud.[28] Trade agreements seem to have eluded the Company and the Armenian trading firms for a variety of reasons. According to Ferrier, there does not seem to have been a time when the interests of both groups coincided to an extent where wide-reaching collaboration was achievable.[29] The Armenian agreement with the Company formalised a much higher level of communication and cooperation between both parties, enhancing the existing trade with the Armenians that took advantage of the Company's markets and shipping.

The various advantages derived from association between the Company and the Armenians, however, never succeeded in redirecting the all-important silk trade from the Ottoman Empire to the Gulf. It is clear from Ferrier's analysis that while the Armenian community was more than happy to assist, guide and be employed by the Company, they were not self-sacrificial and therefore never relinquished their hold over the silk trade from Persia through either Russia or Turkey.[30] This reinforces the idea of the Armenian community being a self-supporting society, with the necessary structural rigidity to resist and coerce both state power, in the case of the Persians' or commercial pressure, as exerted at varying times by the Company and Dutch. In appreciating this fundamental strength, it is possible to build a balanced picture of the relationship enjoyed by the Armenians and the Company as one of mutual assistance and benefit,[31] rather than a Western organisation taking advantage of a downtrodden and servile sub-class within Persian society. As already shown in other parts of this book the Company learned to recognise its own fundamental limitations to expansion politically, militarily, commercially or financially and, in the Armenian example, the power of entrenched local commercial interest. We see again the Company accepted the situation for what it was and created a partnership to make the best of these circumstances. This state of affairs would see a fundamental shift after the Company became the paramount military and trading power after the Battle of Plassey in 1757. This affected its relationship with both the Persian state and the Armenian traders operating between Persia, India and the wider world.

The close relationship between the Armenians and the Company can be traced through a variety of different practices undertaken by both groups in support of the other. The East India Company's freedom from paying customs and duties at Bandar Abbas was one of its most valuable privileges, meaning that goods that they imported could be sold cheaper, undercutting their competitors, especially the Dutch.[32] Yet again, this advantage highlights the significance to the Company of their privileges through the *Farman* and the value of a continued presence in Persia. Early attempts to extend this privilege to Armenian merchants and freighters coming from India met with sanctions when the Persians found out, usually with Dutch assistance. In one instance in 1737, the Dutch actively informed upon the Company, damaging their relationship with Nader Shah's subordinate, Taqi Khan.[33] The Company persisted, however, in negotiating advantageous terms for those Armenians who worked for and with them, making clear the value of Armenian merchants to the Company's business while reciprocally showing how useful Company patronage could be. This came in various guises such as Armenian merchants being allowed to land goods at a lower rate of customs than would normally be charged, or the right to land goods and have them processed and customs calculated at the Company's factory.[34] These attempts to ease or circumvent Persian restrictions and charges for Armenians using the Company's ships appear to show a desire by the Company to gain a further edge against their competitors in the Asian carrying trade between India and the Gulf.

This facilitation of Armenian trade was part of a wider effort to co-opt the Armenians more fully into the Company's trade and business, encouraging Armenians to settle in the Company's Indian settlements. Armenians who took up residence in the Company's possessions in India were given a tranche of other rights, including the right to worship freely in their traditional manner, to trade and freight on Company ships, and to hold office.[35] Armenians, albeit Christians, belonged to a separate religious tradition, and were viewed by the Company as a safer and more reliable population for Madras and Bombay, likely to invest in and defend the cities in which they lived. Stern suggests that the Company was consciously mimicking the resettlement policies of Shah Abbas

I in their treatment of the Armenians.[36] While Stern is almost certainly right that the Company was inspired by the success of New Julfa, their choice of who to emulate seems unfortunate. The Company evidently believed that the Armenians would take well to the idea of relocation, as historically they had done so before. It is hard to believe that the Company could be so callous and crass to imagine that any repetition of this experience would be profitable. Those Armenians who did decide to move to the Company's Indian settlements no doubt did it for pragmatic reasons, such as the explicit military protection offered by the Company from local oppression and financial extortion. Implicitly, the Company was also providing the Armenians with a home base and shipping ready to transact their own trade. The Company's main benefit from the Armenian presence in its settlements appears to have been access to financial instruments which the Armenians were able to make available in return for the benefits they received from the Company. Stern shows that the Company believed that by co-opting the Armenians into its settlements they could use them to counter the 'falsitys and untruths' propagated by the Company's commercial and political adversaries in India, which surrounded the Company's dealings in Asia.[37]

The Company suffered, over the course of its history, from a lack of ready cash and available capital with which to transact its trade in the Indian Ocean. The Armenians were seen by the Company as a pool of investors with established financial instruments and networks, which could be deployed to back the mercantile aspirations of the Company and their Armenian backers.[38] The Julfans in Persia were themselves not short of credit when the Armenians required extra support; their merchants were capable of attracting vast financial backing from their own family firms and communities or could take advantage of modern European banking methods. A letter from Danvers Graves, the Company's Kerman factor, shows a group of Armenian merchants trading in Isfahan in 1750 using 70,000 toman in cash and credit supplied by bankers in Venice.[39] This reveals the truly vast sums that Armenian merchants could call upon from across considerable distances, as well as showing the Company's awareness, not to mention jealousy, of such transactions. It also became common practice in Persia for Armenian traders to pay for the goods they were purchasing with bills and writs on fellow Armenians living in Madras and Bombay, rather than Julfa.[40] This demonstrates the extensive links and relationships garnered by the Armenian community across Europe and Asia, the likes of which the Company simply could not replicate.

The co-option of the Armenian trading community into the fabric of the Company's Indian possessions was therefore a shrewd strategic decision, as it provided not only an educated corps of men with local experience and fluent in local languages but also a vast reserve of cash and credit. The same process, as has been shown above, was happening in India, where Armenians had been encouraged to migrate to the Company's cities and take part in the financial and administrative life of the Company's settlements. Armenian and Banian bankers were incentivised by the Company to shift their working capital to the protection of Company settlements including India. These valuable concessions and Company protection included the promise of freer trade across existing networks. In the Company's settlements, the protection of the Company was more tangible, however, as the case of Bandar Abbas makes clear, the intangible protection of the Company's privileges and advocacy in Persia was just as attractive. Venice had for centuries been the centre of the banking world of Europe, only in the seventeenth and eighteenth centuries being eclipsed by the exchanges in London and Amsterdam. As already noted, it was possible for Armenian merchants to draw credit from far away and in large amounts. But perhaps more interesting is that Madras and Bombay were also becoming nodes of commercial credit for the Armenian family firms. With the arrival of the Company in the early seventeenth century and the efforts of Abbas I to stimulate Persia's trade, Bandar Abbas was also part of a growing network of trade, functioning as an entrepôt for European goods imported by the VOC and Company, as well as an outlet for Persian commerce flowing to India.[41] Aslanian does not consider or attribute the importance of Bandar Abbas as the connection between the Armenians of Persia and the wider Indian Ocean trading world, especially the Company settlements at Madras and Bombay. I contend that Bandar Abbas, and by extension the Company and VOC factories there, formed a vital link between the Armenians and their trade partners and lines of credit in India and Europe. As we have seen, the shift from 'old world' sources of finance, such as Venice, to closer, Indian settlements under the Company's jurisdiction is central to understanding the relative positions of the Company and the Armenians in the eighteenth century. The research for this book, along with the work of Aslanian and Stern, shows that the Armenians were capable of linking these two circuits of trade together, drawing credit from one side to the other, facilitating both their own commercial ventures and providing the Company with a source of capital and income through freighting. This meant that the Company's ships travelling between Europe and India, their factories at Isfahan and Bandar Abbas and their settlements at Madras, Bombay and Calcutta, had become as indispensable to the good management of Armenian business as the Armenians had for the Company.

Their various financial facilities led Armenians to be directly employed by the Company for a number of tasks. Their facility with Middle Eastern and European languages also made them ideally suited to employment by the Company as translators and interpreters. For their part, the Armenians who worked for the Company in Persia were doubly protected as they were subject to the privileges granted in the treaty signed in 1688 by the Company on the Armenian community, while also benefitting from the conditions of the Company's *Farmans*, which guaranteed their safety explicitly. These privileges included protection of physical property from theft, damage or seizure, and freedom from taxation and extortion by the Persian government. This was a marked departure for many Armenians who were often targeted by the Persian authorities for 'gifts' and extortions.[42] The Company also provided for their servants' physical well-being: They were fed and clothed by the Company from their allowance, which was limited and audited by the authorities in Bombay and London. They were also given gifts at Christmas.[43] In this way the Armenians were granted a measure of 'state power' protection that they had previously lacked.

The Armenians hired by the Company were forced to navigate between two identities that did not always mix comfortably. While the Company's protection was evidently valuable and trusted, the translators were still considered by the Persians as being subjects of the Shah. Therefore any benefit or defence derived from association with the Company was secondary to this status. Indeed, according to the Company's records, sometimes claiming European protection was a significant disadvantage. The Dutch *Vakil* at Kerman, 'Owanooze' (most likely Hovhannes, the Armenian rendering of John), was repeatedly beaten during Nader Shah's occupation of the city in 1747; he was also extorted by Persian and Afghan soldiers on the Shah's orders. On being targeted in this way and brought before the Shah when he was unable to pay what was demanded, he was beaten severely and only worsened this chastisement when he protested that he was under Dutch protection.[44] Owanooze may have only tried to use his Dutch connection in extremis, but it clearly did not have the desired effect. This incident reveals Nader Shah did not feel obliged to stay his hand concerning the lives of his subjects by outside influence. Owanooze was beaten because he was considered uncooperative and the attempt to use his Dutch status was seen only as a further impertinence. Considering the brutality with which Nader Shah extracted money from the general population, it seems likely, in this case, that Owanooze's race was not at issue, but his inability to comply and then claim protection of a foreign power was.

As well as being viewed as subjects by Persian officials, the Armenians' position was made somewhat precarious as they had to communicate with officials who might not like the messages they received and thus ran the risk of being punished as proxy for their masters, who as Europeans were much less likely to be physically threatened. The Company's *Farmans* also covered this eventuality, promising protection and good treatment for those carrying messages for the Company.[45] At least notionally, the Armenian linguists were given protection by the Company's *Farman* against punishment or rebuke by their Persian interlocutors, although, as the case with Owanooze demonstrates, that may not always have been effective. This again shows that the Company's employees derived significant protections and benefits from their service. These benefits also included a regular salary, often calculated on the rupee, rather than the shahi, which was desirable to those working in Persia due to the advantageous exchange between the rupee and the often debased Persian currency.

The benefits that both the Company and Armenian communities brought to one another appear to have created an exceptionally durable connection. The case of Sultan David, an Armenian merchant trading between Persia and the Coromandel Coast, in the 1740s provides a clear example of how the relationship could be stretched, both in terms of time and distance.[46] The incident is first mentioned as a simple transaction for cloth, which was paid for by a bill on Sultan David in Madras for the sum of 14,800 rupees. This is a considerable sum, representing the wages of the Company's Agent in Persia for twelve years, demonstrating the trust in and durability of financial instruments agreed between Armenian family firms and the Company across large distances and long periods of time. The disbursement of the bills seems to have been complicated by Sultan David having left Madras for Pondicherry, at the time still under French rule, and the Company therefore being unable to reach him.[47] It is a testament to the relationships maintained between the Company and the Armenians that the bill was not invalidated immediately after the failure of Sultan David to pay it. Eventually, it was agreed that 'Shawmeer' (most likely Shah Amir), Sultan David's son, would be permitted to go to India and secure the payment from his father, with the interest that had been accruing over the previous six years. The Company was evidently capable of tracing sums of money accurately across a variety of currencies in a wide geographical area and calculating the appropriate interest over long periods of time. Equally, the value of Armenian credit, both in India and Persia, is made clear by the willingness of the Company to risk allowing Shawmeer to leave Persia to pursue the debt further.[48]

There were times, however, when the Company's relations with the Armenian community were significantly weakened by bad practice on one side or the other. There are recorded cases, for example, of the Company's linguists having abused their positions and therefore the good name of the Company. This is illustrated by the case of 'Stephen' who served as the Company's linguist at Isfahan while the city was under siege by Safavid Loyalists attempting to oust the Afghans in 1730. Stephen appears to have colluded with the Afghans to keep the Company's employees in Isfahan, rather than allowing them to leave to avoid the siege, according to the account in the Company's minutes. In so doing he betrayed the confidence of his employer and was dismissed, as well as being banned from any further Company service.[49] After 1730, the Company employed Joseph Hermet as their linguist and members of his family as interpreters and assistants. The Hermet family were of French descent and appear to have had no connection to any of the local communities in Persia.[50] This seems to signal a break in trust with the Armenians of Isfahan as interpreters. The Armenians are also reported to have been caught misleading inexperienced Company servants into making poor decisions amounting to fraud and deception in their business and signing off added expenses.[51] One instance of this was discovered during a case for incompetence made by the Company against two of its employees. It transpired that they had borrowed huge amounts of ready money on credit and then attempted to cover up their fraud with deception.[52] From the letter outlining the trial, it appears that the two employees, Peirson and Blandy, had been incompetent to start with, but had then been badly advised by some Julfans into making poor investments and financial transactions that benefitted the Armenians to the detriment of the Company's credit.[53] In this report, the Armenians were accused of having stolen gifts destined for the Persian Court and withholding deliveries from the Company's servants under the licence of the factory.[54] It is unclear whether these accusations against the Armenians were substantiated, or whether they represented an attempt by Peirson to shift the blame away from himself (Blandy had died before being charged with misconduct). In either case, the privileged position of Armenian merchants as advisors, partners and suppliers at Isfahan is clear from the fact that accusations against them could be deemed realistic enough to be a defence for Peirson. Conversely, the Company was equally capable of manipulating their relationship with the Armenians to their own advantage. Sometimes cargoes carried on Company ships and charters were directed to be landed at Bandar Abbas, rather than other ports preferred by the freighters, in order to collect a share of the customs the Armenians were liable to pay there.⁵⁵ In this way, the Company was seen to be augmenting the trade to the port, while lining their own pockets both in carrying freight to Persia and receiving their cut of customs from the goods landed there.

The compact of 1688 between the Company and the Armenian community resident in India presents a set of complex questions concerning legal sovereignty and subjecthood with regard to the Company's European servants. The agreement recognised Armenians as having all the same rights as 'Englishmen Born', thus opening positions within the Company's hierarchy and civil service to them and permitting them to trade and travel without restriction between the Company's cities and factories. It would appear from this that the Company was granting citizenship, of a sort, to the Armenians. Nevertheless, the idea of citizenship in this context is problematic on several levels. Stern has put forward the argument that the Company constituted 'government, state, and sovereign in Asia'.⁵⁶ While this is true, especially for the Company's large settlements in India which were under the direct jurisdiction of the Governors, Presidents and Councils, in Persia it was not nearly so simple. The Persian factory was a small, distant outpost of the 'Company-State' and therefore lacked the mechanisms by which state-like functions could be enforced. This was as true for the Armenians in Company service there as for the Company's English employees. Essentially, the realities of communication and extending authority over long distances made the Company's nominal rights for its servants moot in the face of immediate threats and concerns.

The position of the Armenians in particular was further complicated by the claim of Nader Shah to be sovereign over all Armenians, not just those in his empire but also those who lived outside of it.⁵⁷ While Nader Shah was unlikely to be able to assert his status as ruler over all Armenians, whether they were living in the Russian Empire, Poland or just across the border in the Ottoman Empire, for those Armenians living in Persia, the message was clear. How then, could the Company contend that the Armenians of India, and those in their employment elsewhere, were citizens of a trading organisation based in London, rather than of a resurgent Persian Empire? In reality, Nader Shah could only assert his claim of rulership over the Armenians who were physically or evidentially financially present in his domain. The Company could likewise use its physical and legal presence to counter any attempt by Nader Shah to attack or dispossess the Armenians in the Company's employ. The Persian recognition of the Company's rights granted in the *Farman* to extend the non-payment of tax and other benefits to the Armenians shows how the legal sovereignty of the

Shah could be curtailed within his own realm, while abroad, Persian rulership could only be notional.[58]

For much of its existence, the Armenian community had lacked a state of its own. In this way, the claim by Nader Shah to rule over all Armenians has questionable merit. Nader Shah did rule Armenia itself and therefore most Armenians, including their religious leaders, and they lived as his subjects and paid him tax. The East India Company did, however, fulfil some state-like functions for the Armenian community, which was not limited to only their employees. The most commonly documented of these functions, excluding the nominal protection offered by the Company to those Armenians who worked for it, was the administration and disbursement of the wills and estates.[59] The evidence for this comes from copies of the contents of packets sent between Bombay and Bandar Abbas, as well as notifications of the disbursements of money from the wills of Persian Armenians in the Bandar Abbas Consultations. There is no easy explanation as to why the Company was entrusted with this task, nor why they agreed to carry it out. While the Company was willing to carry out various legal functions for its English employees, including the administration of wills and disbursement of payments and estates, doing so for Armenians would seem a long jurisdictional stretch. A possible reason for these transactions could be that the Company was attempting to secure debts that it was owed by the merchants, effectively making the Company a priority investor in the estate of the merchant and guaranteeing, as far as was possible, that the Company received its due.

The Armenians, along with other minority groups, had no protection for their goods against seizure by the local Khan or the Shah on their deaths. It was Persian custom that anything belonging to a Persian subject ultimately belonged to the Shah and was held by his subjects only for as long as it pleased that Shah. This being the case, when a Persian subject died, their property was liable to be repatriated to the Shah through local officials. By using the Company as a guarantor and executor, the estates of wealthy merchants could instead be safely disbursed through the Europeans, whose property was not liable to confiscation by officials. Between 1700 and 1750, there were five reports of the Company actively being involved in the management of the estates of deceased Armenians, one of whom, 'Yakub John' (Ya'qub is the Arabic derivation of Jacob), appears to have made the Company his executor, or possibly the Agent in his capacity as the Company's representative. Demands and payments on his will appear six times between May 1729 and July 1732 in the Company's consultations.[60] Unfortunately, there is no stated reason as to why Yakub John decided to make either the Company or one of its officials his executor, although it can be imagined that he may have chosen to do so to protect his estate from seizure by the Persian authorities.

This leads to the question of whether the Company in Persia, as Stern suggests was the case in India,[61] was undertaking state-like functions with regard to the Armenian population or whether this was a more personal arrangement. The Company was often the agent for the estates of its employees who died while abroad, organising the sale of personal items and goods to be sent back to the deceased's family as cash.[62] It is possible that the Armenians who worked for the Company, including brokers, were aware of this, and thereafter the benefits of the custom spread through the community. This does not mean that the Company viewed the Armenians as being subjects, though as employees of the Company they were bound by certain codes of conduct, nor does it suggest that the Armenians considered themselves to be so. In this way, the Armenians appear to have been using the Company as a sort of tax-haven, whereby they could avoid losing a portion or all of their estate after death to the Persian authorities and therefore guaranteeing the continuation of their family firm.

Aslanian tracks the movements of Armenian merchant families from Persia to Europe and India during and after the oppressive reign of Nader Shah. Many Armenians from influential families are shown by his research to have moved to Madras[63] and Calcutta;[64] indeed, Aslanian suggests these as possible foci for a new commercial circuit around which the Armenians could rebuild their wealth and society. Both of these cities were governed by the Company, which seems too much of a coincidence to avoid comment, though Aslanian does not mention this specifically in his work. It appears that the Armenians, on seeing the collapse of Persian and then Mughal power, gravitated towards the Company cities and authorities in India most closely aligned with their business interests. Looking back at the long connections between the Armenians and the Company this is no surprise. Aslanian seems to suggest that stateless and vulnerable, the Armenians were forced to comply with the Company's 'intense monopolising rivalry' and ceased to be independent traders.[65] That being said, Aslanian's later description of a flourishing trade, not to mention the first Armenian printing press in Madras, demonstrates that the Armenians took advantage of their privileged relationship with the Company.[66]

Unlike the relatively homogeneous Armenians, the 'Banians'[67] were a collection of itinerant merchants from a wide variety of religious, social and caste groups. James Onley explains the many divisions within the Banian community, while also stressing that this term was accepted and used ubiquitously when talking about the Indian community in the Gulf.[68] As such, it is difficult to speak of 'the Banians' as a whole, but to try and cover every caste, family and ethnicity from the *Lawatiyya* to the *Mappilla*, or *Memon* to *Kshatriya*, would become impossibly cumbersome. Unlike the Armenians, the Banians do not appear to have had any recognisable political relationship with the Safavids. Having voluntarily migrated and settled in the Gulf region, they appear to have simply been treated as subject peoples, in a similar way to the Arab tribes. This differs from the Armenians, who were recognised as their own 'nation' as discussed above; their long history, Christian religion and strong communal ties demarcated them from the looser, more fragmented Banian groups, or the fiercely independent Arabs. The Banians also appear to have been considerably more numerous in the Gulf region than the Armenians. This is perhaps unsurprising, considering that the Armenians' traditional homeland, as well as their post-migration homes, were in the North and West of Persia, and the Banians, coming from India, arrived in the Southeast.

The Company, by 1710, with its connections between the Subcontinent and the Gulf, rapidly discovered and cultivated useful relationships with Banian merchants, who acted most often as brokers, while also sometimes assisting with translation and interpreting.[69] The Company's broker at Bandar Abbas appears to have always been a Banian merchant who as a Company employee gained certain rights and protections from the Persian authorities, such as freedom from taxation for his household, or Company intervention in legal disputes.[70] Serving the Company in this capacity was therefore very attractive and potentially very profitable to the broker, over whom the Company was able to extend its patronage and protection.[71] The connection with the Company could also be familial, with the position of broker being passed down from father to son on at least one occasion.[72] Other positions were also passed down within families. This family connection with the Company was not simply notional, as demonstrated by the giving of gifts by the Company on special occasions, including Christmas, but also family events, such as the marriage of the broker's son, who received a princely 50 tomans.[73]

The Company made it a condition of the employment of 'Sankhar' as broker in 1730 that he would pay a stipend to the family of the former broker 'Noqua Chittra'.[74] This suggests that Sankhar's family would, in turn, receive a similar pension should Sankhar be unable to support them. The broker was also given rooms from which he could carry out his business within the new factory completed in 1750.[75] This gave him security for his goods and cash, while also giving him a place of business separate from his house, which was vulnerable to occupation by avaricious Persian officials.[76] In one particular instance in 1732, the Company paid

> 100 Venetians for a Rogum to get Chitrah's house back from Mirza Mahomett who took possession of it without any consent or privity which villain promised to repay and therefore you must see that he does it.[77]

This was not the first time the Company had been forced to intervene to protect their broker's property, which had been seized twice during the Afghan occupation of Persia in 1729.[78] The Afghans had been evicted with an order from the Court and the withdrawal of the Company's assistance and collaboration in the running of the port, upon which they seem to have been reliant.[79] Eventually, Baru Khan, the offending Afghan, sent his son to beg the Company's pardon, bestowing a *khalat*, or robe of honour, upon the broker for his pains.[80] As was the case with the Armenians, the Company could use its political position to the benefit of the Banian merchants in its service, paying bribes to Nader Shah's officials or withdrawing support from the Afghan administration.

The Company's broker was a vital member of the factory's staff. He not only provided ready cash with which the Company could carry out its various transactions but was also a major purchaser of their imported cloth.[81] As the Company's broker, the legal protections extended to him could be invaluable as a safeguard against extortion, which was not uncommon,[82] and also against spurious criminal charges. On one occasion in 1732, the Banian community at Bandar Abbas was held collectively responsible for the death of a thief, despite the fact he had been beaten to death by the *Katwal*, the local constable.[83] In response, the Company demanded a public apology and restitution for those taken prisoner,[84] while only half of what was taken was ordered to be returned.[85] The broker was also reimbursed for his work on behalf of the Company, as he was entitled to a 1% levy on all transactions carried out in the factory for which he and the Agent were responsible.[86] In return for these privileges, the broker was very often the sole purchaser of the Company's shipments of cloth, which he then sold off as best he could. Eventually, the opportunity was taken to end the brokering system at Bandar Abbas in preference for direct payments, triggered by the resignation of Sankhar from the post. In return for his service, Sankhar was given considerable time and leeway to repay the money he owed the Company, including a facility for credit on the Company to bring his own business back into order before leaving his position in 1739.[87]

The Banians, like the Armenians, provided the Company with a ready network of financial support, predicated and guaranteed by the status and good credit both of the Company and their broker in Bandar Abbas. The business of the Armenians and Banians overlapped geographically but did not necessarily form competing interests. The Armenians, with their major commercial enterprises lying in the land-bound trade carrying silk to the Ottoman Empire and Russia then onwards to Europe, only rarely competed directly with the Banians, who traded a wide variety of goods between the Gulf and India. In terms of the Company's finances, the Armenians could provide credit based on Europe, while the Banians could do likewise via India.

The Company's reliance on the Banians for access to ready cash again highlights the important trust relationships formed between the Company and its native intermediaries. In only one year, 1728–9, the Company exchanged money with fifteen Banians from Bandar Abbas and Kerman: this does not count transactions where the individuals are not named and mostly consists of bills being issued for 'black money', adulterated silver coinage, with which the wool trade at Kerman could be carried out. The broker, as the premier lender to the Company, sometimes had to be paid with bills of exchange (credit notes) on the Company's office in Bombay, rather than being satisfied with cash or cloth at Bandar Abbas. This demonstrates both the level to which the Company was indebted to, and therefore relied upon, its brokers, while also showing the reach of the broker as an individual. The broker would have to have an agent at Bombay for the transaction to work, as well as the capital to support himself through the long wait between being debited in the Gulf and then receiving his credit from India. An example of the amounts and distances of these transactions can be seen when in 1734, Sankhar drew a bill for 15,000 rupees on the Company in Bombay while also being provided with bills for Bombay himself for 550,000 shahis to cover the Company's wool investment for that year.[88] This is evidence for a business, if not familial, connection back to Bombay, where such large withdrawals on the Company suggest either adequate security or a trusted intermediary to make good on the sums being exchanged.

The bills of exchange presented to the Company at Bandar Abbas also provide valuable information about the geographical extent of the Banian community. Stephen Dale's work sheds light on the truly vast reach of Indian merchants throughout Eurasia, penetrating not only into the Persian hinterland to Kerman and Mashhad but also through Persia to Central Asia, the Caucasus and the Caspian littoral.[89] The distance travelled by these merchants was considerable, though not necessarily exceptional when considering the long distance travelled by the Armenians, Portuguese, English and Dutch. It is also important to consider the numbers of people involved. Onley has outlined the size of the Indian population in the Gulf, suggesting that as many as 3,000 Banians lived in and around Hormuz and Bandar Abbas, though this number fluctuated considerably with the shipping season.[90] The size and apparent wealth of the Banian community does not appear to have translated into political power. Whereas the Armenians had been able to gain positions of significance in the Persian hierarchy, the Banians do not seem to have done so. This may have been due to the Persian distaste for Hinduism, though some of the Banian groups were Muslims, including Shi'a groups like the *Lawatiyya*.

The Banians were often targets of extortion and bribery by the Persian authorities, therefore the ability of the Company to mediate in disputes between the community and Persian officialdom, even with the Shah himself, was invaluable to them as a method of influencing key political figures. One can see here again how the Company's ability to deploy its political power, as granted by the *Farman*, could be used to the advantage of the Asian merchant communities. This was perhaps more important to the Banians, who unlike the Armenians had no entrenched elite within Persian society on whom they could call in times of difficulty or danger. These efforts were not always effective and could sometimes lead to unexpected circumstances, such as in 1747 when 'Lecheram', the Company's broker in Kerman, was burned to death by Nader Shah's soldiers.[91] This seems to have been not only partly punishment for his inability to pay various bribes and demands but also as a show of disregard by Nader Shah for the Company and the protection they were believed to offer. The Armenians, despite being Christians, were still arguably 'native' to Persia, while the Banians seem to have remained essentially foreign.

The last significant group employed by the Company were local Persians, who worked in a variety of specialised roles. While the Armenians were trusted to represent the Company's interests to Persian officials and to translate faithfully for them, Persians were generally not employed to do so. As brokers, Persians tended to lack the connections with India which so benefitted the Banians in their ability to circulate cash and credit. There were advantages to hiring Persians for certain tasks, for example, only a Persian would have been an appropriate Mullah, while Persian local merchants employed as brokers had a more intimate knowledge and connection with local suppliers, traders and buyers. The Company seems to have been able to provide enough encouragement to attract otherwise wealthy and locally influential men to their service in order to facilitate the Company's trade. Service with the Company was, however, a potentially fraught life for those who chose it. Persians, rather than Armenians, Banians or Englishmen, were more vulnerable to intrigue, coercion and reprisal by the local authorities, not to mention pressure to spy and inform upon their European employers.

Persians fulfilled a number of functions within the Company's organisation, the most prominent of which was the brokerage at Kerman. Kerman was a vital arena for the Company, as the wool from this region was particularly highly prized and was exported in bulk to Europe, mostly for the trade in felts and hats. Kerman was therefore a centre of considerable investment for the Company and as such required constant supervision. Over the course of the period between 1700 and 1750, the brokerage at Kerman was under the supervision of a pair of Persian merchants named 'Cosroe' (Khosrow, d. 1732)[92] and 'Seawax' (probably 'Siavush', d. September 1747).[93] The Company's minutes for the meeting on 14 March 1732 report that Khosrow's estate was to be taken into the charge of William Cordeux, who was sent to take over the wool investment when Khosrow died. This again shows the Company's ability to keep assets out of the hands of the Persian authorities, even when the estate belonged to an irrefutably Persian subject. While it is not recorded when Khosrow was appointed to his station, the terms of Siavush's employment with the Company are listed in their consultations. It is reported that Siavush was paid at the same rate as Khosrow, 1 toman per month, as well as being given a *khalat* to show that he was now in the Company's favour and therefore under their protection.[94] Not only was the Kerman broker paid more than most of the Company's servants in Persia, he was also responsible for three other Persians hired by the Company there, two assistants Sevan and Rostam, and a wool merchant named Kasim. The broker was therefore evidently a trusted individual, undertaking business worth 1,400 toman in 1733,[95] managing other employees and negotiating with the Khan of Kerman on the Company's behalf.

While the Company was able to extend some of its legal and diplomatic privileges to its Persian agents in Kerman, there were limitations on how effectively these could be upheld. During Nader Shah's visit to the city, this became particularly clear. Not only was the Dutch Armenian Vakil, Owanooze, beaten to death, but Siavush, Esfandiar (Siavush's son-in-law) and Mohammed, the Company's linguist in Kerman, were all beaten and financially ruined.[96] While the Company's representative in Kerman, Danvers Graves, was never harmed, he was equally unable to do anything to protect Siavush, who eventually died from his wounds, nor to gain financial reprieve for the other two men. Nader Shah, when challenged by Graves, made it clear that he wished the Company no ill will, nor did he wish any conflict with the British. Nader Shah insisted, however, that Siavush and the other men, as Persians, were his subjects and therefore his to do with as he pleased.[97]

While Graves' inability to intercede effectively for Siavush reveals a fundamental weakness in the Company's ability to uphold its promises of protection to its employees, the incident also reveals the extent of Siavush's own wealth. Siavush alone appears to have paid over 600 toman to Nader Shah, showing that he was a man of considerable means in his own right, if not among the highest-ranking merchants in Persia. It also highlights how violence was an ever-present theme in Persia at this time, as it was throughout the Early Modern world. The total and arbitrary rule of the Shah and therefore the authority of his subordinates permitted for little to no resistance unless money, political will or physical force could be brought to bear, *Farman* or no. The fear of retaliation in any of these forms by the Company appears to have often been enough to protect its European servants, though the native employees of the Company were still expected, at times, to submit to threats and demands as Persian subjects.

The Company employed Persians for more than directly commercial purposes, as demonstrated by repeated mentions of the 'Company Mullah'. This means that the Company hired a local Persian cleric, but it is unclear exactly why they chose to do so. Sadly, no reason is given for the periodical appearances of this individual, who seems to have mostly worked as an intermediary or negotiator.[98] It is possible that he was contracted to interpret Islamic law for the Company and/or provide religious succour for its Muslim employees. The Mullah was paid with a *khalat* worth 1,000 shahis per year as payment, which amounts to rather less than most of the Company's other native employees.[99] Apart from his function as a negotiator and someone to greet visiting officials, it is not clear what the Mullah was employed for, nor why the Company felt employing a Muslim holy man would be advantageous. One can imagine that this was an attempt to make their guests and visiting Persian officials feel more at home when dealing with the Company, or as a way of demonstrating sensitivity to local religious beliefs.

Lastly, the Company employed a man called 'Mullah Zenaul' (possibly either Zaynal, or a fragmentation of a compound name such as *zayn al-haqq*, etc.), who was listed in the Company's payroll as their 'Persian Writer'. The duty of this man seems to have been to translate the messages from the Company from simple replies to something framed in the correct courtly language and in a pleasing hand.[100] Presumably the writer would have provided neat copies in the correct register of letters both from the Agent to regional officials and also, when necessary, any correspondence to the Shah. If this is the case it goes some way to proving the relative weakness of the Company's European employees' acquisition of Persian, which is also partly evidenced by their constant need for interpreters. The Persian Writer was paid 1,400 shahis a year, or three and a half times the wage of a European Writer and could expect the customary gifts given to all the Company's servants at Christmas. On the death of Mullah Zenaul, his son Mohammad Jafer (more correctly rendered as Ja'far) was employed in his father's stead and on the same terms. On his accession to the role he was also given the traditional *khalat*, publicly demonstrating his attachment to the Company.[101] The rationale for this decision is indicative of the Company's attitude, both to its servants and to the conception of itself: 'As We apprehend [he] will be more Firmly attached to the Hon. Co.'s Interest than a Stranger, Who has never Experienced the advantages their Family have for many years received from that Employ.'[102] This quotation demonstrates that the Company believed that they were a benefit to their employees, not only in as much as they paid them a salary but also of more notional advantage in status, to the individuals themselves and also their families.

The Armenian involvement with the Company in Persia and the interactions between these two groups reveal a great deal about the perceptions of both communities. The enduring uniqueness of the Armenian community, which resisted full assimilation into either the Persian or Company sphere, is a demonstration of the durability of non-state links before the modern period. This uniqueness, derived from religious freedom granted by both the Company and the Persians, was reinforced by shared mercantile interests garnered and spread across the globe. While such business necessitated cooperation with European shipping, this was predicated on the acceptance and recognition of entrenched norms within Armenian society. The merchants of Armenian family firms used European ships and beneficial rates of freighting and duties to further their own goals, while some also served the Company as intermediaries with officials in India and Persia as translators and brokers. In many ways, by seeking to integrate with the Company, the Armenians repeated the same process they had undergone while finding a place within the Safavid Empire: finding and fulfilling a range of functions that were required but did not fit in with religious or social norms. In Persia, they formed an international trading network based around silk, an industry that directly financed the Royal Treasury, while for the Company they acted as interpreters and a source of capital. In both cases they formed a kind of 'service gentry' and in return received protection for their cultural heritage and religion. Under the Company's administration, the Armenians were granted further rights, amounting to legal equality with their English interlocutors, while not sacrificing their own commercial interests, as seen by the continuation of the silk trade through the Ottoman Empire. Eventually, the interests of the Armenians would drive them into the Company's Indian possessions, fleeing the barbaric cruelty of Nader Shah and the interregnum and chaos that followed his death in 1747.

The East India Company is often described as an impressive combination of European innovation, mercantile prowess and military power; however, the Company was far more complex than this. The Company may have been chartered in London and under the control of English merchants and officials from the Court of Directors all the way to the factory agents, but the Company did not always have a European face. Most business in the Gulf factory was transacted through an Armenian or Persian interpreter, while the hard currency necessary for everything from paying for the wool investment in Kerman to the salary roll was provided by an Indian Banian. The letters composed and written to Persian officials were prepared by a local artisan, while a Mullah was employed to provide guests and visitors with a familiar interlocutor. Indeed, for a long time the Company's largest investment, the Kerman wool trade, was overseen by a local merchant of independent means. The Company was English, but its investors and customers were relatively unlikely to have had much to do with the *kullah-pushan* who lived in the factory.

The Company provided the Banians and Armenians with legal protections they would never have otherwise enjoyed, while in return, these merchants supplied capital and advice to the Company in their business. The Armenians were happy to assist the Company in their endeavours but never lost sight of their own communal interest, scuppering any attempt by the Company to redirect meaningfully the silk trade away from the Ottoman Levant. The Company, Banian and Armenian communities, sharing common links and even living as neighbours and in-laws in Bandar Abbas, Bombay and Madras, formed a mutually supportive bond which would continue to benefit both until the eventual collapse of the Company's organisation. The Company's ability to use its *Farman* as a means by which to protect the wealth and well-being of its local servants was a heretofore unforeseen boon to the Banian and Armenian merchant communities, even if there were practical limitations to this notional protection. The Company could practically protect the person and property of people who were not even directly employed by them, as demonstrated in the execution of the wills of Khosrow and Yakub John, without recourse to the Persian legal system, under which their estates might have been taken as forfeit by the Shah.

The established trading relationships of the Armenian and Banian communities between Persia and India were a necessity for the often capital-poor Company, for whom the well-established financial instruments deployed across the continents were of vital benefit. The ability to exchange large sums of money over great distances and considerable lengths of time facilitated the purchase of the Company's goods, providing much-needed ready cash in Persia. Such instruments also required trust, evident from the case of Sultan David and the debts accrued by his family firm. The ability to borrow large sums of money also made it possible for the Company to finance large investments in goods for shipment back to Europe, most clearly demonstrated in the case of Kerman wool. This particular investment required the local, specialist knowledge of Persian merchants and brokers, who worked for the Company over long periods of their lives; Siavush worked for the Company for fifteen years before his death.

The Company made itself an attractive employer, garnering the goodwill of its workers through generous salaries and regular gifts, which were not only financially attractive but also demonstrated an understanding of local culture in the presentation of *khalats*. The Company also provided security for the relatives of their people, insisting on stipends for their widows and offering work to their sons on generous terms. In this way, the Company was consciously building a system of support in which they were accruing the loyalty and service of capable individuals in areas where they lacked the required skills.

Conclusion

The chapters of this book have explored the important relationship between the East India Company and Persia through a period of significant, often volatile, change. Far from being a 'glassy tideway',¹ the decades after 1700 in Persia are shown to have been a period of dynamic engagement between the Company and Persia's changing regimes. The climactic joint Persian and Company campaign at Hormuz in 1622 enabled the Company to displace their Portuguese rivals from this vital pivot of their Indian Ocean Empire. At Hormuz, the Company added its significant naval power to the Persian assault against the Portuguese fortifications and warships in and around this island city. Shah Abbas I, in recognition of this contribution, bestowed a *Farman* on the Company that proved to be the foundation stone of a long-lasting relationship. Over time, the Persians were to update the *Farman* through a combination of mutual or exchangeable, political, strategic and commercial interests. This *Farman* stayed in force for well over a century, surviving the accession of four Safavid Shahs through whom it was renewed twice, the Afghan invasion and occupation, Safavid restoration and the reign of Nader Shah. The *Farman*, far from being a literary fiction, was the core of the Persian state's relationship with the Company. Shah Abbas I must be credited with initiating the relationship as he recognised the new strategic, technological potential that European naval powers represented to restore and maintain the balance of Persian power in the Gulf and protect their trade interests.

Ogborn gives an accurate characterisation of the Company's use of the written word to create its own reality. Importantly, through this book, it can now be seen that the Company was not the only power capable of doing so.² This book contradicts Barendse's view that successive Persian rulers were either incapable of controlling their trade or alternatively completely disinterested, even in a time of upheaval like that experienced after 1722.³ The Company's role as a 'navy for hire' in the Persian Gulf and the central part they played in the formation of Nader Shah's navy in the Gulf is a continued demonstration of the intertwined interests that existed between the Company and the Persian state. This book is the first time this aspect of the Company's presence in the Gulf has been explored and represents a far more active and cooperative role for the Company. What began, under the rule of Shah Abbas I, with a campaign to eject the Portuguese from the Gulf developed over a century into a complex web of naval services, through the blockade of ports, capture of fugitives and attacks on rebels.

As we have seen, the Company did not limit its maritime assistance to Persia for solely military purposes. Indeed, the Company's ships were an integral part of Persian strategy to project diplomatic influence around the Indian Ocean. Occasionally reimbursed, the Company provided ships to carry embassies to the states of the Indian subcontinent and beyond. It is evident that the Company actively used the good favour of these services to gain and maintain their trading privileges, as enshrined in the *Farman*, when these were threatened. Although Floor, Axworthy and Lockhart write about the creation of Nader Shah's fleet they do not recognise the Company's key role. There can be no doubt that the Company continually sought and was sought out by the Persians for maritime capability. In this way, the Company filled a strategic niche and became a ubiquitous, useful presence in the Gulf. The Company's privileges in Persia gave it a number of advantages in its trade. The Company had hoped that silk would provide a valuable luxury export for the markets of Europe, but this never fully met expectations, so other goods and sources of income were found. The Company's exportation of Kerman wool to Europe, sometimes in huge quantities, helped make up for the vicissitudes of the Persian silk trade. The Company also prioritised the production of wine and rose water at their house in Shiraz, using these goods not only as tradable commodities but also as prestigious gifts both to European employees of the Company, in India, and foreign dignitaries.

In addition to Matthee's work on the place of wine in the Persianate world, we can now say that the Company both elevated production and increased demand through wider exportation of Shiraz wine. This was important revenue for both the Company and even more so for the Persians who had few exportable commodities, especially ones considered of premium quality. While it is true that Persia did not yield the same scale of trade as that of India, Persia did provide a steady market for English cloth. On top of these benefits were the cash income from port duties, consulage and trading passes. Another reason for the continued interest in Persia is that the Company's servants found a variety of lucrative private avenues of personal trade. The Company, who permitted private trade, unlike its Dutch rival, therefore took advantage of this situation, charging fees and consulage to private merchants in exchange for extending the Company's freedom of customs. Private merchants benefitted from paying a significantly lower customs rate than they would have at the Persian customs house, and the Company drew a steady cash income from these fees.

In this way, the Company used the terms of the *Farman* to gather revenue that was clearly against the spirit of the agreement; however, the Persians in turn failed to provide the Company with its full share of the customs of Bandar Abbas. The argument as put forward by Floor identifies the collection of customs and the Persians' default as a major issue, but while it may have been an irritation, it was hardly terminal. Company records show that the payment of its share of the Bandar Abbas customs was not the be all and end all of its financial interests. The Company gained an income from both the payments they received from the Persians for well over a century, as well as the lucrative taxation of private trade. It is useful to reflect how important liquidity was to the Company and how they could use ready money to magnify its value through trading. While the Company was using its position and favour in Persia to gather revenue which circumvented the Persians' own system of customs, it should not be imagined that the Persian state was not also benefitting from the Company's presence. On the contrary, the Persians continually used the terms of the *Farman* and the granting of fresh privileges to promote their own goods. The state monopoly of hing represents just one example of this tactic and the lengths Nader Shah went to press for its trade.

The Persians gained significantly from the Company's presence, whether this was through investment in the wine industry of Shiraz or the creation of new markets for Persian wool in Europe and for copper from Kerman's mines to India. Both sides benefitted symbiotically from the presence of the other, with the provisions of the *Farman* acting as a guideline to both sides. Both failed to live up to the full demands of the document, and although there are disputes and disagreements, the relationship is too important to be broken by either party. The Company's position and relationship with the Persian state necessitated a close relationship with other ethnic groups in the region. The Armenians, who had carved an important place for themselves in the Persian and intra-Eurasian trade in silk and other goods, were especially important to the Company. The Armenians provided access to capital, financial instruments and local expertise without which the Company would have continued to find it difficult to operate in Persia. While much work has been done exploring the connection between the Armenians and the Company,[4] the reciprocal benefits to the Armenians that the Company represented, especially legal protection through the *Farman*, have never been considered before. The 1688 agreement made between the Company and the Armenian community resulted in a concerted effort to forge strong ties with the Armenians, from Persia to India and on to London. The Company in Persia, the port in Bandar Abbas and the major trading hub they represented form the most vital communication link in the Armenians' web of commercial bases. The Company, by granting specific protections to Armenians in their employment, as well as allowing Armenian goods to benefit from the Company's freedom from taxation, was highly prized by the Armenian community.

As well as the Armenians, the Company also made significant efforts to provide its Banian employees with more than just a salary. The Company used the *Farman* to afford this community protection against taxation, the seizure of goods, property and physical violence. The Company gained significantly from the Banians' ability to move money between India and Persia, while the legal protection that the Company could afford the community, as well as extending the same benefits in trade as it did to the Armenians, made for a reciprocally beneficial relationship. In Persia, the rights and privileges which the Company could extend to its employees and their families made it an attractive employer and business partner. The Company's employment of local Persian merchants as brokers in the wool trade, as well as artisans and scribes to create official documents in the Persian style and register of language, meant that the Company was a significant employer in Bandar Abbas. Because of the large amounts the Company spent monthly on feeding and clothing its employees, the presence of the Company also boosted the local Persian economy.

The conspicuous consumption in which Company servants indulged was only a part of the wider life of the Company's factory. The factory was a home, workplace and market for a small number of English merchants, whose lives have been left unexplored by historians. Unlike in India, where the Company established its own fortresses, cities and ports, the Persian factory was a small community under the direct rule of a foreign power, very unlike the situation in India, Stern has so ably illuminated in his work.[5] The Company's *Farman* was all that stood between the Company's Factors and direct Persian rule. In many cases, disagreements arising in the factory were much less likely to be due to any issues with the Persians, with whom the factory's Agent or Chief Factor appears to have maintained cordial relations. Instead, disputes seem to have arisen from within the factory owing to the opacity and developmental nature of the Company's own rules when applied at a remove from the central authority of Bombay or London. The remoteness of the factory in the Gulf made communication with the higher levels of the Company's hierarchy in Bombay slow at best, but despite this, many cases and conflicts were referred to the higher echelons of the Company's leadership in Bombay.

The Company employees in their various Persian factories had considerable business and personal contact with local Persian people and officials. The merchants in the factory adapted to local customs, maintaining a garden, as well as a store of luxury goods, for the comfort of their Persian interlocutors. The Company invested heavily in the creation of gardens elsewhere to emulate the Persian style of polite social interactions and adopted habits such as the drinking of coffee and smoking of qalyan. Adoption of such social practices helped to provide Persian officials with a familiar setting through which they could negotiate with the Company and in turn the Company could gain favour by pampering its guests in a manner that was familiar to them. Life for the Company's employees, on the other hand, could be hard, painful and short due to the prevalence of disease and the harshness of the climate. However, despite these problems, the factories could keep their presence, while turning a profit for the Company. Chaudhuri has suggested that the Company's distant factories functioned merely as a mechanism.[6] This underplays the significant adaptation and improvisation through autonomous action required by the staff in the Company's factories. It is evident that both the Company mechanism and the ability of the servants were able to overcome major issues. A good example can be seen through the occasion when all the senior factory employees in Bandar Abbas died in less than a fortnight, but junior Company servants continue the work. Far from an engine turning over, the Company was far more flexible due to the ability of the individual employees to adapt closely to their own tasks and surroundings. John Keay's assertion that the period between 1710 and 1740 was calm and profitable clearly does not take account of the life and times of the Company in Persia. While the Company's business in India may have been stable, Persia was a hive of activity. The new research conducted for this book, revealed from the Company's own records, demonstrates how the factory at Bandar Abbas and the Company's staff there actively took part in and witnessed major events, especially those transpiring during the death throes of the Safavid Empire and its eventual dissolution. It is impressive how nimbly the Company servants adapted to culture, regime and ruler change, making themselves equally relevant both to the Afghan invaders who toppled the Safavids in 1722, then just as quickly forging bonds with the regime of Nader Shah.

Lastly, there remains the question of the dynamic of power between the Company and the Persians. This is impossible to quantify, nor was it a zero-sum game. In many ways, the Persians had every advantage over the Company, from the strength of a state with complex bureaucratic functions, desirable goods that the Company wanted and the ability to deploy overwhelming force. The Company, on the other hand, had only its ability to deploy naval power to offer; however, the Company's employees were able to effectively harness this to gain and maintain their privileges through the *Farman*. The power relationship was therefore based on mutually beneficial exchanges, as well as the strength of the attachment felt by both parties to the terms of the *Farman* itself. Both parties stood to gain from a long-term settlement, which is what was managed through the written letter of the document, as well as the tacit removal of problematic aspects, such as the ever-troublesome silk contracts. The wealth of new information researched and catalogued for this book concerning the Company in Persia reveals the way in which the Company adapted to situations beyond the Indian subcontinent, finding innovative ways of working with local powers to the betterment of the Company's trade. The Company was an instrumental link in the connections between the Persian Empire and the world of the Indian Ocean and beyond, while providing them with assistance and services that were not replicated anywhere else that the Company did business.

Notes

Author's Notes

1 Rudi Mattee, Willem Floor and Patrick Clawson, *The Monetary History of Iran* (London: I.B. Tauris, 2013), p. 3.
2 Edmund Herzig, 'The Volume of Raw Silk Exports in the Safavid Period', *Iranian Studies*, vol. 25 (1992): 61–79, 67.

Prologue

1 Even though he went by a variety of different names over the course of the period covered by this book, he will be referred to consistently by this regnal title for ease of reading. The only exception to this is where we discuss his rise to power and his subsequent adoption of different appellations.

Introduction: Historiographical Essay

1 Couto and Loureiro liken the mythologisation of Hormuz to similar myths about Sri Lanka, known as 'Taprobane', which had a similar air of mystery, wealth and cosmopolitanism.
2 Throughout this book, the English Company will be referred to as 'the Company'.
3 William Foster, *The English Factories in India* (London: Clarendon, 1908–26).
4 For a very recent and excellent overview of current trends in Company history, I recommend David Veevers, *The Origins of the British Empire in Asia* (Cambridge: Cambridge University Press, 2020).
5 Philip Stern, *The Company-State: Corporate Sovereignty and the Early Modern Foundations of the British Empire in India* (Oxford: Oxford University Press, 2011).
6 Holden Furber, 'Asia and the West as Partners before "Empire" and After', *Journal of Asian Studies*, vol. 2, no. 4 (August 1969): 711–21.
7 There is a great deal of literature on the Early Modern Persian silk trade, but for the Armenians' role in it see Edmund Herzig, *The Armenian Merchants of New Julfa, Isfahan: A Study in Pre-modern Asian Trade* (Oxford, 1991).
8 Sanjay Subrahmanyam, *The Political Economy of Commerce: Southern India 1500–1650* (Cambridge: Cambridge University Press, 1990), p. 297.

9   K. N. Chaudhuri, *The Trading World of Asia and the East India Company, 1660–1760* (Cambridge: Cambridge University Press, 1978), pp. 111–14.
10 Adam Clulow, *The Company and the Shogun: The Dutch Encounter with Tokugawa Japan* (New York: Columbia University Press, 2014); and Bhawan Ruangsilp, *Dutch East India Company Merchants in the Court of Ayutthaya* (Leiden: Brill, 2007), p. 221.
11 Ruangsilp, *Dutch East India Company Merchants*, p. 221.
12 Clulow, *The Company and the Shogun*, p. 259.
13 This difficulty is not limited only to archival sources. Availability and access to Persian language publications and scholarship are also extremely limited.
14 See Chaudhuri, *The Trading World*.
15 Rene Barendse, *The Arabian Seas: The Indian Ocean World in the Seventeenth Century* (London: Routledge, 2016).
16 Ibid., p. 1570.
17 Willem Floor, *The Persian Gulf: A Political and Economic History of Five Port Cities, 1500–1700* (Washington, DC: Mage, 2006), p. 601.
18 Willem Floor and Edmund Herzig, eds. *Iran and the World in the Safavid Age* (London: I.B. Tauris, 2012).
19 Michael Axworthy, *Sword of Persia* (London: I.B. Tauris, 2007); Willem Floor, *The Rise and Fall of Nader Shah: Dutch East India Company Reports, 1730–1747* (Washington, DC: Mage, 2009).
20 Axworthy, ed., *Crisis, Collapse, Militarism and Civil War: The History and Historiography of 18th Century Iran* (Oxford, 2018), p. 23.
21 Ibid., p. 31.
22 Alexander Hamilton, *A New Account of the East-Indies: Being the Observations and Remarks of Capt. Alexander Hamilton Who Resided in Those Parts from the Year 1688, to 1723, Trading and Travelling, by Sea and Land, to Most of the Countries and Islands of Commerce and Navigation, between the Cape of Good-Hope, and the Island of Japan. The Second Edition.* Volume I, 1739 and John Fryer, *A New Account of East-India and Persia in Eight Letters* (London, 1698) and Charles Lockyer, *An Account of the Trade in India* (London, 1711).
23 Jonas Hanway, *An Historical Account of the British Trade over the Caspian Sea: With a Journal of Travels through Russia and into Persia*, 4 vols (London, 1753) and Engelbert Kaempfer, *Am Hofe des Persischen Großkönigs 1684–85*, trans. Walter Hinz (Leipzig, 1940).
24 John O'Kane, *The Ship of Sulaiman* (London: Routledge), p. 27.
25 Sheikh Mohammed Ali Hazin, *The Life of Sheikh Mohammed Ali Hazin*, trans. F. C. Belfour (London, 1830), p. 215.
26 A slang term for Europeans, meaning Hat Wearers, amusingly adopted by the English in some of their correspondence with Persian-speaking polities, rendered as 'hat men'.

27 Iskander Beg Munshi Turkoman, *Tarikh 'Alam Ara-ye 'Abbasi*, 2 vols, paginated as one, ed. Iraj Afshar, Amir Kabir, 1350 AH/1971, p. 981, Also available in an English translation by Roger Savory.
28 Mirza Mohammed Khalil Mar'ashi Safavi, *Majma al-Tavarikh dar Tarikh-i Inqiraz-i Safaviyeh va vaqa'i-ye ba'd ta sal-eh 1207 h.q.*, ed. Abbas Eqbal (Tehran, 1328 H.S.) and Mahdi Khan Astarabadi, William Jones, trans. *The history of the life of Nader Shah: King of Persia. Extracted from an Eastern manuscript, with an introduction, containing, I. A description of Asia II. A short history of Persia and an appendix, consisting of an essay on Asiatick poetry, and the history of the Persian language. To which are added, pieces relative to the French translation* (London, 1773).
29 Mar'ashi Safavi, *Majma al-Tavarikh*, p. 40.
30 Whether the Gulf is Persian, Arabian or another combination of terms is a matter of considerable political debate in the region; for the purposes of this book it will be known as the Persian Gulf, in common with most scholarship, sometimes shortened to 'the Gulf'.
31 Lawrence G. Potter, *The Persian Gulf in History* (London: Palgrave Macmillan, 2009), p. 7.
32 Mohammad Bagher Vosoughi, 'The Kings of Hormuz', in *The Persian Gulf in History*, edited by Lawrence Potter (Palgrave Macmillan, 2009), p. 93.
33 Ibid.
34 Fernandes Couto and Miranda Loureiro, *Revisiting Hormuz: Persian Interactions in the Persian Gulf Region in the Early Modern Period* (Harrassowitz, 2008), p. 1.
35 Elio Brancaforte, 'The Italian Connection: Pietro Della Valle's Account of the Fall of Hormuz (1622)', in Couto and Loureiro, *Revisiting Hormuz* (Harrassowitz, 2008), p. 196.
36 Ibid.
37 IOR/G/29/1 ff.18–18v, letter from John Purifie at Jask to the Factory at Isfahan, 14 December 1621.
38 IOR/G/29/1 f. 18v, letter from John Weddell to the Factory at Isfahan, 14 December 1621.
39 David Blow, *Shah Abbas: The Ruthless King Who Became an Iranian Legend* (London: I.B. Tauris, 2009), p. 69 and Brancaforte, *Della Valle*, p. 196.
40 Floor, *Five Port Cities*, p. 229 and Niels Steensgaard, *Carracks, Caravans and Companies: The Structural Crisis in the European-Asian Trade in the Early 17th Century* (Studentlitteratur Lund, 1973), p. 341.
41 Foster, William. *The English Factories in India, 1618–1621(–1669): A Calendar of documents in the India Office,* British Museum and Public Record Office (Clarendon, 1906–27), p. ix.
42 Ibid.

43 IOR/G/29/1 ff.23v–25 Letter from the Commanders of the Fleet at Hormuz to Isfahan, 6 April 1622.
44 The letters are stored in the India Office Records, IOR/G/29/1.
45 IOR/G/29/1 ff.23v–25 Letter from the Commanders of the Fleet at Hormuz to Isfahan, 6 April 1622.
46 IOR/G/29/1 ff.36v–37v Letter to Richard Blythe and John Weddell at Bandar Abbas from Edward Monnox on 27 April 1622.
47 Ibid.
48 Ibid.
49 IOR/G/29/1 ff. 26–28, Letter from Edward Monnox at Hormuz to Isfahan, 8 April 1622.
50 William Foster, *The English Factories in India 1622–23* (London: Clarendon, 1908), p. xi.
51 Ibid.
52 K. N. Chaudhuri, *The East India Company* (London: Routledge, 1999), p. 64.
53 Foster, *1618–21*, pp. xiii and 223.
54 Ibid., p. xiii.
55 Ibid.
56 Ibid.
57 Ibid.
58 Foster, *1622–23*, p. xii.
59 Halil Inalcik, ed. *An Economic and Social History of the Ottoman Empire* (Cambridge: Cambridge University Press, 1994), p. 194 and Michael Talbot, *British-Ottoman Relations, 1661–1807* (Woodbridge: Boydell, 2017).
60 Ibid.
61 Foster, *1618–21*, p. xiii.
62 Ibid., p. xix.
63 For a more complete exploration of the *Farman* and its various terms, see Peter Good, 'The East India Company's Farmān, 1622-1747', *Iranian Studies*, vol. 52, nos 1–2 (2019): 181–97.
64 IOR/G/29/1 ff.234–9 Terms of the Company's Treaty with Shah Abbas I.
65 Ibid.
66 R.W. Ferrier, 'The Terms and Conditions under which English Trade was Transacted with Safavid Persia', *Bulletin of the School of Oriental and African Studies*, vol. 49, no. 1 (1986): 48–66.
67 Ibid., p. 50.
68 Ibid., p. 53.
69 Ibid.
70 Cambridge History of Iran, volume 6, 1986, p. 297.
71 IOR/G/29/4 f.5 Summary of Business, March 1727.

72 IOR/G/29/1 ff.189v–193v Stipulations of the *Farman* of Abbas I-Granted Shavval 1036, 42nd Year of the reign of Abbas I (1627).
73 Ibid.
74 Ibid.
75 IOR/H/628 f.31 Privileges from the Company's *Farman*.
76 IOR/H/628 ff.19–33v Collection of the Company's Farmāns in Persia, *Farmān* from Shah Soltan Husayn to the East India Company.
77 Two forms of taxation.
78 Urban officials.
79 The poll tax on non-Muslims.
80 Ibid.
81 IOR/G/29/5 f.350–351 List of Rogums granted to the Company in Consultation on 12 August 1736.
82 R. W. Ferrier, *British-Persian Relations in the 17th Century*, Unpublished Dissertation, University of Cambridge, 1970, pp. 81–2.
83 IOR/G/29/5 f.350–351 List of Rogums granted to the Company in Consultation on 12 August 1736.
84 The Company's *Farman* was a collection of *Irqam*, s. *Raqam*. The latter term, though taxonomic with *Farman*, was used in the Company's records to denote the individual *Capitula* or 'chapter' within the document. The Company's merchants used both 'phirmaund' and 'rogums' interchangeably when talking about their privileges.
85 Miles Ogborn, *Indian Ink: Script and Print in the Making of the English East India Company* (Chicago: University of Chicago Press, 2007), p. 36.
86 For regional diplomacy in the Mughal Empire, see 'Diplomacy in a Provincial Setting: The East India Companies in Seventeenth-Century Bengal and Orissa', in Adam Clulow and Tristan Mostert (eds), *The Dutch and English East India Companies: Diplomacy, Trade and Violence in Early Modern Asia* (Amsterdam: Amsterdam University Press, 2018), 55–78.

1 Life in the Company's Persian factory

1 Abd al-Amir Muḥammad Amin, *British Interests in the Persian Gulf* (Leiden: Brill, 1967), p. 41.
2 Stern, *The Company-State*, p. 19.
3 John Keay, *The Honourable Company* (London: HarperCollins, 1993), p. 251.
4 The Company's records refer to the town, now known as Bandar Abbas in English by a variety of names, *Bunder Abbasee, Gamron, Gombroon*. For ease and clarity, the current spelling has been used.

5 Floor, *Five Port Cities*, p. 1.
6 Cornelius Le Bruyn, *Travels into Muscovy, Persia and Part of the East Indies* (London, 1737), vol. 2, p. 73.
7 Ibid.
8 Le Bruyn, *Travels*, p. 74.
9 Ibid.
10 IOR/G/29/7 f.59 Consultation on Tuesday 29 May 1747.
11 Tim Blanning, *The Pursuit of Glory: Europe 1648–1815* (Penguin, 2008), p. 57.
12 Keay, *The Honourable Company*, p. 135.
13 IOR/G/29/2 f.21 Consultation on 10 July 1710.
14 Stern, *The Company-State*, p. 101.
15 IOR/G/29/15 f.139 Letter to the Court of Directors from Isaac Housaye on 23 July 1723.
16 IOR/G/29/15 f.150v Letter to the Court of Directors from Owen Phillips, John Horne and William Cockell on 4 December 1723.
17 IOR/G/29/15 f.157 Letter to the Court of Directors from Isaac Housaye on 2 January 1724, for a fuller account of these events, see Laurence Lockhart, *The Fall of the Safavi Dynasty* (Cambridge, 1958), p. 416 and for a perspective from the Dutch records see Willem Floor, *The Afghan Occupation of Safavid Persia 1721–1729*: v.19 (Cahiers de Studia Iranica, 1998), pp. 214–18.
18 IOR/G/29/15 f.163 Letter to the Court of Directors from Henry Fowler and Martin French 24 June 1724.
19 IOR/G/29/5 f.82v Consultation on Friday 29 August 1729.
20 *World Health Organization, Guidelines for Drinking-Water Quality Third Edition Volume I* (WHO, 2006), p. 276.
21 Roger Savory, *Iran under the Safavids* (Cambridge, 1980), pp. 155–6.
22 IOR/G/29/17 f.30 Letter to the Court of Directors, 7 June 1745.
23 IOR/G/29/5 f.330v Consultation on Thursday 25 March 1736.
24 IOR/G/29/5 f.180v Consultation on Tuesday 10 June 1732.
25 IOR/G/29/5 f.331 Consultation on Wednesday 31 March 1736 and IOR/G/29/5 f.345 Consultation on Wednesday 28 July 1736.
26 IOR/G/29/5 ff.358v–9 Consultation on Saturday 20 November 1736.
27 IOR/G/29/5 f.366 Consultation on Wednesday 9 January 1737.
28 Philip Lawson, *The East India Company: A History* (London: Routledge, 1993), p. 72. The Factor was the lowest rank of 'covenanted' servant, who had entered into a contractual relationship with the Company to serve, while providing a security and references in support of that contract.
29 Ogborn, *Indian Ink*, p. 72.
30 IOR/G/29/5 f.206v Consultation on Wednesday 13 June 1733.
31 IOR/G/29/5 f.261 Consultation on Saturday 28 December 1734.

32 IOR/G/29/5 f.261v Consultation on Saturday 28 December 1734.
33 Ibid.
34 Ibid.
35 Rudi Matthee, *Christians in Safavid Iran*, Studies on Persianate Societies (vol. 3 2005/1384), p. 20.
36 Hamilton, *A New Account*, p. 222.
37 IOR/G/29/17 ff.18–v Letter to the Court of Directors 20 February 1745.
38 Ibid.
39 Amin, *British Interests*, p. 45.
40 William Dalrymple, *White Mughals* (London: Viking, 2003), p. 134.
41 Ibid.
42 IOR/G/29/5 ff.230v–1v Consultation on Monday 1 March 1734.
43 IOR/G/29/5 f.216v Consultation on Monday 20 August 1733.
44 IOR/G/29/5 f.217 Consultation on Saturday 25 August 1733.
45 IOR/P/341 f.396 Letters in a packet from Bandar Abbas received at Bombay on 13 June 1733.
46 IOR/G/29/15 ff.69v–70 Letter from Isaac Housaye and Edmund Wright to the Court of Directors on 20 January 1723.
47 Stern, *The Company-State*, p. 102.
48 IOR/G/29/15 ff.69v–70 Letter from Isaac Housaye and Edmund Wright to the Court of Directors on 20 January 1723.
49 Keay, *The Honourable Company*, p. 42.
50 Ferrier, *British-Persian Relations*, p. 264.
51 For more on Iran's wine culture: Rudi Matthee, *The Pursuit of Pleasure: Drugs and Stimulants in Iranian History, 1500–1900* (Princeton, NJ: Princeton University Press, 2005).
52 IOR/G/29/4 f.72 Consultation on 5 July 1727.
53 IOR/G/29/5 f.41 Consultation on Tuesday 11 February 1729.
54 David Hancock, '"An Undiscovered Ocean of Commerce Laid Open": India, Wine, and the Emerging Atlantic Economy, 1703–1813', in *The Worlds of the East India Company*, ed. Bowen, Lincoln and Rigby (Boydell, 2003), p. 159.
55 IOR/G/29/5 f.59 Consultation on Saturday 3 May 1729.
56 IOR/G/29/5 f.84 Consultation on Saturday 13 September 1729.
57 IOR/G/29/3 Consultation on Monday 26 December 1726.
58 IOR/G/29/6 f.116v and f.121 Consultation on Wednesday 15 October and Monday 10 November 1740.
59 IOR/G/29/5 f.261 Consultation on Saturday 28 December 1734.
60 IOR/G/29/4 f.77v Consultation on Wednesday 12 July 1727.
61 Ibid.

62 Stern, *The Company-State*, p. 68. Richard Keigwin, a settler in Bombay, was named governor after the garrison of the city revolted against the Company's council after having their wages cut.
63 IOR/G/29/5 f.6v Consultation on Monday 25 November 1728.
64 Ibid.
65 IOR/G/29/5 f.145v Consultation on Thursday 20 January 1732.
66 IOR/G/29/5 f.349v Consultation on Monday 9 August 1736.
67 IOR/G/29/5 f.88 Consultation on Saturday 25 October 1729.
68 Ferrier, *British-Persian Relations*, p. 263.
69 Tupas, Topas, a Eurasian of Portuguese ancestry.
70 IOR/G/29/7 f.132v Consultation on Sunday 17 January 1748.
71 Stern, *The Company-State*, p. 86.

2 Governance, information management, reporting, communication and control

1 Hamilton, *A New Account*, p. 94.
2 The location of the garden will be referred to by this English derivation of the place name.
3 IOR/G/29/4 f.10 Consultation on Saturday 1 April 1727.
4 IOR/G/29/7 f.287 Consultation on 30 November 1750 Consultation on Friday 30 November 1750.
5 IO/G/29/4 f.47v Consultation on Thursday 15 June 1727.
6 Stern, *The Company-State*, p. 31.
7 IOR/P/341/2 f.106 Letter to the Committee of Victualing at Bombay 19 January 1705 and f.211 Consultation at Bombay Castle on 5 June 1705.
8 IOR/G/29/6 f.108 Consultation on Saturday 16 August 1740.
9 IOR/G/29/5 f.227 Consultation on Friday 1 March 1734.
10 Hamilton, *A New Account*, p. 94.
11 IOR/G/29/17 f.30 Letter to the Court of Directors, 7 June 1745.
12 IOR/P/341/2 f.106 Letter to the Committee of Victualing at Bombay 19 January 1705 and f.211 Consultation at Bombay Castle on 5 June 1705.
13 IOR/G/29/5 f.134 Consultation on Monday 17 October 1731.
14 IOR/G/29/5 f.218v Consultation on Wednesday 10 October 1733.
15 IOR/G/29/6 f.28 Consultation on Thursday 27 April 1738.
16 IOR/G/29/6 f.63 Consultation on Tuesday 30 October 1739.
17 This is the Persian word for the water pipe, called hookah in India and shisha or nargileh in Arabic.
18 Rudi Matthee, 'Smoking in Iran', in *Smoke: A History of Smoking*, ed. Gilman and Xun (New York: Reaktion, 2004).

19 IOR/G/17/1 f.5 Indents for Ships *Blenheim and Donnegall* landed at Mocha, August 1710.
20 IOR/G/29/3 f.12 Accounts and stocks for 1726.
21 Matthee, 'Smoking', p. 60.
22 IOR/G/29/6 f.4 Consultation on Tuesday 9 August 1737.
23 See Matthee, *Pursuit*, especially concerning the development of tobacco smoking.
24 Niels Steensgaard, *The Asian Trade Revolution* (Chicago, 1974), p. 66.
25 IOR/G/29/6 f.63 Consultation on Tuesday 30 October 1739.
26 IOR/G/29/5 f.235v Consultation on Thursday 9 May 1734.
27 IOR/G/29/6 f.210v Consultation on Thursday 20 May 1742.
28 IOR/G/29/16 f.242v Letter to the Court of Directors from the Council at Gombroon 8 June 1742.
29 IOR/G/29/15 ff.29–30v, Promise of payment to the Company on a loan to Ceasar Devaux, 15 March 1722.
30 For a more thorough exploration of the Rahdar system, see John Emerson, 'Rahdars and Their Tolls in the Safavid and Afsharid Periods', *Journal of the Economic and Social History of the Orient*, vol. 30, no. 3 (1987): 318–27.
31 IOR/G/29/17 f.66v Letter to the Court of Directors from the Council at Gombroon from 10 February 1749.
32 IOR/G/29/6 f.254 and IOR/G/29/7 f.141 Consultation on Wednesday 2 March 1748.
33 IOR/G/29/17 f.66v Letter to the Court of Directors from the Council at Gombroon from 10 February 1749.
34 IOR/G/29/16 f.192v Letter to the Court of Directors from the Council at Gombroon from 15 December 1737.
35 IOR/G/29/4 f.72 Consultation on Wednesday 5 July 1727.
36 IOR/G/29/7 f.18v Consultation on Friday 24 October 1746.
37 IOR/G/29/4 f.52 Consultation on Saturday 24 June 1727.
38 Rudi Matthee, *Persia in Crisis* (London: I.B. Tauris, 2012), p. 153 and Emerson, 'Rahdars and Their Tolls', p. 319.
39 http://www.iranicaonline.org/articles/capar-or-capar-turk and http://dsalsrv02.uchicago.edu/cgi-bin/philologic/contextualize.pl?p.0.hobson.1444099. Accessed 1 January 2018.
40 IOR/G/29/5 f.61v Consultation on Thursday 15 May 1729.
41 IOR/G/29/7 f.18v Consultation on Friday 24 October 1746.
42 IOR/G/29/5 f.293 Consultation on Monday 4 August 1735.
43 IOR/G/29/7 f.18v Consultation on Friday 24 October 1746.
44 IOR/G/29/5 f.105 Consultation on Saturday 7 March 1730.
45 IOR/G/29/7 f.186 Consultation on Friday 28 October 1748.
46 http://www.iranicaonline.org/articles/capar-or-capar-turk. Accessed 13 November 2015.

47 See Willem Floor, 'The Chapar-Khana System in Qajar Iran', *Iran*, vol. 39 (2001): 27–291, 257.
48 Ibid.
49 IOR/G/29/5 f.42v Consultation on Wednesday 19 February 1729 and f.5 Consultation on Saturday 23 November 1728.
50 IOR/G/29/6 f.123–v Consultation on Wednesday 4 November 1740.
51 IOR/G/29/15 f.88 Letter to William Phillips from Edmund Wright from 3 November 1722.
52 IOR/G/29/15 f.192 Letter to the Court of Directors from Isaac Housaye from 12 December 1724.
53 IOR/G/29/7 f.176v Consultation on Saturday 20 August 1748.
54 Blanning, *Pursuit of Glory*, p. 6.
55 IOR/G/29/7 f.217 Consultation on Thursday 13 April 1749.
56 IOR/G/29/7 f.250v Consultation on Monday 31 July 1750.
57 Ogborn, *Indian Ink*, pp. 80–3.
58 IOR/G/29/4 ff.53–61 Consultations on Wednesday 28 June–Saturday 1 July 1727.
59 Ibid.
60 Ibid.
61 IOR/G/29/4 ff.67v–8 Consultation on Tuesday 4 July 1727.
62 IOR/G/29/4 f.62v Consultation on Sunday 2 July 1727.
63 IOR/G/29/4 ff.67v–8 Consultation on Tuesday 4 July 1727.
64 Blanning, *Pursuit of Glory*, p. 22.
65 Stern, *The Company-State*, p. 11.
66 IOR/G/29/15 f.262 Letter to the Court of Directors from Henry Draper, William Cordeux and John Fotheringham from 25 March 1727 and f.265 Letter to the Court of Directors from Henry Draper from 25 March 1727.
67 IOR/G/29/15 ff.7–10v Letter from Anthony Beavis to the Secret Committee, 25 January 1719 and Letter from John Lock to the Court of Directors January 25 January 1719.
68 Santhi Hejeebu, 'Contract Enforcement in the English East India Company', *Journal of Economic History*, vol. 65, no. 2 (June 2005): 499–500.
69 IOR/G/29/6 f.143v Monday 20 April 1741.
70 IOR/G/29/5 f.361v Consultation on Wednesday 15 December 1736.
71 IOR/G/29/5 f.381 Consultation on Saturday 25 June 1737.
72 IOR/G/29/5 f.335 Consultation on Monday 3 May 1736.
73 IOR/G/29/5 f.257v Consultation on Monday 2 December 1734.
74 Ibid.
75 IOR/G/29/5 ff.314–314v Consultation on Friday 26 December 1735.
76 IOR/G/29/5 f.315v Consultation on Friday 9 January 1736.
77 IOR/G/29/5 f.230 Consultation on Monday 8 April 1734.

78 IOR/G/29/5 f.239v Consultation on Monday 20 May 1734.
79 Ibid.
80 IOR/G/29/5 f.232v Consultation on Wednesday 10 April 1734.
81 Robert Bickers, *The Scramble for China* (London: Penguin, 2011), p. 62.
82 IOR/G/29/5 f.228 Consultation on Tuesday 14 March 1734.
83 IOR/G/29/16 ff.150v–1 Letter to the Court of Directors from Gombroon 15 August 1733.
84 IOR/G/29/5 f.231 Consultation on Monday 1 March 1734.
85 Op. cit. ff.172v–3 Consultation on Friday 11 August 1732.
86 Ibid.
87 IOR/G/29/15 f.250v Letter from William May to the Court of Directors on 25 March 1727.
88 Ibid.
89 Ibid.
90 Ibid.
91 Ogborn, *Indian Ink*, p. 72.
92 IOR/P/341/2 ff.174–5 Consultation at Bombay Castle 24 April 1705.
93 Ibid.
94 Ibid.
95 Ferrier, *British-Persian Relations*, p. 333.
96 Clulow, *The Company and the Shogun*, p. 34.
97 Rudi Matthee, 'Between Aloofness and Fascination: Safavid Views of the West'. *Iranian Studies*, vol. 31, no. 2 (Spring 1998): 219–46, 233.
98 Ibid.
99 IOR/H/628 f.28 The Terms of the Company's *Farman*.
100 Keay, *The Honourable Company*, p. 226.
101 IOR/G/29/5 f.236 Consultation on Monday 13 May 1734.
102 IOR/G/29/7 f.88v Consultation on Saturday 14 March 1747.
103 IOR/G/29/6 f.97 Consultation on Tuesday 4 May 1740.
104 IOR/G/29/6 f.5 Consultation on Tuesday 23 August 1737, for more on Ottoman-Safavid gift exchange, see Rudi Matthee, *Gifts and Gift-Giving in Safavid Persia* (Encyclopaedia Iranica).
105 Clulow, *The Company and the Shogun*, p. 110.
106 Hejeebu, 'Contract Enforcement', pp. 499–501.

3 Trade's increase: The Company's commerce in Persia

1 See Steensgaard, *The Asian Trade Revolution*.
2 See Rudi Matthee, *The Politics of Trade in Safavid Iran* (Cambridge: Cambridge University Press, 1999).

3 Ibid., p. 7.
4 Stephen Dale, *Indian Merchants and Eurasian Trade, 1600–1750* (Cambridge, 1994).
5 Sanjay Subrahmanyam, ed. *Merchant Networks in the Early Modern World* (Variorum, 1996), p. xvii.
6 Keay, *The Honourable Company*, p. 104.
7 IOR/G/29/1 ff.232–233v Samples of silk. IOR/G/29/1 ff. 19v–20v, Copy of letter from Mr. Monox [Edward Monnox], Ormuz [Hormuz] received in Spahan [Isfahan], 12 March 1621–5 May 1621.
8 IOR/G/29/6 ff.219v–220 Consultation on Thursday 1 July 1742.
9 For a fuller story of the Russia trade from the perspective of those who undertook it, see John Stilman, *A Journey through Russia to Persia* (London, 1742) and Matthew Romanello, *Enterprising Empires. Russia and Britain in Eighteenth-Century Eurasia* (Cambridge, 2019).
10 Ibid.
11 IOR/G/29/6 f.338v–9 Letter from Danvers Graves at Serjune (Likely Sirjan) to the Agent and Council at Bandar Abbas 1 July 1746.
12 Ibid.
13 Rudi Matthee, 'Christians in Safavid Iran: Hospitality and Harassment', *Studies on Persianate Societies*, vol. 3 (2005/1384 AH): 3–43, 48.
14 IOR/P/341/2 f.51 Consultation at Bombay Castle on 21 December 1704.
15 IOR/P/341/2 f.194 Consultation at Bombay Castle on 19 May 1705.
16 Matthee, *Politics of Trade*, p. 74.
17 IOR/G/29/5 ff.350–51 List of Rogums in Consultation on the 12 August 1736.
18 IOR/G/29/6 f.203v Consultation on Tuesday 13 April 1742.
19 For the trade in silk through Russia in the seventeenth century, see Herzig, *Armenian Merchants*, pp. 141–3 and Stefan Troebst, 'Sweden, Russia and the Safavid Empire', in *Iran and the World in the Safavid Age* (London: I.B. Tauris, 2012), pp. 253–9.
20 Letter to a Member of Parliament relating to The Bill for the Opening of Trade with Persia through Russia 1741, RSS Tracts 5 vol. 17, p. 6.
21 Ibid.
22 Ibid.
23 Letter to Parliament, 1741, p. 14.
24 Ibid., p. 17.
25 IOR/G/29/6 f.152 Consultation on Monday 20 April 1741.
26 Ibid.
27 IOR/G/29/6 f.178v Consultation on Wednesday 18 November 1741.
28 Ibid.
29 IOR/G/29/6 f.190v Consultation on Saturday 6 January 1742.
30 IOR/G/29/6 ff.192v–3 Consultation on Monday 15 February 1742.

31 IOR/G/29/6 f.208 Consultation on Friday 7 May 1742.
32 IOR/G/29/6 f.208 Consultation on Friday 7 May 1742 and IOR/G/29/7 f.31v Consultation on Thursday 11 December 1746.
33 Ibid.
34 Ibid and Ferrier, *Terms and Conditions*, p. 385, for a thorough examination of the production and trade in wool from Persia, see Willem Floor, *The Persian Textile Industry in Historical Perspective 1500–1925* (Paris, 1999), pp. 335–79.
35 IOR/G/29/3 f.4v Consultation on Friday 25 November 1726 and IOR/G/29/5 f.74 Letter to William Cordeux from the Council at Bandar Abbas 16 June 1729.
36 Matthee, *Kerman Wool*, p. 343.
37 Ibid.
38 Matthee, *Kerman Wool*, p. 347.
39 IOR/G/29/5 f.73v Letter to William Cordeux from the Council at Bandar Abbas 16 June 1729, IOR/G/29/5 f.358v Consultation on Saturday 20 November 1736 and IOR/G/29/6 f.24v–25 Consultation on Tuesday 21 March 1738.
40 IOR/G/29/5 f.200v Consultation on Thursday 15 March 1733.
41 IOR/G/29/5 f.74–74v Letter to William Cordeux from the Council at Bandar Abbas 16 June 1729.
42 IOR/G/29/4 f.48v Consultation on Friday 16 June 1727, IOR/G/29/5 f.41 Consultation on Friday 11 February 1729, IOR/G/29/5 f.38v Consultation on Monday 3 February 1729. For a fuller exploration of the phenomenon of Persian gift-giving, see Assef Ashraf, 'The Politics of Gift Exchange in Early Qajar Iran, 1785–1834', *Comparative Studies in Society and History*, vol. 58, no. 2 (2016): pp. 550–76 and Rudi Matthee's entry GIFT GIVING iv. In The Safavid Period – Encyclopaedia Iranica (iranicaonline.org).
43 IOR/G/29/6 f.22 Consultation on Friday 17 February 1738.
44 Ibid.
45 IOR/G/29/4 f.73v Consultation on Sunday 9 July 1727 and IOR/G/29/6 f.22 Consultation on Friday 17 February 1738.
46 IOR/G/29/5 f.367v Consultation on 19 February 1737.
47 IOR/G/29/5 f.89 Consultation on Thursday 27 November 1729.
48 Matthee, *Kerman Wool*, p. 364.
49 IOR/G/29/5 ff.145–v Consultation on Friday 28 January 1732.
50 IOR/G/29/5 f.147v Consultation on Tuesday 8 February 1732.
51 IOR/G/29/5 f.193v Consultation on Friday 19 January 1733.
52 IOR/G/29/5 f.358v Consultation on Saturday 20 November 1736.
53 IOR/G/29/5 f.78v–9 Consultation on Saturday 26 July 1729. The natural colours of Kerman wool vary between shades of white, black and a russet brown or red.
54 IOR/G/29/5 f.358v Consultation on Saturday 20 November 1736.
55 IOR/G/29/7 f.44v Consultation on Wednesday 17 December 1746.

56 IOR/G/29/5 f.194 Consultation on Friday 19 January 1733.
57 IOR/G/29/15 f.69.
58 Matthee, *Persia in Crisis*, p. 106.
59 IOR/G/29/16 f.161 Letter to the Court of Directors from Gombroon 27 May 1735 and IOR/G/29/16 f.156 Letter to the Court of Directors from Gombroon 10 February 1735.
60 IOR/G/29/16 f.119v Letter to the Court of Directors from Gombroon 20 August 1732.
61 IOR/G/29/16 f.156 Letter to the Court of Directors from Gombroon 10 February 1735.
62 IOR/G/29/17 f.15v Letter from Danvers Graves at Isfahan on 31 October 1749.
63 Matthee, *Kerman Wool*, p. 382.
64 Floor, *The Rise and Fall of Nader Shah*, p. 239.
65 IOR/G/29/15 f.174v Letter to the Court of Directors from Edmund Edlyne and Martin French on 25 September 1724.
66 Lockyer, *An Account of the Trade in India*, p. 247.
67 Ibid.
68 Ibid.
69 Wines made from grapes gathered later than the general harvest, characterised by a sweeter flavour.
70 IOR/G/29/5 f.285v Consultation on Thursday 10 July 1735 and IOR/G/29/7 f.153v Consultation on Monday 2 May 1748.
71 Alexander, *A New Account*, p. 98.
72 Sir John Chardin, *Travels in Persia, 1673–1677* (Dover, 1988), p. 243.
73 Ibid., p. 242.
74 IOR/G/29/17 f.30.
75 IOR/G/29/6 f.155 Consultation on Saturday 2 May 1741 and IOR/G/29/7 f.11v Consultation on Wednesday 24 September 1746. For advance on production see IOR/G/29/15 f.8.
76 IOR/G/29/15 f.240.
77 Matthee, *The Pursuit of Pleasure*, p. 48.
78 Hamilton, *Account of Trade*, p. 98.
79 Matthee, *The Pursuit of Pleasure*, p. 48.
80 IOR/G/29/5 f.94v Consultation on Sunday 21 December 1729.
81 IOR/P/341/4 Consultation on 22 April 1711 and IOR/P/341/4 Consultation on the 8 December 1711.
82 IOR/G/29/5 f.307v Consultation on Saturday 15 November 1735. Arak or arrack was produced by the Company in India and shipped to Persia and elsewhere to supply the factories.
83 IOR/G/29/5 f.59 Consultation on Saturday 3 May 1729.

84 IOR/P/341/2 f.51 Consultation at Bombay Castle on 21 December 1704.
85 Ruangsilp, *Court of Ayutthaya*, p. 130.
86 IOR/P/341/2 f.36 Letter to Surat from Bombay 4 October 1704.
87 See John Hancock, *An Undiscovered Ocean*.
88 James Mills and Patricia Barton ed., *Drugs and Empire: Essays in Modern Imperialism and Intoxication, c.1500-c.1930* (London: Palgrave, 2007), p. 1.
89 Matthee, 'Christians in Safavid Iran', p. 48.
90 Hancock, *An Undiscovered Ocean*, p. 156.
91 Ibid.
92 Herzig, *Armenian Merchants*, p. 144.
93 Keay, *The Honourable Company*, p. 173.
94 Ferrier, *British-Persian Relations*, p. 370.
95 Ibid.
96 Ibid.
97 Ibid.
98 IOR/G/29/5 f.183 Consultation on Monday 13 November 1732.
99 Ferrier, *British-Persian Relations*, p. 371.
100 IOR/G/29/16 f.241 Letter to the Court of Directors from Gombroon 8 June 1742.
101 IOR/P/341/7b f.358 Letter received from Gombroon at Bombay on Saturday 19 October 1734.
102 Floor, *Five Port Cities*, p. 315.
103 Ibid.
104 Floor, *Five Port Cities*, pp. 312–15.
105 Ibid.
106 Ibid.
107 IOR/G/29/16 f.218v Letter to the Court of Directors from Gombroon 3 June 1740.
108 Asafoetida is a gum or resin extracted from the roots of the *Ferula* genus or plants; the name means 'foetid smell', but it is a common addition to South Asian cuisine.
109 IOR/G/29/7 f.43 Consultation on Wednesday 18 February 1747.
110 IOR/G/29/16 f.27 List of the Company's Rogums made in March 1730.
111 IOR/G/29/5 f.304v Consultation on Monday 20 October 1735.
112 Floor, The and Fall of Nader Shah, Dutch East India Company Reports, 1730–47 (Mage, 2009), p. 236.
113 Ibid.
114 Matthee, *Politics of Trade*, p. 68.
115 IOR/G/29/6 f.249 Consultation on Monday 23 May 1743.
116 Rudi Matthee, 'The Career of Mohammed Beg, Grand Vizier of Shah Abbas II', *Iranian Studies*, vol. 24, no. 1 (1991): 17–36, 27.
117 Floor, *Five Port Cities*, p. 315.

4 A navy for hire: The continuing maritime operations of the East India Company in the Persian Gulf 1727–43

1. An abridged version of this chapter was published as 'The East India Company and the foundation of Persian Naval Power in the Gulf under Nader Shah, 1734-47', in the volume The Dutch and English East India Companies, edited by Adam Clulow and Tristan Mostert in 2019. I am very grateful to Amsterdam University Press for their permission to reuse this material.
2. Laurence Lockhart, 'The Navy of Nadir Shah', in *The Proceedings of the Iran Society* (London, 1936).
3. Willem Floor, 'The Iranian Navy in the Gulf during the 18th Century', *Iranian Studies*, vol. 20, no. 1 (1987): 31–53.
4. Michael Axworthy, 'Nader Shah and Persian Naval Expansion in the Persian Gulf, 1700-1747', *Journal of the Royal Asiatic Society*, vol. 21 (2011): 31–9.
5. Michael Axworthy, *The Sword of Persia* (Penguin, 2006), p. 124.
6. Lockhart, 'Navy of Nadir Shah', p. 5.
7. Ibid.
8. IOR/G/29/4 ff.17–17v Consultation on Wednesday 26 April 1727.
9. IOR/G/29/5 f.97 Consultation on Friday 2 January 1730.
10. IOR/G/29/5 f.106v Consultation on Tuesday 19 March 1730.
11. IOR/G/29/5 ff.106-v Consultation on Thursday 19 March 1730.
12. IOR/G/29/5 f. 185 Consultation on Thursday 7 December 1732.
13. IOR/G/29/5 f.225 Consultation on Sunday 3 February 1734.
14. IOR/G/29/5 f.233 Consultation on Wednesday 10 April 1734 and Floor, 'The Iranian Navy', p. 39. For a Dutch perspective, see Willem Floor, 'The Revolt of Shaikh Ahmad Madani in Laristan and the Garmsirat (1730-1733)', *Studia Iranica*, vol. 12 (1983): 63–93.
15. IOR/G/29/5 f.235v Consultation on Thursday 9 May 1734, Lockhart, 1934, p. 7.
16. For a list of the Directors of the VOC's operations in Persia, see Floor, *The Rise and Fall*, pp. xiii–xiv.
17. IOR/G/29/5 ff.235-v Consultation on Wednesday 8 May 1734.
18. IOR/G/29/5 ff.236v-7 Consultation on Tuesday 14 May 1734.
19. Ibid.
20. IOR/G/29/5 f.238 Consultation on Friday 17 May 1734.
21. Ibid.
22. Ibid.
23. Axworthy, *Sword of Persia*, p. 107.
24. IOR/G/29/5 f.335 Consultation on Monday 3 May 1736.
25. Ibid.
26. Ibid.

27 Floor, 'The Iranian Navy', p. 33.
28 Ibid., p. 32.
29 Lockhart, 'Navy of Nadir Shah', p. 10. The 'Arab Shore' is a somewhat loose term for the south coast of the Gulf, which encompassed much of what is now the UAE, Oman, Bahrain, Qatar and Saudi Arabia.
30 IOR/G/29/6 f.17 Consultation on Saturday 31 December 1737.
31 IOR/G/29/5 f.377 Consultation on Tuesday 3 April 1737 and Wednesday 4 April 1737.
32 IOR/G/29/6 f.14v Consultation on Tuesday 20 December 1737.
33 Ibid.
34 IOR/G/29/6 f.16 Consultation on Tuesday 27 December 1737.
35 IOR/G/29/6 ff.37v–38 Consultation on Tuesday 13 June 1738.
36 IOR/G/29/6 ff.39v–40 Consultation on Wednesday 21 June 1738.
37 Ibid.
38 Ibid.
39 IOR/G/29/6 f.44 Consultation on Wednesday 19 July 1738.
40 IOR/G/29/6 f.45v Consultation on Friday 21 July 1738.
41 IOR/G/29/6 f.48v Consultation on Friday 28 July 1738.
42 IOR/G/29/6 f.49 Consultation on Monday 31 July 1738
43 Ibid.
44 IOR/G/29/6 f.73v Consultation on Friday 7 December 1739.
45 Ibid.
46 IOR/G/29/6 f.74v Consultation on Saturday 22 December 1739.
47 Denis Wright, *The Persians among the English* (London: I.B. Tauris, 1985), pp. 2–3, See also R. W. Ferrier, 'The European Diplomacy of Shah Abbas I and the First Persian Embassy to England', *Iran*, vol. 11 (1973): 75–92.
48 Wright, *The Persians among the English*, p. 4.
49 Ibid., pp. 5–6.
50 Ibid.
51 Rudolph Matthee, *The Politics of Trade in Iran* (Cambridge: Cambridge University Press, 1999), p. 141.
52 Stern, *The Company-State*, p. 77.
53 Riazul Islam, *Indo-Persian Relations: A Study of the Political and Diplomatic Relations between the Mughal Empire and Iran* (Tehran, 1970), p. 55.
54 Sanjay Subrahmanyam, 'An Infernal Triangle: The Contest between the Mughals, Safavids and Portuguese 1590–1605', in *Iran and the World in the Safavid Dynasty* (London: I.B. Tauris, 2012), p. 105.
55 IOR/G/29/5 f.105v Consultation on Saturday 14 March 1730.
56 IOR/G/29/5 f.106 Consultation on Thursday 19 March 1730.
57 Ibid.

58 IOR/G/29/5 f.109 Consultation on Friday 17 April 1730.
59 IOR/G/29/5 f.109 Consultation on Saturday 18 April 1730.
60 IOR/G/29/5 f.109v Consultation on Monday 20 April 1730.
61 IOR/G/29/5 f. 111v Consultation on Wednesday 29 April 1730 (dated incorrectly in text as 27).
62 IOR/G/29/5 f. 111v Consultation on Wednesday 29 April 1730.
63 IOR/G/29/5 f. 111v Consultation on Wednesday 29 April 1730 and IOR/G/29/5 f.112v Consultation on Saturday 2 May 1730 and Monday 4 May 1730.
64 Ibid.
65 IOR/G/29/5 f.115 Consultation on Monday 31 May 1730.
66 Ibid.
67 IOR/G/29/5/ f.118v Consultation on Wednesday 22 July 1730.
68 Ibid.
69 IOR/G/29/5/ f.118v Consultation on Wednesday 22 July 1730.
70 IOR/G/29/5/ f.118v Consultation on Wednesday 22 July 1730.
71 IOR/G/29/5/ f.120 Consultation on Wednesday 22 July 1730.
72 IOR/G//29/5/ f.120 Consultation on Sunday 26 July 1730.
73 IOR/G/29/5 f.139v Consultation on Wednesday 14 December 1730.
74 IOR/G/29/5 ff.181–v Consultation on Saturday 28 October 1732.
75 IOR/G/29/5 f.184 Consultation on Monday the 27 November 1732.
76 IOR/G/29/5 f.193 Consultation on Saturday 13 January 1733.
77 IOR/G/29/5 f.255 Consultation on Saturday 9 October 1734.
78 IOR/G/29/5 f.263 Consultation on Wednesday 15 January 1735.
79 IOR/G/29/5 f.274v Consultation on Tuesday 6 May 1735.
80 IOR/G/29/5 f.275 Consultation on Friday 9 May 1735.
81 Ibid.
82 IOR/G/29/5 f.289 Consultation on Thursday 17 July 1735.
83 IOR/G/29/5 f.300 Consultation on Saturday 6 September 1735.
84 IOR/G/29/5 f.302 Consultation on Tuesday 16 September 1735.
85 IOR/G/29/5 f.306v Consultation on Thursday 13 November 1735.
86 IOR/G/29/5 f.307 Consultation on Thursday 13 November 1735.
87 IOR/G/29/5 f.310 Consultation on Monday 1 December 1735.
88 IOR/G/29/5 f.310v Consultation on Thursday 4 December 1735.
89 IOR/G/29/5 f.315 Consultation on Saturday 3 January 1736.
90 IOR/G/29/5 f.359v Consultation on Tuesday 30 November 1736.
91 IOR/G/29/5 f.234v Consultation on Thursday 2 May 1734, Lockhart, 'Navy of Nadir Shah', p. 6, Lockhart provides this quotation but failed to give a reference for it.
92 Lockhart, 'Navy of Nadir Shah', p. 6n.1.
93 IOR/G/29/5 ff.240v and 241 Consultations on the 28 May 1734 and 29 May 1734.
94 IOR/G/29/5 f.241 Consultation on Wednesday 29 May 1734.

95 Ibid.
96 Lockhart, 'Navy of Nadir Shah', p. 7.
97 IOR/G/29/5 f.242 Consultation on Sunday 2 June 1734.
98 Lockhart, 'Navy of Nadir Shah', p. 7 and IOR/G/29/5 f.257v Consultation on Monday 2 December 1734.
99 Ibid.
100 Ibid.
101 Lockhart, 'Navy of Nadir Shah', p. 7.
102 IOR/G/29/5 ff.336–v Consultation on Friday 21 May 1736.
103 Axworthy, 'Naval Expansion', p. 35.
104 IOR/G/29/5 ff.340v–342 Consultation on Thursday 6 July 1736, consisting of letters between the Agency at Bandar Abbas and Eustace Peacock and Captain Robert Mylne.
105 IOR/G/29/5 f.357v Consultation on Friday 19 November 1736.
106 IOR/G/29/5 f.361v Consultation Saturday 18 December 1736.
107 Floor, 'The Iranian Navy', p. 41n. 46; Lockhart, 'Navy of Nadir Shah', p. 9.
108 IOR/G/29/5 ff.38v–9 Consultation on Tuesday 3 March 1737.
109 IOR/G/29/6 f.189v Consultation on Wednesday 27 January 1742 and f.190 Consultation on Sunday 31 January 1742.
110 IOR/G/29/6 ff.188v–9 Consultation on Sunday 24 January 1742.
111 IOR/G/29/6 f.183v Consultation on Wednesday 30 December 1741.
112 IOR/G/29/6 f.187 Consultation on Thursday 21 January 1741.
113 IOR/G/29/6 f.204v Consultation on Monday 19 April 1742.
114 Jean Sutton, *The East India Company's Maritime Service* (Boydell, 2010), p. 108.
115 IOR/G/29/6 f.201 Consultation on Tuesday 23 March 1742.
116 IOR/G/29/6 f.204 Consultation on Tuesday 13 April 1742.
117 IOR/G/29/6 f.204v Consultation on Monday 19 April 1742.
118 IOR/G/29/5 f.282v Consultation on Monday 23 June 1735 and Lockhart, *The Navy of Nadir Shah*, p. 11.
119 IOR/G/29/6 f.14 Consultation on Friday 16 December 1737.
120 IOR/G/29/6 f.215v Consultation on Friday 28 May 1742.
121 Ibid.
122 IOR/G/29/6 f.233v Consultation on Sunday 14 November 1742.
123 IOR/G/29/5 f.367v Consultation on Monday 21 February 1737.
124 IOR/G/29/6 f.274v Consultation on Wednesday 20 December 1743.
125 IOR/G/29/6 f.249 Consultation on Monday 23 May 1743.
126 Ibid.
127 IOR/G/29/6 f.108v Consultation on Tuesday 26 August 1740.
128 Ibid.
129 Ibid.

130 IOR/G/29/6 f.115v Consultation on Sunday 12 October 1740.
131 Lockhart, 'Navy of Nadir Shah', p. 12.
132 IOR/G/29/5 f.282v Consultation on Monday 23 June 1735.
133 J. C. Sharman, *Empires of the Weak* (Princeton, 2019).

5 Brokers, Khwajas and country Christians: The Company's employment of non-Europeans in Persia

1 Vahé Baladouni and Margaret Makepeace, *Armenian Merchants of the Seventeenth Century and Early Eighteenth Centuries: English East India Sources* (Philadelphia, 1998); Herzig, *Armenian Merchants* and R. W. Ferrier, 'The Armenians and the East India Company in Persia in the Seventeenth and Early Eighteenth Centuries'. *Economic History Review*, vol. 26, no. 1 (1973): 38–62. .
2 Aslanian Sebouh, 'Diaspora vs. Colonial State: Armenian Merchants, the English East India Company and the High Court', *Transnational Studies*, vol. 13, no. 1 (Spring 2004): 37–100.
3 Ibid., p. 65.
4 Ibid.
5 Ferrier, 'The Armenians and the East India Company', p. 54.
6 See Haneda, 'Les compagnies des Indes orientales et les interprètes de Bandar 'Abbās', in *Eurasian Studies*, ed. Michele Bernardini, Masashi Haneda and Maria Szuppe (Liber Amicorum. Études sur l'Iran médiéval et moderne offertes à Jean Calmard, vol. V/1-2, 2006), pp. 175-93.
7 James Mather, *Pashas: Traders and Travellers in the Islamic World* (New Haven, CT: Yale University Press, 2009), p. 98.
8 Baladouni and Makepeace, *Armenian Merchants of the Seventeenth Century*, p. 26.
9 Ibid., p. 186.
10 Stephen Dale, *Indian Merchants and the Eurasian Trade 1600-1750* (Cambridge: Cambridge University Press, 1994).
11 K. N. Chaudhuri, *Trade and Civilisation in the Indian Ocean* (Cambridge: Cambridge University Press, 1985), pp. 137-8.
12 Baladouni and Makepeace, *Armenian Merchants of the Seventeenth Century*, p. xx.
13 Matthee, *The Politics of Trade*, p. 6.
14 IOR/G/29/15 f.115v Letter to the Court of Directors 20 June 1723.
15 Keay, *The Honourable Company*, p. 224.
16 Aslanian, *Trade Diaspora*, p. 42.
17 Matthee, *Politics of Trade*, p. 84.
18 Ibid.

19 R. W. Ferrier, 'The East India Company in Persia in the Seventeenth and Early Eighteenth Centuries', *Economic History Review*, vol. 26, no. 1 (1973): 39.
20 IOR/H/Misc/634 ff.581-94 Text of agreement between the East India Company and the Armenian Nation, 22 June 1688.
21 Ferrier, 'The Armenians and the East India Company', p. 50.
22 Baladouni and Makepeace, *Armenian Merchants of the Seventeenth Century*, p. xxvi.
23 Ibid., p. 86.
24 Floor and Herzig, *Iran and the World*, p. 450.
25 Baladouni and Makepeace, *Armenian Merchants of the Seventeenth Century*, p. 86.
26 Ibid.
27 Ibid.
28 Ibid., p. 116.
29 Ibid., p. 56.
30 Ibid., p. 61.
31 Ibid., pp. 86-90.
32 IOR/H/628 f.23 *Farman* from Abbas I to the East India Company.
33 Floor, 'The Iranian Navy', p. 43.
34 IOR/G/29/16 f.241 Letter to the Court of Directors 8 June 1742.
35 Stern, *Company State*, p. 39.
36 Ibid.
37 Ibid.
38 Ferrier, 'The Armenians and the East India Company', p. 55.
39 IOR/G/29/17 f.98 Letter from Danvers Graves at Isfahan on 31 October 1749.
40 IOR/G/29/16 f.259, IOR/G/29/6 f.276v Consultation on Tuesday 26 December 1743.
41 Aslanian, 'Diaspora vs. Colonial State', p. 44.
42 IOR/G/29/5 f.350-351 List of Rogums in Consultation on 12 August 1736.
43 IOR/G/29/15 f.237 and IOR/P/341 f.240.
44 IOR/G/29/7 f.82 Consultation on Monday 2 March 1747.
45 IOR/H/628 f.29 *Farman* from Abbas I to the East India Company.
46 IOR/G/29/7 f.61 Consultation on Tuesday 3 June 1747.
47 IOR/G/29/7 f.127v Consultation on Sunday 20 December 1747.
48 While Aslanian devotes a chapter of his book on the question of trust, he limits it to Armenians dealing with each other through contracts like the *commenda*, rather than looking at those relating to business with outsiders. For the various types of contracts used by Armenian merchants see Aslanian, *From the Indian Ocean*, pp. 122-36.
49 IOR/G/29/5 f.119 Consultation on Monday 13 July 1730.
50 Ibid.
51 IOR/G/29/17 f.99v-100 Letter to the Agent from the Court of Directors 31 October 1747.

52 Ibid.
53 Ibid.
54 Ibid.
55 IOR/G/29/16 f.190v Letter to the Court of Directors 15 December 1737.
56 Stern, *The Company-State*, p. 3.
57 IOR/G/29/6 f.324 Consultation on Saturday 8 March 1746.
58 IOR/G/29/5 f.350–v List of the Company's Rogums 1730.
59 IOR/G/29/7 f.7v List of items in a packet to the Bombay Presidency from Persia Friday 22 August 1746 and IOR/G/29/5 f.57 Consultation on Thursday 1 May 1729 and f.169 Consultation on Friday 7 July.
60 IOR/G/29/5 f.57 Consultation on Thursday 1 May 1729 and f.169 Consultation on Friday 7 July.
61 Stern, *The Company-State*, p .13.
62 IOR/G/29/1 ff. 26–28, Letter from Edward Monnox at Hormuz to Isfahan, 8 April 1622.
63 Aslanian, *From the Indian Ocean*, p. 208.
64 Ibid., p. 213.
65 Ibid., p. 220.
66 Ibid., pp. 208 and 51.
67 Banyan, Vania, Bania, a caste or occupational designation in India for merchants, bankers and those involved in commerce generally. Most commonly rendered as 'Banian' in the Company's sources.
68 Onley James, 'Indian Communities in the Persian Gulf', in *The Persian Gulf in Modern Times*, ed. Lawrence Potter (Palgrave, 2014), p. 240.
69 IOR/G/29/2 f.19 Consultation on 15 June 1710.
70 IOR/G/29/5 f.350–351 List of Rogums granted to the Company in Consultation on the 12 August 1736.
71 IOR/G/29/2 f.7 Consultation on 6 May 1709.
72 IOR/G/29/4 f.75v Consultation on Wednesday 12 July 1727.
73 IOR/G/29/5 f.363v Consultation on Friday 7 January 1737.
74 IOR/G/29/5 f.110 Consultation on Monday 27 April 1730.
75 IOR/G/29/16 f.176v Letter to Court of Directors 28 January 1737.
76 IOR/G/29/5 f.189v Consultation on Sunday 24 December 1732.
77 Ibid.
78 IOR/G/29 ff.44v–45 Consultation on Saturday 22 February 1729.
79 IOR/G/29/5 f.48 Consultations on the 12–21 March 1729.
80 Ibid.
81 IOR/G/29/5 f.364 Consultation on Thursday 13 January 1737.
82 IOR/G/29/5 f.382 Consultation on Monday 4 July 1737.
83 IOR/G/29/5 f.172v–3 Consultation on Friday 4 August 1732.

84 Ibid.
85 Ibid.
86 IOR/G/29/16 f.251v Letter to the Court of Directors 18 November 1742.
87 IOR/G/29/6 f.58v Consultation on Thursday 4 October 1739.
88 Ibid. f.242v Consultation on Friday 11 June 1734 and f.253 Consultation on Saturday 21 September 1734.
89 Dale, *Indian Merchants and Eurasian Trade*.
90 Onley, 'Indian Communities', p. 242.
91 IOR/G/29/7 f.70 Letter to Thomas Grendon at Basra 2 July 1747.
92 IOR/G/29/5 f.200 Consultation on Wednesday 14 March 1732.
93 IOR/G/29/17 f.39v Letter to the Agent at Bandar Abbas 25 September 1747.
94 IOR/G/29/5 f.204 Consultation on Thursday 26 April 1733.
95 IOR/G/29/5 f.200 Consultation on Wednesday 14 March 1732.
96 IOR/G/29/7 f.86v–7 Consultation on Sunday 8 March 1747.
97 Ibid.
98 IOR/G/29/6 f.278v Consultation on Sunday 14 January 1743.
99 IOR/G/29/6 f.93v Consultation on Friday 9 May 1740.
100 IOR/G/29/5 f.117v Consultation on Friday 10 July 1730.
101 IOR/G/29/7 f.124 Consultation on Tuesday 1 December 1747.
102 Ibid.

Conclusion

1 Keay, *The Honourable Company*, p. 220.
2 Ogborn, *Indian Ink*, p. 36.
3 Barendse, *The Arabian Sea*, p. 1570.
4 As we have seen, Aslanian and Ferrier both consider this relationship, but did not cover the stipulations in the *Farman* granting the Armenians protection under the aegis of the Company's own extraterritorial concessions.
5 See Stern, *The Company-State*.
6 Chaudhuri, *The Trading World*, p. 39.

Bibliography

Primary sources

Archival sources

Harley Collection: MSS. 109 Persian *Farman*.
India Office Records: Persian Factory Records (IOR/G/29/1, 2, 3, 4, 5, 6, 7, 15, 16, 17), Bombay Proceedings (IOR/P/341/2, 3, 5 7a, 7b).
Letter to a Member of Parliament relating to The Bill for the Opening of Trade with Persia through Russia 1741, RSS Tracts 5, vol. 17.
Miscellaneous Collection of *Farman*s and Treaties (IOR/H/628).

Printed primary sources

Ansari, Mohammed Rafi ad-Din. *Dastur al-Moluk: A Safavid State Manual*. Edited by Willem Floor and Mohammad Faghfoory. Mazda, 2007.
Astarabadi, Mahdi Khan, and William Jones, trans. *The History of the Life of Nader Shah: King of Persia. Extracted from an Eastern manuscript, with an introduction, Containing, I. A Description of Asia II. A Short History of Persia and an Appendix, Consisting of an Essay on Asiatick Poetry, and the History of the Persian Language. To Which Are Added, Pieces Relative to the French Translation*. London, 1773.
Chardin, Sir John. *Travels in Persia, 1673–1677*. New York: Dover, 1988.
Fryer, John. *A New Account of East-India and Persia in Eight Letters*. London, 1698.
Hamilton, Alexander. *A New Account of the East-Indies: Being the Observations and Remarks of Capt. Alexander Hamilton who resided in Those Parts from the Year 1688, to 1723, Trading and Travelling, by Sea and Land, to most of the countries and Islands of Commerce and Navigation, between the Cape of Good-Hope, and the Island of Japan. The Second Edition*. Volume I, 1739.
Hanway, Jonas. *An Historical Account of the British Trade over the Caspian Sea: With a Journal of Travels through Russia and into Persia*, 4 vols. London, 1753.
Hazin, Sheikh Mohammed Ali. *The Life of Sheikh Mohammed Ali Hazin*. Translated by F. C. Belfour, London, 1830.
Kaempfer, Engelbert. *Am Hofe des Persischen Großkönigs 1684–85*. Translated by Walter Hinz. Leipzig: Koehler, 1940.

Le Bruyn, Cornelius. *Travels into Muscovy, Persia and Part of the East Indies*, vol. 2, London, 1737.
Lockyer, Charles. *An Account of the Trade in India*. London, 1711.
Minorsky, Vladimir, trans. and ed. *Tadhkirat Al-Mulūk, A Manual of Safavid Administration*. London, 1943, reprinted 1980.
Nasiri, Mirza Naqi. *Titles and Emoluments in Safavid Iran*. Translated by Willem Floor. Washington, DC: Mage, 2008.
O'Kane, John. *The Ship of Sulaiman*. London: Routledge, 1972.
Safavi, Mirza Mohammed Khalil Mar'ashi. *Majma al-Tavarikh dar Tarikh-i Inqiraz-i Safaviyeh va vaqa'i-ye ba'd ta sal-eh 1207 h.q.* Edited by Abbas Eqbal. Tehran, 1328 H.S.
Tavernier, Jean-Baptiste. *Travels in India*. 2 vols, London, 1889.
Turkoman, Iskander Beg Monshi. *Tarikh-i Alam-ara-yi Abbasi*, 2 vols paginated as one. Edited by Iraj Afshar. Tehran, 1350AH/1971AD.

Secondary sources

Alam, Muzaffar, and Subrahmanyam, Sanjay. *Indo-Persian Travels in the Age of Discoveries 1400–1800*. Cambridge: Cambridge University Press, 2007.
Amin, A. *British Interest in the Persian Gulf*. Leiden: Brill, 1967.
Antunes, Catia, and Gommans, Jos, eds. *Exploring the Dutch Empire*. London: Bloomsbury, 2015.
Arjomand, Said Amir. 'Coffeehouses, Guilds and Oriental Despotism Government and Civil Society in Late 17th to Early 18th Century Istanbul and Isfahan, and as seen from Paris and London'. *European Journal of Sociology*, vol. 45, no. 1 (2004): 23–42.
Ashraf, Assef. 'The Politics of Gift Exchange in Early Qajar Iran, 1785–1834'. *Comparative Studies in Society and History*, vol. 58, no. 2 (2016): 550–76.
Aslanian, Sebouh. *From the Indian Ocean to the Mediterranean: The Global Trade Networks of Armenian Merchants from New Julfa*. Berkeley: University of California, 2011.
Aslanian, Sebouh. *From the Indian Ocean to the Mediterranean: The Global Trade Networks of Armenian Merchants from New Julfa*. Berkeley: University of California, 2012.
Aslanian, Sebouh. 'Trade Diaspora vs. Colonial State: Armenian Merchants, the English East India Company and the High Court'. *Transnational Studies*, vol. 13, no. 1 (Spring 2004): 37–100.
Avery, Peter, Hambly, Gavin and Melville, Charles, eds. *Cambridge History of Iran in 7 vols*, vol. 7. Cambridge, 1991.
Axworthy, Michael. *Iran: Empire of the Mind: A History from Zoroaster to the Present Day*. Penguin, 2008.

Axworthy, Michael. 'Nader Shah and Persian Naval Expansion in the Persian Gulf, 1700–1747'. *Journal of the Royal Asiatic Society*, vol. 21 (2011): 31–9.
Axworthy, Michael. *The Sword of Persia: Nader Shah, from Tribal Warrior to Conquering Tyrant*. I.B. Tauris, 2006.
Babaie, Sussan et al. *Slaves of the Shah: New Elites of Safavid Iran*. London, 2004.
Baladouni, Vahé, and Makepeace, Margaret. *Armenian Merchants of the Seventeenth Century and Early Eighteenth Centuries: English East India Sources*. Philadelphia, 1998.
Barendse, Rene. *The Arabian Seas: The Indian Ocean World in the Seventeenth Century*. Routledge, 2002.
Bayly, C. A. *Empire and Information: Intelligence Gathering and Social Communication in India, c 1780–1870*. Cambridge, 1996.
Bayly, C. A. *Imperial Meridian: The British Empire and the World 1780–1830*. London, 1989.
Bernardini, Michele, Haneda, Masashi, and Szuppe, Maria, eds. 'Études sur L'Iran Médiéval et Moderne Offertes à Jean Calmard'. *Eurasian Studies*, vols 1–2 (2006): 175–93.
Bhattacharya, Bhaswati. 'Armenian European Relationship in India, 1550–1800: No Armenian Foundation for European Empire?' *Journal of Economic and Social History of the Orient*, vol. 48, no. 2 (2005): 277–322.
Bill, James A. 'The Plasticity of Informal Politics: The Case of Iran'. *Middle East Journal*, vol. 27, no. 2 (Spring 1973): 131–51.
Blanning, Tim. *The Pursuit of Glory: Europe 1648–1815*. Penguin, 2008.
Blow, David. *Shah Abbas: The Ruthless King Who Became an Iranian Legend*. I.B. Tauris, 2009.
Bose, Sugata. *A Hundred Horizons*. Harvard, 2006.
Bowen, Huw, Lincoln, Margaretta and Rigby, Nigel, eds. *The Worlds of the East India Company*. Boydell, 2003.
Bowen, Huw, Mancke, Elizabeth and Reid, John, eds. *Britain's Oceanic Empire: Atlantic and Indian Ocean Worlds c.1550–1850*. Cambridge, 2012.
Bruce Watson, I. 'Fortifications and the "Idea" of Force in Early English East India Company Relations with India'. *Past and Present*, vol. 88 (1980): 70–87.
Bruijn, J. R., and Gaastra, F. S. eds. *Ships and Spices East India Companies and Their Shipping in the 16th, 17th and 18th Centuries*. Amsterdam: Neha, 1993.
Cain, Peter, and Hopkins, A. G. 'Gentlemanly Capitalism and British Expansion Overseas I. The Old Colonial System, 1688–1850'. *Economic History Review, New Series*, vol. 39, no. 4 (November 1986): 501–25.
Cain, Peter, and Hopkins, A. G. 'The Political Economy of British Expansion Overseas 1750–1914'. *Economic History Review*, Second Series, vol. 33, no. 4 (November 1980): 463–90.
Casale, Giancarlo. *The Ottoman Age of Exploration*. Oxford, 2010.
Chaudhuri, K. N. *The East India Company*. Routledge, 1999.

Chaudhuri, K. N. 'The Emergence of International Business, 1200–1800', vol. 4, in *The English East India Company*, 7 vols. Routledge, 1965.

Chaudhuri, K. N. *The Trading World of Asia and the English East India Company 1660–1760*. Cambridge: Cambridge University Press, 1978.

Chaudhuri, K. N. *Trade and Civilisation in the Indian Ocean*. Cambridge: Cambridge University Press, 1985.

Chaudhury, Sushil. 'Companies and Rulers: Bengal in the Eighteenth Century'. *Journal of Economic and Social History of the Orient*, vol. 31, no. 1 (1988): 74–109.

Chaudhury, Sushil, and Kevonian, Keram, eds. *Armenians in Asian Trade in the Early Modern Era*. Lisbon, 2008.

Chew, E. *Arming the Periphery: The Arms Trade in the Indian Ocean during the Age of Global Empire*. Palgrave, 2012.

Clark, Hugh R. 'Maritime Diasporas in Asia before da Gama: An Introductory Commentary'. *Journal of the Economic and Social History of the Orient*, vol. 49, no. 4: *Maritime Diasporas in the Indian Ocean and East and Southeast Asia (960–1775)* (2006): 385–94.

Clulow, Adam. 'European Maritime Violence and Territorial States in Early Modern Asia 1600–1650'. *Itinerario*, vol. 33, no. 3 (November 2009): 72–94.

Clulow, Adam. *The Company and the Shogun: The Dutch Encounter with Tokugawa Japan*. New York: Columbia University Press, 2014.

Couto, Fernandes, and Loureiro, Miranda, eds. *Revisiting Hormuz: Portuguese Interactions in the Persian Gulf Region in the Early Modern Period*. Harrassowitz Verlag, 2008.

Crone, Patricia. *Pre-Industrial Societies: Anatomy of the Pre-Modern World*. 2nd edn. Oxford, 2003.

D'Souza, Rohan. 'Crisis before the Fall: Some Speculations on the Decline of the Ottomans, Safavids and Mughals'. *Social Scientist*, vol. 30, nos. 9/10 (September–October 2002): 3–30.

Dale, Stephen. *Indian Merchants and Eurasian Trade, 1600–1750*. Cambridge, 1994.

Dale, Stephen. *The Muslim Empires of the Ottomans, Safavids and Mughals*. Cambridge, 2010.

Dalrymple, William. *White Mughals*. Viking, 2003.

Dodwell, H. H., ed. *The Cambridge History of India*, 7 vols. Vol. 4. Cambridge, 1929.

Dodwell, H. H., ed. *The Cambridge History of India*, 7 vols. Vol. 5. Cambridge, 1929.

Duindam, Jeroen. *Dynasties*. Cambridge, 2016.

Emerson, John. 'Rahdars and Their Tolls in Safavid and Afsharid Iran'. *Journal of the Economic and Social History of the Orient*, vol. 30, no. 3 (1987): 318–27.

Erikson, Emily. *Between Monopoly and Free Trade: The East India Company 1600–1757*. Princeton, 2014.

Ferguson, Niall. *Empire*. Penguin, 2004.

Ferrier, R. W. *British-Persian Relations in the 17th Century*. Unpublished Dissertation, University of Cambridge, 1970.

Ferrier, R. W. 'The Armenians and the East India Company in Persia in the Seventeenth and Early Eighteenth Centuries'. *Economic History Review*, vol. 26, no. 1 (1973): 38–62.

Ferrier, R. W. 'The East India Company in Persia in the Seventeenth and Early Eighteenth Centuries'. *Economic History Review*, vol. 26, no. 1 (1973): 39.

Ferrier, R. W. 'The Terms and Conditions under which English Trade Was Transacted with Safavid Persia'. *Bulletin of the School of Oriental and African Studies*, vol. 49, no. 1 (1986): 48–66.

Floor, Willem. *The Economy of Safavid Persia*. Wiesbaden, 2000.

Floor, Willem. 'The Iranian Navy in the Gulf during the 18th Century'. *Iranian Studies*, vol. 20, no. 1 (1987): 31–53.

Floor, Willem. 'The Office of Muhtasib in Iran'. *Iranian Studies*, vol. 18, no. 1 (Winter 1985): 53–74.

Floor, Willem. *The Persian Gulf: A Political and Economic History*. Washington, DC: Mage, 2006.

Floor, Willem. *The Persian Gulf: A Political and Economic History of Five Port Cities, 1500–1700*. Washington, DC: Mage, 2006.

Floor, Willem. *The Persian Gulf: Dutch-Omani Relations*. Washington, DC: Mage, 2014.

Floor, Willem. *The Persian Gulf: The Hula Arabs of the Shibkuh Coast*. Washington, DC: Mage, 2014.

Floor, Willem. *The Persian Gulf: The Rise and Fall of Bandar-e Lengeh*. Washington, DC: Mage, 2010.

Floor, Willem. *The Persian Gulf: The Rise of the Gulf Arabs*. Washington, DC: Mage, 2007.

Floor, Willem. 'The Revolt of Shaikh Ahmad Madani in Laristan and the Garmsirat (1730–1733)', *Studia Iranica*, vol. 12 (1983): 63–93.

Floor, Willem, and Clawson, Patrick. 'Safavid Iran's Search for Silver and Gold'. *International Journal of Middle East Studies*, vol. 32, no. 3 (August 2000): 345–68.

Foran, John. 'The Long Fall of the Safavid Dynasty: Moving Beyond the Standard Views'. *International Journal of Middle East Studies*, vol. 24, no. 2 (May 1992): 281–304.

Foran, John. 'The Making of an External Arena: Iran's Place in the World System, 1500–1722'. *Review (Fernand Braudel Centre)*, vol. 12, no. 1 (Winter 1989): 71–119.

Foster, William. *The English Factories in India, 1618–1621(-1669): A Calendar of Documents in the India Office*, British Museum and Public Record Office. Clarendon, 1906–27.

Fragner, Bert, Kauz, Ralph and Schwartz, Florian, eds. *Wine Culture in Iran and Beyond*. OAW, 2014.

Furber, Holden. 'Asia and the West as Partners before "Empire" and After'. *Journal of Asian Studies*, vol. 2, no. 4 (August 1969): 711–21.

Gilman, Sander, and Xun, Zhou, eds. *Smoke: A History of Smoking*. Reaktion, 2004.

Gommans, Jos. *Mughal Warfare: Indian Frontiers and High Roads to Empire, 1500–1700*. London, 2002.

Gommans, Jos, and Kolff, Dirk, eds. *Warfare and Weaponry in South Asia 1000–1800*. Oxford, 2001.

Gregorian, Vartan. 'Minorities of Isfahan: The Armenian Community of Isfahan 1587–1722'. *Iranian Studies*, vol. 7, nos. 3/4 *Studies on Isfahan: Proceedings of the Isfahan Colloquium Part II* (Summer–Autumn 1974): 652–80.

Haneda, Masashi, ed. *Asian Port Cities, 1600–1800*. Kyoto University Press, 2009.

Haneda, Masashi, ed. 'Bandar Abbas and Nagasaki: An Analysis of the Reaction of the Safavid Government to Europeans from a Comparative Perspective'. *Annals of Japan Association for Middle East Studies*, vol. 20, no. 2 special issue II: Ports, Merchants and Cross-cultural Contacts (2005): 119–30.

Haneda, Masashi, ed. *Le Chah et les Qizilbach: Le Système Militaire Safavide*. Berlin, 1987.

Haneda, Masashi, ed. 'Les Compagnies Les Indes Orientales et les Interprètes de Bandar Abbas'. *Eurasian Studies*, vol. 1–2 (2006): 175–93.

Hang, Xing, and Andrade, Tonio, eds. *Sea Rovers, Silver, and Samurai: Maritime East Asia in Global History, 1550–1700*. Hawaii, 2016.

Harding, D. F. *Smallarms of the East India Company 1600–1856*, vols I and II. Foresight, 1997.

Hejeebu, Santhi. 'Contract Enforcement in the English East India Company'. *Journal of Economic History*, vol. 65, no. 2 (June 2005): 499–500.

Herzig, Edmund. *The Armenian Merchants of New Julfa, Isfahan: A Study in Pre-modern Asian Trade*. Oxford, 1991.

Herzig, Edmund. 'The Volume of Iranian Raw Silk Exports in the Safavid Period'. *Iranian Studies*, vol. 25, nos. 1/2 (1992): 61–79.

Herzig, Edmund, and Floor, Willem, eds. *Iran and the World in the Safavid Age*. London: I.B. Tauris, 2012.

Herzig, Edmund, and Kurkchiyan, Marina, eds. *The Armenians*. Routledge Curzon, 2005.

Hodgson, Marshall G. *The Venture of Islam: Conscience and Civilisation in a World Civilisation*, 3 vols. Chicago, 1974.

http://www.iranicaonline.org/articles/abbasi.

http://www.iranicaonline.org/articles/capar-or-capar-turk.

Inalcik, Halil ed. *An Economic and Social History of the Ottoman Empire*, 2 vols. Cambridge, 1994.

Islam, Riazul. *Indo-Persian Relations: A Study of the Political and Diplomatic Relations between the Mughal Empire and Iran*. Tehran, 1970.

James, Lawrence. *Raj: The Making and Unmaking of British India*. Abacus, 1997.

Karim, A. 'Murshid Quli Khan's Relations with the English East India Company from 1700–1707'. *Journal of Economic and Social History of the Orient*, vol. 4, no. 3 (December 1961): 264–88.

Katouzian, Homa. *The Persians: Ancient, Medieval and Modern Iran*. Yale, 2009.

Keay, John. *India: A History*. Harper Perennial, 2000.

Keay, John. *The Honourable Company*. London: HarperCollins, 1993.
Keddie, Nikki, and Matthee, Rudi, eds. *Iran and the Surrounding World*. Washington, DC, 2002.
Klein, Rüdiger. *Trade in the Safavid Port City of Bandar Abbas and the Persian Gulf Area ca. 1600–1680: A Study of Selected Aspects*. PhD Dissertation, University of London, 1993.
Kuran, Timur. 'The Economic Ascent of the Middle East's Religious Minorities: The Role of Islamic Legal Pluralism'. *Journal of Legal Studies*, vol. 33, no. 2 (June 2004): 475–515.
Lambton, Ann K. S. 'The Impact of the West on Iran'. *International Affairs*, vol. 33, no. 1 (January 1957): 12–25.
Langer, Axel, ed. *The Fascination of Persia: The Persian-European Dialogue in Seventeenth-Century Art and Contemporary Art of Teheran*. Chicago, 2013.
Lawson, Philip. *The East India Company, A History*. Routledge, 1993.
Lockhart, Laurence, ed. *The Cambridge History of Iran*, 7 vols, vol. 6. Cambridge, 1991.
Lockhart, Laurence, ed. *The Cambridge History of Iran*, 7 vols, vol. 7, Cambridge, 1991.
Lockhart, Laurence, ed. *The Fall of the Safavīd Dynasty and the Afghan Occupation of Persia*. Cambridge, 1958.
Lockhart, Laurence, ed. 'The Navy of Nadir Shah'. *Proceedings of the Iran Society*, 1936.
Maktabi, Hadi. 'Under the Peacock Throne: Carpets, Felts and Silks in Persian Painting, 1736–1834'. *Muqarnas*, vol. 26 (2009): 317–47.
Marcinkowski, Ismail. 'The Iranian-Siamese Connection: An Iranian Community in the Thai Kingdom of Ayutthaya'. *Iranian Studies*, vol. 35, nos. 1/3 (Winter–Summer 2002): 23–46.
Marshall, P. J. *East Indian Fortunes, the British in Bengal in the Eighteenth Century*. vol. 1. Oxford, 1976.
Marshall, P. J. *The Oxford History of the British Empire: The Eighteenth Century*. vol. 2, 5 vols. Oxford, 1998.
Mather, James. *Pashas: Traders and Travellers in the Islamic World*. New Haven, CT: Yale University Press, 2009.
Mathew, John. *Margins of the Market: Trafficking and Capitalism across the Arabian Sea*. California, 2016.
Mathew, K. M. *History of the Portuguese Navigation in India, 1497–1600*. Mittal, 1988.
Matthee, Rudi. 'Alcohol in the Islamic Middle East: Ambivalence and Ambiguity'. *Past and Present* (2014): Supplement 9.
Matthee, Rudi. "Anti-Ottoman Politics and Transit Rights: The Seventeenth Century Trade in Silk between Safavid Iran and Muscovy'. *Cahiers du Monde Russe*, vol. 35, no. 4 (October–December 1994).
Matthee, Rudi. 'Between Aloofness and Fascination: Safavid Views of the West'. *Iranian Studies*, vol. 31, no. 2 (Spring 1998): 219–46.
Matthee, Rudi. 'Between Arabs, Turks and Iranians: The Town of Basra, 1600–1700'. *Bulletin of the School of Oriental and African Studies*, vol. 69, no. 1 (2006): 53–78.

Matthee, Rudi. 'Between Venice and Surat: The Trade in Gold in late Safavid Iran'. *Modern Asian Studies*, vol. 34, no. 1 (February 2000): 223–55.

Matthee, Rudi. 'Christians in Safavid Iran: Hospitality and Harassment'. *Studies on Persianate Societies*, vol. 3 (2005/1384AH): 3–43.

Matthee, Rudi. 'From Rhubarb to Rubies: European Travels to Safavid Iran (1550–1700)'. *Harvard Library Bulletin*, vol. 23, nos. 1–2 (Spring–Summer 2012): 10–25.

Matthee, Rudi. 'Mint Consolidation and the Worsening of the Late Safavid Coinage: The Mint at Huwayza'. *Journal of the Economic and Social History of the Orient*, vol. 44, no. 4 (2001): 505–39.

Matthee, Rudi. *Persia in Crisis*. I.B. Tauris, 2012.

Matthee, Rudi. 'The Career of Mohammed Beg, Grand Vizier of Shah Abbas II'. *Iranian Studies*, vol. 24, no. 1 (1991): 17–36.

Matthee, Rudi. *The East India Trade in Kerman Wool, 1658–1730*. Etudes Safavide, 1993.

Matthee, Rudi. 'The Imaginary Realm: Europe's Enlightenment Image of Early Modern Iran'. *Comparative Studies of South Asia, Africa and the Middle East*, vol. 30, no. 3 (2010): 449–62.

Matthee, Rudi. *The Politics of Trade in Safavid: Silk for Silver 1600–1730*. Cambridge, 1999.

Matthee, Rudi. *The Pursuit of Pleasure: Drugs and Stimulants in Iranian History, 1500–1900*. Princeton, 2009.

Matthee, Rudi. 'The Safavids under Western Eyes: Seventeenth Century European Travellers to Iran'. *Journal of Early Modern History*, vol. 13 (2009): 137–71.

Matthee, Rudi. 'Was Safavid Iran an Empire?' *Journal of Economic and Social History of the Orient*, vol. 53 (2010): 233–65.

Matthee, Rudi, Floor, Willem and Clawson, Patrick. *The Monetary History of Iran*. I.B. Tauris, 2013.

McPherson, Kenneth. *The Indian Ocean: A History of People and the Sea*. Oxford University Press, 1993.

Melville, Charles. *Safavid Persia*. I.B.Tauris, 2009.

Mentz, Søren. *The English Gentleman Merchant at Work*. Copenhagen: Museum Tusculanum Press, 2005.

Mills, James, and Barton, Patricia, eds. *Drugs and Empire: Essays in Modern Imperialism and Intoxication, c.1500–c.1930*. Palgrave, 2007.

Mukherjee, Ramkrishna. 'The Rise and Fall of the East India Company'. *Monthly Review Press*, 1974.

Murphey, Rhoads. *Ottoman Warfare 1500–1700*. New Brunswick, 1999.

Newman, Andrew. *Safavid Iran: Birth of a Persian Empire*. London, 2006.

Newman, Andrew. *Society and Culture in the Early Modern Middle East*. Leiden: Brill, 2003.

Nierstrasz, Christopher. *In the Shadow of the Company: The Dutch East India Company and Its Servants in the Period of Its Decline, 1740–1796*. Leiden: Brill, 2012.

Nierstrasz, Christopher. *Rivalry for Trade in Tea and Textiles*. Palgrave, 2015.

Ogborn, Miles. *Indian Ink: Script and Print in the Making of the English East India Company*. Chicago, 2007.
Onley, James. 'Britain and the Gulf Shaikhdoms, 1820–1971: The Politics of Protection'. *CIRS Occasional Paper (SFS, Georgetown University)*, vol. 4, School of Foreign Service, Georgetown University (2009): 1–44.
Onley, James. 'Britain's Native Agents in Arabia and Persia in the Nineteenth Century'. *Comparative Studies of South Asia, Africa and the Middle East*, vol. 24, no. 1 (2004): 129–37.
Onley, James. *The Arabian Frontier of the British Raj*. Oxford, 2007.
Onley, James. 'The Raj Reconsidered: British India's Informal Empire and Spheres of Influence in Asia and Africa'. *Asian Affairs*, vol. 40, no. 1 (March 2009): 44–62.
Parker, Charles, and Bentley, Jerry, eds. *Between the Middle Ages and Modernity. Individual and Community in the Early Modern World*. Rowman and Littlefield, 2007.
Parker, Geoffrey. *Global Interaction in the Early Modern Age, 1400–1800*. Cambridge, 2010.
Parker, Geoffrey. *The Military Revolution: Military Innovation and the Rise of the West 1500–1800*. Cambridge, 1988.
Pearson, Michael N. *The Indian Ocean*. Routledge, 2003.
Pettigrew, William. 'Corporate Constitutionalism and the Dialogue between the Global and Local in Seventeenth Century English History'. *Itinerario*, vol. 39, no. 3 (2015): 487–501.
Potter, Lawrence G. *The Persian Gulf in History*. Palgrave MacMillan, 2009.
Razzari, Daniel. '"The Gulfe of Persia Devours All": English Merchants in Safavid Persia 1616–1650'. PhD Dissertation Submitted to University of California Riverside, 2016.
Ritter, Markus, Kauz, Ralph and Hoffman, Brigitt, eds. *Iran und Iranisch Geprägte Kulturen*. Wiesbaden, 2008.
Ruangsilp, Bhawan. *Dutch East India Company Merchants at the Court of Ayutthaya*. Leiden: Brill, 2007.
Rubies, Joan-Pau. *Estudos sobre Don García de Silva y Figueroa e os "Comentarios" da embaixada à Persia (1614–1624)*. Lisbon, 2011.
Rubies, Joan-Pau. 'Political Rationality and Cultural Distance in the European Embassies to Shah Abbas'. *Journal of Early Modern History*, vol. 20 (2016): 351–89.
Saad Al-Muqadam, Mohammad. 'Omani Relations with Persia 1737–1848'. PhD Dissertation Submitted to the University of Exeter, 1996.
Savory, Roger. *Iran under the Safavids*. Cambridge, 1980.
Steensgaard, Niels. *Carracks, Caravans and Companies: The Structural Crisis in the European-Asian Trade in the Early 17th Century*. Studentlitteratur Lund, 1973.
Steensgaard, Niels. *The Asian Trade Revolution*. Chicago, 1974.
Stern, Philip. *The Company-State: Corporate Sovereignty and the Early Modern Foundations of the British Empire in India*. Oxford: Oxford University Press, 2011.
Subrahmanyam, Sanjay. *Courtly Encounters*. Harvard, 2012.

Subrahmanyam, Sanjay. *Exploration in Connected History: Mughals and Franks.* Oxford, 2005.

Subrahmanyam, Sanjay. *Improvising Empire: Portuguese Trade and Settlement in the Bay of Bengal.* Delhi, 1990.

Subrahmanyam, Sanjay. 'Iranians Abroad: Intra-Asian Elite Migration and Early Modern State Formation'. *Journal of Asian Studies*, vol. 51, no. 2 (May 1992): 340–63.

Subrahmanyam, Sanjay. *Merchant Networks in the Early Modern World.* Variorum, 1996.

Subrahmanyam, Sanjay. *Merchants, Markets and the State in Early Modern India.* Oxford, 1990.

Subrahmanyam, Sanjay. *The Political Economy of Commerce: Southern India 1500–1650.* Cambridge: Cambridge University Press, 1990.

Subrahmanyam, Sanjay. *The Portuguese Empire in Asia, a Political and Economic History, 1500–1700.* Wiley, 2012.

Troebst, Steffan. 'Sweden, Russia and the Safavid Empire', in *Iran and the World in the Safavid Age.* I.B. Tauris, 2012, pp. 253–9.

Tuck, Patrick. *The East India Company: 1600–1858*, vol. 4. Routledge, 1998.

Tuck, Patrick. *The East India Company 1600–1858*, vol. 5. Routledge, 1998.

Tucker, Ernest. 'The Peace Negotiations of 1736: A Conceptual Turning Point in Ottoman-Iranian Relations'. *Turkish Studies Association Bulletin*, vol. 20, no. 1 (Spring 1996): 16–37.

Van Gelder, Maartje. 'Cross-Confessional Diplomacy and Diplomatic Intermediaries in the Early Modern Mediterranean'. *Journal of Early Modern History*, vol. 19 (2015): 93–105.

van Meersbergen, Guido. *Diplomacy in a Provincial Setting: The East India Companies in Seventeenth-Century Bengal and Orissa.* Forthcoming.

White, David, L. *Competition and Collaboration: Parsi Merchants and the English East India Company in 18th Century India.* Munshiram Manoharlal, 1995.

Wilson, C. R. *The Early Annals of the English in Bengal.* London, 1900.

Wilson, Jon. *The Domination of Strangers: Modern Governance in East India 1780–1835.* Palgrave Macmillan, 2008.

World Health Organisation. *Guidelines for Drinking-Water Quality*, 3rd edn, vol. 1. WHO, 2006.

Wright, Dennis. *The English amongst the Persians.* I.B. Tauris, 2001.

Ziglar, Katie M. 'A Persian Banquet'. *Gastronomica: The Journal of Critical Food Studies*, vol. 3, no. 4 (Fall 2003): 8–12.

Index

Abbas I 8, 24, 32, 53, 75, 98, 107, 109, 136, 153
  and the Armenians 130–2
  and the Farman 16–18, 78
  and the Portuguese 11, 12, 153
  and the Shirley brothers 108–9
Abbas II 18, 32, 36, 93
Abbas III 24, 67, 100, 101
Adventure Grab, ship 51
Afghans xvi, 17, 18, 24, 30, 33, 39, 40, 48, 54, 56, 60, 73, 76, 81, 98, 99, 100, 124, 137, 144, 153, 157
Afseen 46–7, 68, 71
Afshar/Afsharid 100
Agent, Company rank xi, 22, 31, 32, 33, 34, 36, 37, 39, 43–6, 48, 49, 50, 51, 56, 57, 58, 59, 60, 61, 62, 66, 67, 71, 90, 102, 113, 116, 118, 119, 120, 138, 144, 148, 150, 156
  autonomy 125
  as consul 69–70
  delegated authority 80, 82
  as executor of wills 141
  legal authority 64
  as private merchant 91
Ahdname 16
Ali Mardan Khan 98, 110–14
Amsterdam 10, 51, 130, 136
Arab Shore 104, 105, 106, 107, 122, 124
  location 24
Arabian Peninsula 10
Arabs 51, 56, 100, 101, 102, 103, 106, 121, 122, 124, 130, 143
  crewing Persian ships 122–3
  and piracy 25, 50, 111
  and trade 51
arak 33, 34, 38, 39, 40, 88
Armenians xii, 27, 37, 87, 89, 91, 127, 128, 130, 131–3, 136, 138. 140, 143, 144, 145, 146, 149, 150, 155
  and the Company 134–5, 141, 156
  overland trade 78, 80
  as service gentry, and banking 135, 137
  as translators 129, 139
  and wine production 87

Bahrain 1, 100, 103, 104
Baluchis 9, 24, 40, 48, 54, 56, 81, 102, 103, 111
Bandar Abbas 13, 17, 20, 24, 25, 27, 33, 35, 36, 38, 39, 42, 46, 47, 48, 58, 72, 69, 76, 83, 93, 102, 105, 106, 111, 112, 113, 114, 115, 118, 119, 120, 122, 124, 129, 132, 136, 141, 143, 145, 150, 157
Banian Community 146
and communications 50, 52, 53–7, 60, 68, 71
conditions 30, 31, 32
customs duties 63, 68, 91, 101, 134, 155
factory 18
geographical position 28, 45
law and order 65, 144
and trade 79, 80–1, 89, 92, 139, 156
in travel narratives 8
water supply 32
weather 29
Bandar Kung 32, 36
Bandar Laft, Laft 28, 122–3
Banians 55, 57, 82, 127, 129, 142–5, 146, 150, 151, 156
  as brokers 7, 65, 130
  and the Farman 20
  and finance 136
  legal protection 90
  transliteration of names xii
Barker, Thomas 14
Baru Khan 144
Basaidu 28
Basra 1, 10, 42, 45, 49, 52, 60, 66, 102, 107, 123
  customs and other duties 90–1
  Resident (*see also* French, Martin) 62
Batavia 10, 51, 68, 102
Bencoolen 29

Index

Bengal 58, 89
Blandy, William 139
Bombay xii, xviii, 3, 25, 28, 30, 43, 61, 62, 63, 66, 85, 110, 113, 117, 137, 145, 150, 157
  and alcohol 87–8
  and Armenians 134–6
  Bombay Council 7, 33, 45, 50
  Bombay Presidency 7, 50, 77, 80, 118
  communication 50–1, 52, 57, 68, 141
  and gambling 40
  gardens 47
  and governance 60, 67, 102, 104
  and law 36–7, 58–9
  and Persian goods 92
  and the Persian Navy 118–20, 125
  urban planning 42
  and wine 38–9
  and the wool trade 81, 84
Britannia (galley), ship 30, 102, 111, 113

Calcutta 25, 28, 128, 136, 142
Callendar, Panous, Armenian merchant 132–3
Cape of Good Hope 38, 53, 79, 88, 89
Captain Forbes 65
caravan/caphila/qafileh 10, 19, 34, 38, 48, 53–4, 81
caravanserai 34, 53
Carmania, *see* Kerman
Caspian Sea 17, 145
  and silk 78–9
Chardin, Jean 49, 87
Charles I 15, 23, 68–9
Charles II 23, 69
Chaudhuri, K. N. 3–4, 5
  and business constitutionalism 59
  and Company governance 157
Chiras, *see* Shiraz
Chittra/Chitrah, Banian broker 143–4
cloth 21, 23, 25, 74, 75–7, 79, 80, 83, 85, 88, 91, 93, 94, 98, 133, 137, 138
  Company brokers as purchasers 144–5, 154
  and the early Company 11
Clulow, Adam 4, 68
Cockayne, William 75
Coddrington, Thomas 35

coffee 16, 157
  and social ritual 48–9, 50
Company garrisons 132
  in Bandar Abbas 7, 30, 41
  and hierarchy 58–9
  in India 40
Cook, Richard, captain of the Ruparell 118, 121
copper xv, 10, 53, 73, 83, 84, 86, 92, 93, 98, 155
  as currency xi, 85
Cordeux, William 35, 36, 39, 83, 147
  and Company orders 58–9, 63, 106
  fraud 61
  murder 64
Cowan, ship 119
customs duties 80, 90, 131
  Company share 17, 45, 89, 91, 94, 101, 140, 155
  and the Farman 13, 20, 21, 124, 134

d'Andrade, Rui Frere 14
Da Gama, Vasco 1
Da'ud, Armenian linguist 133
Darughah 20
de Romade, Laurence 41
della Valle, Pietro 11
Draper, William Henry 39, 58–9, 63, 106
Dutch, Dutch East India Company (VOC) 16, 17, 88, 98, 109, 134, 145
  archival bias 7
  capture of the Spice Islands 25
  and communication 51, 55, 56, 57
  events in Europe 23
  Factory at Bandar Abbas 34
  garden 48
  in historiography 4
  Hofreis 70
  and non-Europeans 84, 133, 137, 147
  and Persian diplomacy 110–12, 114–17, 119
  and the Persian navy 102–3, 123
  and private trade 155
  punch house 39
  relations with Persia 68, 78, 102, 104–5, 126
  rivalry with EIC 74, 75, 81, 94
  socialising 44

sources 5, 6, 99
and wool 81, 83, 84–5

East India Company, wages xi
and alcohol 38–40, 154
and Armenians, *see* Armenians 128, 130–42, 149, 150, 151, 156
and Banians 143–6, 150, 151, 156
and cloth, *see* cloth 75, 85
and colouring 94
and communication 50, 51, 55–6
Company table 33–4
and credit 135–6, 137–9
and crime 60–1, 63–7, 144
and the Crown 15–16, 67
and customs 90–1, 101
and diplomacy 50, 51, 69, 108
and Dutch–Persian relations 104
and empire 23
and entertainment 46–9
Factory 34–5
factory records 7, 52–4
Farman 13, 16–23, 69, 80, 86, 98, 137, 153–4, 158
gardens 46–8
and health 41–2
in historiography 2–6
at Hormuz 13–15
interests in the Gulf 1–2, 11–12
in Kerman 82–4
management 33, 34, 43–5, 50, 57–9, 60–2, 70
and maritime patrols 101–2, 106–7, 110, 117–18, 123, 154
and Nader Shah 79, 80, 92, 93, 101, 102, 110, 124–5, 146
and non-Europeans 81, 82, 84, 127, 150
and Persian diplomacy 111–17, 154
and Persian employees 146–9, 150
and the Persian navy 95, 97, 101, 123, 124–5
in Persian sources 8–9
and private trade 33, 63, 89, 90–1
relations with Muscat 59, 107
relations with Persia 2, 46, 54, 63, 68, 75, 90–1, 92, 97, 98–9, 109, 112, 113, 115, 153
and religion 37
and the Russia Merchants, *see* Russia Merchants 74–6
and ship sales 118–22, 154
and the Shirley family 109–10
and silk 74, 76
and silk, *see* silk 78, 80, 94, 150
treatment of employees 27–8, 30, 38, 144
water security 32
and wine, *see* wine 75, 77, 86, 88, 154
and wool, *see* wool 81, 83–5
Edward, ship 110
Elton, John 76, 79
Esfandiar, wool broker 82, 147
Euston, Ursula 36, 37
Euston, William 36

Fanny, ship 91
Farman 13, 16–23, 25, 32, 38, 48, 63, 64, 65, 68, 77, 86, 98, 104, 116, 124–5, 134, 148, 153–6
acquisition 15
and colouring 94
and contracts 76
Mughal 25, 131
Persian interests 78, 92–3
and power relations 156
protections for non-European employees 20, 128, 137, 138, 140, 146, 150
and royal relationships 69
terms unfulfilled 91
threats of withdrawal 97, 111, 112, 121
as a tradition 113
translation 9
and wine 87
Farrukhsiyar, Mughal Emperor 25, 69, 131
Fath-i Shah, *see* Cowan
Ferrier, R. W. 6, 21, 131, 133
and Armenians 128, 129
and the Farman 17
Floor, Willem xi, 5, 6, 12, 28, 91, 99, 104, 154, 155
Fort St. George Galley, ship 31
Fotheringham, John 58–9, 63, 106
Fowler, Henry 3–31, 58
France, French xvi, 23, 34, 35, 49, 51, 57, 109, 110, 129, 138, 139

Fremlin, William 45
French, Martin 62
Frost, John 30
fruit 46, 47
   as a commodity 54, 77, 89, 92
Fryer, John 8
Furber, Holden 3-4

Garmsir/at 30, 100
Gilan 17, 20, 75, 76, 80, 130, 131, 132
Goa, and the Portuguese 13, 14, 15
   and arak, *see* arak
Gombroon Merchant, ship 63-4
Gombroon, *see* Bandar Abbas
Gostlin, Styleman 30
Graham, Mungo 76, 79
Graves, Danvers xv-xvii, 76, 135, 147

Hajji Tenaul, merchant 103
Halifax, ship 105
Hamilton, Alexander 8
   on the Company garden 34
   on wine 86
Hanway, Jonas 8
Hardcastle, John, surgeon 41
Harris, John 63, 115
Harwich, ship 105, 121
Hermet, Joseph 139
Hill, John 30
hing (asafeotida) 20, 92, 93
Housaye, Isaac 66
Hussein Ali Beg, Persian
   Ambassador 108

Imam Qoli Khan 12, 107
imperialism 3
Indian Ocean 2, 10
   Anglo-Portuguese rivalry 14, 153
   and the Company 1, 5, 25, 89, 94, 108, 118, 158
   and diasporas 127-30, 136
   economics 73, 135
   and Europeans 74
   and free trade 3
   and Persia 5, 94, 97, 99, 117, 154
   and Persian wine 77, 86, 88
   piracy 51
   trade 8, 11
Iran, *see also* Persia

Isfahan xii, 3, 6, 12, 13, 17, 19, 56, 100, 111, 133
   Armenians in 128, 130, 131, 135
   and Bandar Abbas 54
   coffee houses 49
   and cloth 79, 133
   Company's Resident 33
   Company House or Factory 45, 60, 61, 136
   Company Linguist xii, 139
   distance from coast 55
   garden 47-8
   loss to Afghans 45-6
   Russian Embassy 70
   as a silk market 76, 80
   under Abbas I 32, 130
   under siege 31
Iskendrun 52

James I 15, 75
James II 23
James, ship 11
Japan, Japanese 4, 22, 68, 70, 75
Jarun, *see* Hormuz
Jask 11, 12
Jenkinson, Samuel 76
Jesuit xvi, 77
Jews 36-7
Jizya, Company exemption 20
John Geekie 33, 62, 105
John Horne 65, 101, 110
Julfa, New Julfa 61, 130, 132, 135
Julfar 107

Kalantar 64, 82
Kandahar 99, 109
   maund 20
Kasim, wool broker 82, 147
Katwal 64, 144
Kerman 6, 32, 35, 36, 46, 47, 65, 83, 84, 85, 94, 135, 137, 145, 147
   caravan route 10, 53
   Company broker 146-7
   Company House xvi
   Company management in 60-1, 79
   Company Resident in 77
   copper 53, 83, 86, 98
   destruction xv, 77
   and silk 76, 80

wool 21, 53, 61, 64, 76, 81–2, 86, 98,
    150, 151, 154
Khalat 144, 147–9
Khosrow, wool merchant 82, 147
Kish 10, 102

Lahiji, Sheikh Mohammad Ali Hazin 8
Lar 18, 54
Larak 10, 28
Larkin, John 30
Latif Khan, admiral 98, 103, 104, 105,
    106, 115, 116, 117, 118, 119, 121, 122,
    123, 124, 125
Lecheram, Company broker 146
Levant Company 75, 79
Levant, region 150
Livorno 52
Lockyer, Charles 8, 86
London 7, 14, 24, 25, 51, 61, 62, 66, 67,
    68, 69, 70, 75, 137, 140, 150, 157
    and Armenians 130, 132, 156
    Board of Directors 45, 49, 50, 59, 83, 85
    and communication 45, 52
    and finance 136
    Great Fire 42
    and wool 81, 86
Lutf Ali Khan 37

Madeira, wine 38, 88, 89
Madras 28, 40, 42, 43, 150
    and Armenians 128, 134, 135,
    136, 142
    and Sultan David 138
Mahmud Siah Beg 114–16
Manna 35–6, 65
Mary, ship 120–1
Mashhad 53, 79, 145
Matthee, Rudi
    and Armenians 131
    and currencies xi, 84
    and drugs 49
    Euro-Persian relations 68
    and Persian Studies 5–6
    and silk 74
    and wine 77, 87, 89
    and the wool trade 83, 85, 86
May, William 58, 66
Mazandaran 17, 75, 76, 130, 131
Mesopotamia 10

Minab 10, 48, 64
Mir Haidar 40
Mir Mehr Ali 65, 111
Mirza Ismail, Khan of Bandar
    Abbas 92, 102
Mirza Mohsen 116, 120
Mirza Nasser 67, 69, 70
Mocha, city 49
Mohammad Jafar 149
Mohammad Khan Baluchi 102
Mohammad Taqi Khan Shirazi, Taqi
    Khan xii, 33, 98, 103–4, 105, 106,
    107, 120, 121, 122, 123, 124, 134
Monnox, Edward 16
Monsoon 28, 52, 110, 111, 114
Mughal Empire, *see also* India 69, 109,
    110, 113, 116, 120, 131, 142
Muscat/Muscati, *see also* Oman 14, 24,
    32, 51, 58, 73, 99, 100, 102, 104, 105,
    106, 107, 112, 114, 117, 122
Mylne, Robert, captain of the
    Northumberland 118

Naban, Noband 48
Nader Shah 17, 24, 36, 65, 76, 80, 81,
    112, 122, 124, 126, 146, 147, 148,
    150, 157
    and Armenians 137, 140–2
    assent to the throne 100
    campaign in the Gulf 100–1
    description xvii
    destruction of Kerman xv, 77
    and diplomacy 110, 113, 114, 116
    and hing 92, 153
    in historiography 6, 9
    in historiography, and the Farman 18,
    78, 103, 121, 153
    and the navy 62, 63, 98–9, 107, 109
    and reconstruction 54, 56
    relations with the Company 21–2, 93,
    101, 125
    and the Russia Company 76, 79
    and the VOC 137
Naqd Ali Beg 108–9
Nathaniel Whitwell 36, 64, 65, 76, 79, 80,
    120, 121, 125
Newlin, Robert 31
Northumberland, ship 118
nuts 10, 77, 92

Oliphant, Patrick, surgeon 40, 41
Oman/Omani, *see also* Muscat 9, 11, 24, 100, 125
Owanooze (Auwannees), VOC broker 137-7, 147

Pack, George 32
Patna, ship 118
Peacock, Eustace 118, 120
Peirson, John 61, 139
Pembroke, ship 120-2
Pereira, Francis 41
Poland/ Polish-Lithuanian Commonwealth 108, 130, 140
Pondicherry 138
Portugal/Portuguese 12-16, 24, 51, 73, 97, 98, 104, 109, 110, 146, 153, 154
Prescott, Alexander 68
Prince of Wales, ship 102

Qalyan (hookah, shisha, water pipe) 48-50
Qanat 31-2
Qazvin 17, 49
Qeshm 10, 28, 31, 103, 122
Queen Anne 67, 69

Rahdar/Rahdari 13, 17, 18, 53
Raqam/Rogum 19-20, 22, 144
Ras al-Khaymah, *see* Julfar
Rose Galley, ship 63, 106-7, 115
rose water 38, 54, 77, 86, 87, 88, 94, 154
Rostam, wool broker's assistant 147
Ruparell, ship 118, 121
Russia 8, 70, 74, 75, 76, 79, 80, 109, 127, 130, 133, 145
Russia Merchants, *see also* John Elton and Mungo Graham 74, 76, 78, 79, 93

Safavid Empire, *see* Persia
Safi I 17-18, 75, 78
Safi Khan Beg 114-16
Sankhar 143-4, 145
Sarhad, Khwaja 131
Savage, Charles 37
Severn, ship 110
Shah Soltan Husayn 17, 18, 19, 23, 67, 69, 99, 100, 101
Shahbandar 20, 30, 89, 90, 91, 92, 94, 102

Shawmeer (Shah Amir) 138
Sheikh Rashid of Basaidu 100, 103, 117
Shiraz 6, 17, 19, 34, 38, 46, 47, 54, 77, 86, 87, 92, 103, 120, 154
  wine 88, 98, 155
Shirley, Sir Anthony 108, 109, 120
Shirley, Robert 37, 108, 109, 120
Shirley, Teresia 37
Siam 4, 8, 10, 88, 109
Siavush, wool broker 82, 147-8, 151
silk 1, 3, 5, 10, 11, 12, 17, 18, 20, 21, 73-80, 85, 86, 91, 92, 93, 94, 108, 109, 128, 130-2, 133, 145, 149, 150, 154, 155, 158
Silk Road 10
Sind 110, 114, 115, 122
St. Helena 29, 42
Stern, Philip 3, 27, 42, 134, 156
  on Armenians 135, 136, 140, 142
  on gardens 47
  and hierarchy 59
Sultan David 138, 151
Sumatra 29
Surat 12, 13, 43, 45, 50, 52, 90, 108, 115, 117, 120
Surman John 69, 131

Tabriz xii, 10, 49, 79
Tahmasp I 11, 32, 109
Tahmasp II 18, 21, 22, 24, 67, 100, 101
Tahmasp Qoli Khan, *see* Nader Shah
Tavernier, Jean-Baptiste 1, 54, 87
The Ottoman Empire xv, 1, 11, 45, 52, 57, 60, 66, 99, 100, 108, 109, 113
  and Armenians 127, 130, 131, 133, 140
  embassies to Persia 70
  and silk 3, 133, 145, 150
  and trade 16, 78

Venfield, Henry 106, 115
Villiers, George, Duke of Buckingham, Lord High Admiral 14
VOC, *see* Dutch

Weddell, John 12
Weddell, Thomas 118
William Cockell 32, 63, 102, 103, 104, 125
  and hing 93
  and illness 33, 40, 41

and Latif Khan 123
and law and order 64
and Persian embassies 113, 114, 115
and Persian navy 117, 118
Wilmington, ship 105
wine 10, 54, 86–7, 94, 154
   Company use 34, 38–9, 73, 98, 155
   exportation 21, 86
   in the Farman 19, 77
   as a gift 88
   and health 88
   and Islam 89

wool xv, xvii, 21, 73, 76–7, 94, 145, 147, 150, 151, 154, 155
   Company export 53, 61, 81–6, 98, 156
   Company wool investment 64, 74
   in England 75
Wright, Edmund 30, 36

Yakub John 141, 150
Yemen 16

Zahed Ali Mirza 30